0-1

To Darrell

Hope this book helps
you to "Grow Older Gracefully"
and enjoy your golden years.

Deliza a Eller

THE RETIREMENT HANDBOOK

*A Complete Planning Guide
to Your Future*

THE RETIREMENT
HANDBOOK

by Joseph C. Buckley

Sᴉxᴛʜ Rᴇᴠɪsᴇᴅ ᴀɴᴅ Eɴʟᴀʀɢᴇᴅ Eᴅɪᴛɪᴏɴ

by Henry Schmidt

1817

HARPER & ROW, PUBLISHERS

NEW YORK · HAGERSTOWN · SAN FRANCISCO · LONDON

STANDARD BOOK NUMBER: 0-06-010568-2

LIBRARY OF CONGRESS CATALOG CARD NUMBER: 78-138712

77 78 79 80 81 10 9 8 7 6 5 4 3 2 1

Contents

Preface

My purpose in writing this book is to fill a growing need for background information at the practical level to serve as a guide in planning ahead for better living in the retirement years. Successful planning and preparation for retirement requires a sound knowledge of the basic needs of retirees —financial security, good living arrangements, retirement activities, usefulness, health, recreation, good use of leisure time, companionship, religious experience.

Individuals need to evaluate these basic needs in the light of personal desires, ambition and capacities. There is no single solution, no one prescription that meets the needs of all retirees. Planning and effort by the individual himself are so fundamental to getting the most out of retirement that everyone should formulate his own goals and the means for their attainment.

Retirement, approached from its constructive side, is based on the concept that people retire *to* a new way of living rather than retire *from* the present way of life. Retirement is a journey, not a destination.

It is hoped the present volume will be found stimulating and profitable by:

1. Men and women of all ages who are interested in long-range planning for financial and psychological security, for

better living and happiness in retirement. The closer they approach the day of retirement, whether it be on a compulsory or a voluntary basis, the more vital retirement planning becomes. Realizing that both planning and execution can be altered by circumstances, we will attempt to discuss different programs of investment, as well as different levels of risk for different age groups.

2. Those who have retired already or are about to retire. This book may point out to them some shortcomings in their present plans or may confirm the validity of a well-chosen program. Those who have no definite plan will find this book useful for creating a workable program for contentment in later years.

3. Those who have members of the family, relatives and friends retired or about to retire. This book will be helpful as a guide for aiding the retiree to make adjustments with greater facility and happiness.

JOSEPH C. BUCKLEY

Preface to the Sixth Edition

In bringing *The Retirement Handbook* up to date I truly felt the pace of progress in retirement planning. So many aspects of life after fifty are changing—so many new developments to report!

In the last few years there has been a great increase in the awareness of the problems and opportunities offered by the leisure of retirement. In every aspect there is progress in the understanding of the mystique of aging—by the individual, by the cities, states and the Federal Government. Many, many new projects are already under way. Many others are in the planning stage.

The opportunities in retirement housing are multiplying throughout the nation. There is already an exciting variety of choices.

Many aspects of the financial picture keep changing. This is certainly true in the pension field and in Social Security and Medicare.

Progress in health is noteworthy. Many studies have brought new light to good health planning for the later years.

The opportunities for meaningful, creative use of leisure are steadily unfolding.

Second career opportunities are increasing for those who want to put their retirement leisure to profitable use.

Plenty of good living is ahead for people in their advanced years—if they make full use of the opportunities available.

HENRY SCHMIDT

1977

THE RETIREMENT HANDBOOK

1

Know Yourself and Grow Older Gracefully

Many and diverse are the popular fears of aging: loss of vigor, becoming unattractive, becoming unneeded and unwanted, financial insecurity, falling hair, wrinkles, lessening mental capacity, loss of leadership role, loss of the supporting person who loves you, and many others.

If you focus on these debilitations, life can become bleak indeed. But a true understanding of life's cycles, of the special blessings of every age can make each age enjoyable. So too, can preparation for the possibility of avoidance of the foregoing ravages.

Just as there is a new scale of values for the later years there is also a new set of rewards, such as: wisdom, judgment, character, maturity, spiritual fulfillment.

Growing older without growing up in understanding of life's evolution can be tragic. One must have developed a philosophy that enables an all-weather understanding and gives a basic guide to action and reaction.

One of the truths mature people have learned is that we cannot live for ourselves alone—at any age. We must be aware of the world around us—be willing to give of ourselves wherever and whenever we are needed. The wise person has learned also that the sure way to get is to give first.

The person who knows how to be friendly seldom lacks friends, and those who give love usually get it in return, in full measure.

Think Ahead toward Retirement

Your success in retirement and in your later years is largely determined by the attitude toward life that you have developed during your middle years.

It's not that preparation for retirement cannot start in the later years, but the bridge to retirement is easier to build while in your forties and fifties. Crossing the bridge, when retirement time comes, can then be an easier transition. In one's middle years, change and personality expansion come easier. It is also the time of life when people should have, at last, the wisdom and insight to evaluate themselves with realism and accuracy.

By "retirement" we don't mean sitting on the sidelines. We really mean a new period of life, usually signaled by the discontinuance of one's accustomed pattern of employment. We *do not* mean retirement *from* life. We *do not* mean complete disengagement from the working world, or from community contacts, or from old friends and associates, or from all the belonging that has given meaning to one's life.

"To every thing there is a season, and a time to every purpose under the heaven: A time to be born, and a time to die; a time to plant, and a time to pluck up that which is planted." Ecclesiastes 3:1–2.

Planting time is in the early to middle career-building period of one's life. It is during the family-raising years. It is character-building time for the development of the full man, for maturing as an individual, for healthy attitudes toward humanity, toward one's community and nation, and a time for the building of faith in God, faith in himself and faith in his fellow man. It is how we succeed in doing these things in the years before retirement that will set the pattern for the later years—will decide how well we lay the groundwork for happiness after fifty-five, sixty or seventy.

Author Charles M. Crowe said: "The passing years usually do very little to alter our basic character except to intensify it, unless we resolutely take ourselves in hand. If we are close at forty, we likely will be stingy at seventy. If we are skeptical at fifty, we probably will be cynical twenty years later. If we think the world is against us at forty, it will in all likelihood still be against us on our deathbed, only more so. If we take a dim view of our fellow man in our active years, there will be plenty of 'heels' and 'dopes' around later on."

If you seek meaningful friendships in the later years, start building them now. If you wish to emulate some older people whose serenity you admire, you should start now. If you wish to have a storehouse of interests, a strong faith, start to build them now.

"As ye sow, so shall you reap." The rewards of building a good foundation for your life, the rewards of your serenity in the early and middle formative years, will be the easing of the way to a healthy adjustment to the years after your career life and family rearing period has passed.

To a large degree you are the captain of your ship. You can steer your course through rough seas or you can avoid much of the rough water. Not all—for some rough weather comes into everyone's life and can be met with confidence. If the seas were too calm, life might bore you and weaken your strength for living.

What course to steer? What destination? Questions

like these are undoubtedly some of the reasons you had for obtaining this book to read.

It would be nice if I could meet with each one of you. This way I could determine how many plans you already have made—and what steps you have already taken toward their fulfillment.

Not knowing where you stand, we must in good conscience discuss every important aspect of adjustment to retirement we can think of, whether they might apply to you or not. So bear with us.

"As a man thinketh—so is he." The medical profession is pretty much in agreement on the affinity of mind and body. They are inseparable. Right attitudes and mental alertness keep the body in better condition. When our minds retain their curiosity, their eagerness to live and learn, our bodies stay younger longer.

Each person lives in his own universe—which is the complement of all things meaningful in his life: his family, his job, his friends, his community, his nation, etc. His attitude toward his universe is of prime importance to the success of his future. His attitude and respect for the universe of others, especially those close to him, is also of tremendous importance to his success.

What does your universe comprise?

Looking Forward

Some people fear to look forward in their lives. Others take great pleasure in it. Those who fear it may be very content in the present and fear any diminution of their current bliss. Or, they may try to hold on to things of the past. They fear they may be buffeted when their children leave, when old friends die, or when the infirmities of age develop.

Some may be both unhappy in the present and pessimistic about their future. If they could bring themselves to realize how much of their future is in their hands, how much they can do to shape it, they could look on the morrow with happier anticipation.

For those who believe in their ability to shape their course, anticipating the tomorrow of retirement can give them great pleasure today, can often lessen many of today's distasteful aspects. We know of so many people with interesting programs for their later years, who are taking steps now to prepare for new careers, new projects, new goals of achievement. We see the keen pleasure they are getting and the bright horizon they see.

We all know, for instance, how anticipation of an interesting trip or a special summer vacation starts giving one pleasure far ahead. Just so can anticipation of interesting things planned for retirement spread a glow of contentment long in advance.

Sometimes the mere anticipation of going away from aspects of your life that you don't like can enable a happy forward look. Like the man grown discontent with his job or the couple who no longer enjoy living in a community which has changed for the worse. It is all right to shed the aspect of life you don't like, but you must also have *new goals, new destinations,* or else you start to vegetate.

WHERE TO BEGIN:

Rule One—Know thyself.

Where Have You Been Going?

Have you been following a course that pleases you? Or have you picked some wrong roads, and ended up in some dead-end lanes—that is with regard to your job, marriage, hobbies, friends, relatives, your human relations.

Your *determination* to follow a new path is the major factor in achieving new goals. Psychologists will tell you that they have seen quite average people go a lot further than many brilliant people because they made the most of what they had. It's the motivation and the concentration of effort that usually does it.

Evaluate Yourself

It's time for a thorough self-evaluation, asking yourself:

Who you are.
Who you want to be.
Where you have been going.
Where you want to go.

To be specific, ask questions such as:

What have been your greatest satisfactions?
What dreams have been fulfilled?
What dreams remain unfulfilled?
    For many this will take a great degree of soul-search-
    ing, but it may turn up some interesting discoveries.
What abilities have you used?
What abilities have remained unused?
Are you resentful of those who have achieved greater
    success, and isn't it time to stop making comparisons
    with them—or with your dreams?

A captain who sets out to sea must have a destination for his ship and you are the captain of your ship.

So many people live aimless lives because they have not truly sought to get acquainted with themselves. They have not searched their souls for the things that are rich and rewarding and enduring. They therefore fail to live the fuller life that could be theirs.

What Do You Want to Be?

After clarifying your present self-image . . . start to picture an image of yourself for the next decade and the one after, to get a long-range view. You have undoubtedly admired many older people and thought to yourself, "How I would like to be like them some day."

They were probably warm, loving older people who seem well attuned to life, wise in its ways. In contrast, you have also observed folks whose company you avoid. Whichever you are or want to be, now is the time to steer a course toward your new personality goal.

If you think enough about it, so that your conscious mind keeps sending messages to your subconscious mind, you will very likely take on the image you seek.

Who Are the Happy Older People?

Happiness in the later years depends largely on one's focus.

Focus on yesterday and all its glories, while occasionally pleasant for reverie, will not long brighten today's path.

Focus on oneself becomes empty, meaningless and self-defeating. Charles Crowe put it this way: "When we live to get, we lose. When we live to give—we gain. For life offers its fullest measure of happiness to those who are wise enough to forget themselves." Focus on the needs of others, both those near and dear as well as humanity in general, contributes immensely to happiness.

So will a focus on useful and interesting activities which can give you positive reason for existence.

Focus on pleasure is an empty pursuit. One needs only to look about at the often vapid expressions of the pleasure seekers at resorts and vacation hotels to see the disillusionment their pursuit offers.

An acceptance of yourself, as you are—an over-all self respect—is a cornerstone of the door to happiness. William J. Reilly, founder of the Institute for Straight Thinking, said: "I don't mean that people should have an inflated opinion of themselves or should be egotistical or go around bragging or be perfectly satisfied with themselves. What I do mean is that, way down deep inside, happy people have a good opinion of themselves. They're not always picking on themselves and condemning themselves. They're not full of a lot of foolish 'guilt' complexes. They know themselves and their limitations and they still like themselves— in spite of their imperfections. They've got self-respect."

We can't find happiness by going out after it. It is a by-product of right attitudes, of outward looking and then it sneaks up on us unawares.

Other elements in the elixir of happiness, from happiness analysts: "When we maintain our moral integrity, meet our responsibilities, deal fairly with our fellows, and walk hopefully toward the future, we can forget about being happy. For happiness will come in upon us unawares. When we are careful about our appearance, thoughtful of our friends and of the feelings of others, refrain from gossip, take our troubles in stride, and cultivate a healthy interest in the affairs of the world, we create a sound basis for self respect. And when we respect ourselves, we don't need to look in strange places for happiness. It will be ours anyway."

To this, Dr. Martin Gumpert in *The Anatomy of Happiness* adds: "Sunshine, young animals, flowers, the discovery of a book or of a painting, melody, silence, the change from cold to warm, the taste of food, giving to others, being listened to, being well groomed, being liked, sleeping, being well rested, being tired after work, some new knowledge, some usefulness, the viewing of happiness, the absence of hostility, leisure and humor—there is no end to the enjoyment of being alive for those who are willing and able to enjoy and who refuse to play the game of guilt and fear."

No mature person, of course, would expect all honeysuckle and roses. For along the road to the later years there will surely be some problems, some hard times and some worries, but a general serenity will help you tackle these bumpy spots with courage. And the fact that you meet them as part of the inevitable will give you confidence in your ability to cope with life.

Where Do You Want to Go?

New work, hobbies, sports, places to live, travel? Be a better person?

Says career counselor William J. Reilly: "However small your first step in the direction of your new interest, however much the time required to accomplish it, a definite schedule will make the job easier and more certain of achievement."

He advises all to "put themselves down on paper"— information on your assets and qualifications, your hobbies, and your interests, in search of the best potential new career. And if the choice is business, then Reilly recommends picking something which can be owned or controlled lock, stock and barrel, so that you are boss and no one can fire you.

As Sydney Smith wrote: "A great deal of talent is lost in the world for want of a little courage. Every day sends to their graves obscure men whom timidity prevented from making a first effort; who, if they could have been induced to begin, would in all probability have gone great lengths in the career of fame. The fact is, that to do anything in the world worth doing, we must not stand back shivering and thinking of the cold and danger, but jump in and scramble as well as we can."

Will You Choose Work or Service?

During regular employment years, work for some men (and women) is their sole, all-consuming interest in life. To others it has become a boring duty of life, holding little interest or pleasure. For each there is a message in planning for the later years.

The eager beavers in their middle years should remember that "all work and no play makes Jack a dull boy." Another danger in total concentration on work is that many a man burns himself out physically by the dizzy pace of today's business.

Mothers and homemakers need also to be forewarned as to what may happen to their feelings of importance, their ego, when the children are grown and departed and household duties have lessened. It's never too early for them to prepare to replace their function with new activities which can give them a feeling of being needed.

People whose satisfactions derive primarily from their work don't develop the proper rhythm of work and play and may have no aptitude for the leisure of retirement. People in this category have not learned to live with themselves.

Those who have come to *dislike* their work may *at first,* in retirement, rejoice at their freedom from work which retirement allows. However, they soon find that their unstructured days drag along heavily. And then they will probably soon yearn for something useful to do each day to give meaning and purpose to living. Without activity having these values, their egos may take a skid, because they have lost their identity.

Part-time work, developing a little business of their own,

finding a meaningful service, is their answer. It will help them keep their identity and self respect. Otherwise their later years may become terribly boring and, being bored, they will be a bore to their families, friends, and former associates.

There's Plenty to Do

One's new occupation may be an extension of present work—but on a less arduous schedule. It may mean lending your business knowledge on a consulting basis. It may mean a switch of careers for which one has been getting avocational experience on the side.

While many may seek careers offering continuing monetary reward, there is a whole world of opportunities to serve some of the crying needs of humanity—or helping one's neighbors and friends—and one's community. The problems the world faces today are so infinite that there is meaningful, rewarding work for every single retired person—if he is willing to apply himself.

Think how much older people could contribute to the improvement of our communities, the strengthening of our institutions, to education, welfare, toward the solution of teenage problems of narcotics and crime, etc., etc. Charles Crowe said: "Life does not belong to us. It does not begin when we are born or end when we die. Life is timeless and ageless. It moves on. It is a marvelous and wondrous thing. It is given to us to enjoy and use for a time. It is full to the brim with opportunity and privilege and beauty and challenge. To bring its potential to full fruition is the noblest work of man."

Prominent psychologist Dr. Smiley Blanton says: "There can be true self-renewal if one has mutually fruitful relations with other human beings, if he is capable of accepting love and capable of giving it—both more difficult achievements than is commonly thought. If he is capable of depending on others and of being depended upon. If he can see life through another's eyes and feel it through another's heart. The man or woman who cannot achieve these relationships is imprisoned, cut off from a great part of the world of experience. The joy and suffering of those we love are part of our own experience."

As long as you entertain bold dreams for the future, you will never grow old. Life then becomes the exciting adventure it should be.

How Do You Want to Get There?

Good rules for selecting a new career are given by William J. Reilly:

1. It is best to select a business or activity in which you can use the abilities you have developed during your peak earning years.
2. Select a business or activity that you *can get excited about.*
3. Select a business or activity that puts you into everyday relations with the *kind of people you enjoy.*
4. Select a business or activity in which *age or experience are definite assets,* rather than handicaps.
5. Select a business or activity which lends itself to *small-scale operations*—one that you can continue to *direct with ease* as long as you live.

Religion and Faith Can Guide You

A strong faith is one of the best bulwarks against the storms of life in the later years. Belief in a loving, compassionate God can help one go through life serenely.

Dr. Smiley Blanton says: "Every day the psychiatrist is reminded of the importance of faith, because every day he is asked to help people who are suffering from a lack of it. Such people often turn up in my office because they simply do not have the stamina to stand up under the blows that sooner or later life deals to all of us. The unhappiest persons I know are those who almost make a religion of faithlessness. We see such people quite often at the American Foundation of Religion and Psychiatry, full of anxiety, worried about the state of the world, convinced that the country is headed for economic disaster."

We usually live in a larger, more purposeful world, when we seek the perspective of God in our lives. Loneliness is less prevalent when one realizes the constantly available companionship that God offers.

Is Your Spouse Included?

Every plan for retirement of a married person should be blessed by one's spouse—if at all possible. An enduring respect and devotion to each other is the greatest bulwark to retirement contentment.

Here are a few wise words of counsel to wives of new retirees, from the American Association of Retired Persons: "Though your life will be changed, it will not be as changed as his. He will need understanding and sympathy because his whole way of life has changed. He will have lost his usual contacts with the workaday world. Regardless of any demonstrations of 'making like it's wonderful to be free,' he will have problems in trying to adjust.

"You will need to use your feminine intuition to know when to begin to push a bit and when to ask for help with the household chores, even though you may not have had such help for forty years or more. You will need to steer the matrimonial ship past the rocks of despair and into the calmer waters of partnership."

Either the development of joint retirement projects or separate projects mutually respected and admired should be sought. Growth is essential throughout life. Mental growth can and should continue long after physical growth has ended, and there is no reason why we should not continue to grow spiritually until the day we die. Both marital partners should seek to grow together—or they might grow apart.

Dr. Blanton advises: "The best way to avoid rigidity is to check yourself now and then and see how many new ideas or activities or interests have come into your married life during, say, the last six months. Does your marriage partner have a strong interest that you don't share? Try sharing it. Go fishing with the brute, if that's what he likes. Take some dancing lessons and go dancing with your wife, if that's what she loves. Pick out some new and untried activity and explore it together. In marriages where one partner simply grows away from the other—intellectually, socially, or professionally—my observation has been that usually the one who does no growing, the one who stands still, is the woman."

Keep Your Mind Busy

As the world unfolds before your eyes, and the horizons of knowledge keep expanding, it can be exciting to devote your increased time to expanding *your horizon,* maintaining an active interest in the world round about, in other human beings. In other words, in things outside of yourself. If you do, you will never know boredom and never be boring. If you don't—the world will be passing you by as you sit on your shelf.

An alert mind contributes enormously to both health and happiness in the later years.

Keep Up Some Creative Activity

Creativity in any form is essential to maintaining a sense of purpose, of personal value, because you are contributing something of use or pleasure to others. This has always been a prime reward of effort for both men and women. In the later years there need be no cessation of creative effort. A long list could be compiled of outstanding creations by older men and women in the world of music, literature, art, politics, contributions by the famous and the unfamous. Try to keep up a spirit of adventure in everything you do. Welcome new experiences, new ideas, meeting new people. New experiences keep life exciting, help you to stay out of deepening ruts, and keep you from the rigidity from which so many older people suffer.

Keep Up with People

Some people like and need many friends—while others need only a few staunch friends. Whatever a person's social requirements, one should never lose the art of making friends. We should keep adding new friends to replace those who keep departing.

Simply put, the ability to make friends is the desire to be friendly and the ability to remain interested in, and interesting to others. This can be enormously aided by the foregoing recommendations—of keeping the mind alert, remaining interested in new things and of maintaining creativity.

You Need a Philosophy of Life

Emotional maturity, serenity at all periods of life and especially in the later years, requires a self-understanding and a clear feeling of your relation to your fellow human beings and to the world.

The attainment of a philosophy of life is a necessity. It is, however, a slow and intimate process—since it is the sum of many attitudes and beliefs and experiences, acquired over the years.

And when you have a sound philosophy and know yourself—*be yourself* and be happy in knowing *who you are, why you are, where you want to go and how to get there, then . . . you'll be a master!*

2

Getting Ready for Your Harvest Years

The Horizon Brightens

In the last ten years the nation has awakened remarkably to the needs and opportunities in the later years of life.

Millions of dollars of research money have gone into the study of the medical, financial, social and community aspects of life after fifty, sixty and sixty-five. The answers are coming through in many areas, and older people are reaping the rewards.

They are already apparent in a better financial security provided via private pension plans, improvements in Social Security and Medicare. They are certainly coming through in better housing for the later years—a realm where there is a tremendous increase in available facilities. Community opportunities of every kind are also burgeoning in cities and states throughout the nation.

All these trends help to provide a brighter future for our increasing millions of older Americans.

The modern idea calls for retirement *to* a new life rather

than retirement *from* life. When a person retires now he can try to change to a new occupation or a new career in which he can continue to grow in personal value and usefulness.

Today we know it is possible to derive great enjoyment from these years of life, years that can be rich, full and happy. Robert Browning referred to them this way: "The best is yet to be; that last of life, for which the first was made." They are the years for enjoying the harvest of a life's work.

Our Responsibilities as Individuals

One fact we must keep in mind is that profound changes are taking place in the structure of the population of the United States. One significant change is the increase in the number of persons sixty-five years of age and over, due largely to the control of infectious diseases, the discovery of new drugs and advances in public health services.

Because of this lengthening of life expectancy, more people will live to reach retirement and will live longer as retired individuals.

At the same time, more and more people in the lower-income brackets are moving up the scale into a big new middle class where they are getting a larger share of the total income than ever before. This middle class has introduced a new and growing group into the economy with more money and savings than average families had twenty-five years ago. Individuals of this group accept the responsibility, during their productive years, of providing financial protection for their retirement. As we shall see in a later chapter, Social Security benefits and pensions need to be supplemented by private income to assure a secure, worry-free life in retirement.

But, living in the later years presents more than just a money problem. Retirement living is concerned also with the psychological aspects of adjustment, of finding our place in the community, of understanding ourselves and shaping our retirement goals. We should be ready to assume our full share of responsibilities for ourselves, our dependents and society to avoid finding ourselves in critical circumstances that may hinder our pursuit of happiness in retirement.

Plan Your Retirement Ahead

Since neither Social Security nor pension income can solve all the problems faced by the man or woman who is still active at sixty-five or seventy, we must look to additional means to assure happy and productive lives. Just sitting around in a rocking chair without anything to do means being thrown on the scrap pile. Most Americans want to stay useful after they retire. Only a small percentage want complete leisure.

You should begin the planning in a practical and positive way while you are still "in harness." Cultivate a wholesome attitude toward retirement for the day when you find yourself laying down the tools of your trade, business or profession.

In the final analysis, security in retirement is a balance of three things: physical security—reasonably good health to be able to do the things you really want to do; activity security—an engaging program and the opportunity for satisfying and rewarding accomplishments; financial security—having sufficient money to be free of financial worries.

Steps in Successful Retirement Planning

1. *Define Your Concepts of Retirement.* You will be more contented and proud of your accomplishments if you first

clearly understand the meaning, purpose and opportunities of retirement.

2. *Make Decisions on the Basis of Fact.* Find out as much as you can about retirement. Search out friends, acquaintances, friends of friends who have retired and ask them for advice. Analyze their successes and failures. Read books and articles devoted to retirement. Sift all the information you can gather.

3. *Consult Your Wife.* Work out your program with your wife. After retirement, the husband may be around the house a good deal of the time. This will be a new experience for both partners and may require a period of adjustment. Such changes in the mode of living for both husband and wife should be considered and planned for ahead of retirement.

4. *Make a Long-range Plan.* The earlier you make a general plan of what you would like to do, the better off you will be when retirement becomes an actuality. Work out a detailed program, even though it is only tentative. But each time you revise your original plan you will come nearer to developing a program that will be practical for you.

5. *Don't Set Your Financial Goals Too High.* Most people plan for financial independence, or at least financial security to meet the basic living standards and social values suited to their desires. Set down the amount needed monthly to satisfy your minimum standard of living in retirement. See if your projected income is sufficient to cover your minimum requirements. If it is not enough, you will need to adjust your over-all plan to try to provide additional money.

6. *Choose a Location to Live in.* Your decision on where to live when you retire can have a great deal to do with your future happiness. Should you move to a new location, offering a more favorable climate for your health or for better living? Do you want to own your retirement home, rent an

apartment or live in a hotel or boarding house? If your principal hobby is fishing or hunting, where are the best locations for you to follow these pastimes the year round? There are many questions that must be answered before you can finally make your choice of where to live or what to do in retirement.

7. *Follow Through on Your Plan.* Having visualized and worked out a plan of action, follow it through to its conclusion. Set down tentative dates for the completion of the various parts of the entire program. Never hesitate to revise your plan when to go ahead with the original version is obviously foolhardly.

Bibliography

BOOKS

Sociology of Retirement by Robert Atchley (Halsted Press, N.Y.)
The Decision and the Experience (University of Michigan Social Research, Ann Arbor, Mich.)
Executive Retirement and Effective Management by Richard A. Beaumont and James W. Tower (Industrial Relations Press, N.Y.)
Psychological Aspects of Retirement by Harold Geist (Charles C. Thomas, Springfield, Ill.)
Law of Retirement by Libby Jessup (Oceana Publications, Dobbs Ferry, N.Y.)
Plan Your Retirement Now (Money Management Library, U.S. News & World Report, Washington, D.C.)
Marketing Your Skills after Retirement (World Trade Academy Press, N.Y.)
Now It's Your Turn to Travel by Rosalind Massou (Macmillan, N.Y.)
Continue to Circulate Your Talents: How to Live after Retirement by Virginia Moline, (William Frederick Press, N.Y.)
Independent Living for Older People (Institute of Gerontology, University of Florida Press, Gainesville, Fla.)
Choosing Your Retirement Hobby by Norah Smaridge (Dodd, Mead, N.Y.)
Sex and the Senior Citizen by R. Wikler (Frederick Fell N.Y.)
Help Yourself to a Job, A Guide for Retirees by Dorothy Winter (Beacon Press, Boston, Mass.)

PERIODICALS DEALING WITH RETIREMENT AND AGING

Retirement Life, National Assn. of Retired Federal Employees, 1909 Q St., N.W., Washington, D.C. 20009

Retirement Living, 150 E. 58th St., New York N.Y. 10022

Dynamic Maturity, Action for Independent Maturity, 1909 K. Street N.W., Washington, D.C. 20049

Retirement Money Newsletter by Peter Dickinson (Phillips, Washington, D.C. 20015)

Retired Officer, 1625 Eye St., Washington, D.C. 20006

Retirement Counselor, 99 Madison Ave., New York N.Y. 10006

Modern Maturity, 215 Long Beach Blvd., Long Beach, Calif. 90801

Aging. Newsletter of H.E.W. Adm., Washington, D.C. Send $4.50 to Superintendent of Documents, Government Printing Office, Public Documents Dept., Washington, D.C. 20402.

U.S. GOVERNMENT PUBLICATIONS

Social Services—Aging, Medicaid, nursing homes, pensions and retirement, Social Security and social welfare. Send for free bibliography and price list of books and pamphlets on these subjects to Superintendent of Documents, Government Printing Office, Washington, D.C. 20402.

3

Health and Long Life

One of the most interesting statements on the subject of aging is by Senator Thomas C. Desmond, former Chairman, New York State Joint Legislative Committee on Problems of the Aging. In the legislative document, *Age Is No Barrier,* Senator Desmond writes:

> Old age is preventable only by death. The outward signs, such as the weathering of the skin, the dimming of the eye's focus, or the tiring of the legs are inevitable as the years progress. But it is the inner self that largely determines one's own true age.
>
> The thermostat of true aging is set by one's mind, by serenity of spirit, by continued "growth," and by purposeful activity. And underlying these, financial security.
>
> These are for the most part responsibilities of the self. One cannot legislate peace of mind, nor can youthfulness be allocated like roads and bridges and post offices by legislative fiat.

If your health is reasonably good, the chances are that you can expect, if a man, to live to be about 68.2 years old;

if a woman, to the age of seventy-four (75.9). Life expectancy has increased only slightly during the past ten years. We cannot be optimistic about a further increase unless people change their habits of living to those conducive to a better life expectancy. However, a major breakthrough in the battle against cancer and heart disease could greatly accelerate the trend to longer life in the later years.

Life expectancy varies considerably in different parts of the country. In 1969–71, the latest period for which such data are available, the leading state in this respect was Hawaii, where the expectation of life for men aged 65 was 14.8 years. Florida followed with 14.1 years, and Utah was next with 13.9. At the other extreme, the corresponding figure was only 12.1 years in Delaware and 12.2 years in Washington, D.C.

Average Life Expectancy Today

Recent data reveal that the remaining average life expectancy for selected age groups is as follows:

At Age of	Years Remaining for Men	Years Remaining for Women
Birth	67.0	74.6
35	36.0	42.2
40	31.5	37.6
45	27.2	33.1
50	23.1	28.8
55	19.4	24.6
60	16.0	20.6
65	13.0	16.8
70	10.4	13.4
75	8.1	10.3
80	6.3	7.7
85	4.7	5.6

(Readers are advised to check new census figures for new data that may have come out since this book was published.)

A man fifty years old today has a 74 percent chance to survive to the normal retirement age of sixty-five. And having lived until he reaches sixty-five, he has a 60 percent chance to survive to the age of seventy-five. Recent advances in geriatrics offer good prospects for further retarding illness and mortality of senior citizens.

The excellent chance that a middle-aged man has of surviving to retirement age, and the number of years he can then expect to live, point up how important it is to plan and prepare for the basic wants and needs of retirement living.

Each year about half a million wives in the United States become widowed. This fact should be taken into account by married couples contemplating retirement. A personal program should take into consideration the needs and problems that may confront the widow upon the death of her husband. At the husband's death, major income sources are reduced or vanish. Unless some provision has been made for the widow, she may have to face a future filled with fear, want and anxiety.

The expectation of life is a ranking index of a nation's well-being. It is the key to measuring man's progress in controlling his biological environment. Before 1900, only one of every twenty-five citizens in the United States was over 65. In 1960, one of every eleven was over 65.

Next to the expectation of life, another important index of a nation's social and economic welfare is the expectation of working life. Sixty years ago there was little difference between total life span and working life among men. In 1900, one out of five youths aged 10–15 years were already in the labor force; with a life expectancy of 48.2 years they spent about 32 years of their life as workers. Only a few lived long enough to spend time in retirement.

The 20 years of additional life expectancy available to men since 1900 is divided between from 4 to 8 years more spent in education and training; approximately 10 more years in the labor force; and from 2 to 6 years in retirement.

Factors in Longevity

Gerontologists point out that the number of years we live is largely tied up with heredity, environmental factors, the use we make of our creative capacities, how we use our strength and energy and the degree of our optimism.

At present, we can do little about heredity as it applies to the longevity characteristics inherited from our ancestors. Geriatrics and other branches of medical science, however, are working on ways to compensate for lack of hereditary factors in longevity.

We can do a great deal about environmental conditions. We can move to a climatic location that is more beneficial to our physical and emotional well-being. We can make psychological adjustments to changes in economic and social status. We can guard against contracting diseases and take precautions against accidents. We can take advantage of new achievements of medical science to prolong life after sixty-five. It is natural to assume that those who receive and follow the best in medical care should live longer than the ones who do not. We can regulate our lives to minimize the strains of emotional pressures. We can be ever watchful of our diet, securing the right kinds and quantities of foods, the best nutrition.

We can develop to the maximum our intellectual, creative and constructive capacities and abilities, learn new skills and interests. We can apply our energy to keeping active at an easy pace within the limits of our physical strength and mental capacity in a new career better fitted to our age. We can guide our thinking along channels that are positive, beneficial and optimistic.

Earlier attention to diagnosis and treatment, improved public health facilities, and an aggressive health education program at the community level will add more years to the lives of our senior citizens. Long life in itself, however, is not enough. Without health, vitality, creative activity and recreation, the opportunity of being useful and financial security, longevity can be a personal tragedy.

Old Age Is Not a Disease

Old age is not in itself a disease. Aging is merely a phase of the life cycle. Senior citizens are not suddenly afflicted with chronic illness upon retirement and should not be treated as if they were.

A decline in physical capacities occurs in all adult age groups and varies greatly with individuals, irrespective of age groups. Even during middle age, practically everyone has to make many adjustments to gradually declining physical powers. These might be wearing glasses, using a hearing aid, giving up vigorous sports or cutting down on specific items in food and drinks. These adjustments to aging are natural and the necessity for them should not be looked upon with grave concern and fear. Older persons may not be as competent in certain activities as they were in their youth. This should not imply that they are totally incompetent. Senility begins when we close the mind to new knowledge and the heart to new emotional experiences. It is most important to keep on growing, to keep moving forward, in intellectual and emotional vigor.

One of the worst diseases of senior citizens is the fear of old age itself. We must realize that we cannot stop aging. But we can enjoy much health and happiness in our senior years if we learn to grow old intelligently and gracefully. Physicians maintain that fear of disease is often a greater menace to a healthful and happy life than the disease itself.

Other mental attitudes that shatter the peace of mind of our aging population are the fear of being poor, worry about losing the attractiveness and physical vigor of youth, fear of losing social prestige, hate and resentment against individuals or circumstances, worry about what the future may bring and resistance to taking a back seat in running things.

The University of Wisconsin recently made an extensive study of worry and fear. Here are the results of this scientific study. First, about 40 percent of our normal worries turn out to be over things that never happen. Second, 30 percent of our worries and frustrations are over things that happened in the past. They are things about which nothing can be done now. These are the things we hatch up in our discouraged moods. Third, 22 percent are the little, petty and needless fears. These three lists together account for 92 percent of our worries and fears. Fourth, this leaves only 8 percent for the things which might be considered legitimate worries to which individuals must give care and attention.

Health and disease, happiness and despair, have their roots in thought. Fear, hate, jealousy and anger will express themselves through a sickly body. One of the New York City hospitals reportedly conducted a special examination of sixteen hundred patients and found that 79 percent of the patients evidenced a strong element of hate and resentment. This is good evidence of the truth that the body mirrors the condition of the mind.

Aspects of Aging

Dr. Albert L. Lansing, of Washington University in St. Louis, an authority on the problems of aging, reported in *Scientific American,* April, 1953, that some theorists attribute aging to a breakdown of the blood vessels or connective tissue; others maintain that organisms age because their cells wear out, as automobiles or shoes do. Lansing points out that the body will continue to rebuild its cells as long as it lives. It is his contention that "in all probability the main reason that organisms age is not a wearing out of cells, but a decline in the body's cell-building efficiency." The organs of the human body do not operate and function independently of each other. Many of them control the activities of other organs and tissues. An abnormal change in a controlling organ can start abnormal changes in an organ associated with it. In this way are formed circles of retrogression which complicate and aggravate the process of aging.

A new branch of medical specialization, geriatrics, is concerned with the physiologic and disease problems of our older people. Geriatric physicians deal with the health of the aged much as pediatric physicians care for the health of infants and children. Medicine never will be able to prevent and cure the diseases incident to old age to the extent that it can control the diseases of childhood. But definite gains are being made.

With greater frequency we learn of new discoveries—a new treatment for stubborn arthritis, new chemicals being tested as inhibitors of cancer, new nutritional aids which take the stiffness out of age, experiments with insulin, cortisone and testosterone to improve the stability of the body. Out of these medical advances will come the benefits of new techniques and treatments. Senior citizens of tomorrow will be healthier, stronger, less susceptible to premature senility and premature death.

Education for better living will probably contribute as much as scientific knowledge to any great new advance in aging.

Chronic Diseases and the Older Age Group

There are few diseases that afflict senior citizens that are not found also in other age groups. Illness is no respecter of age, but older persons are subject to more illness than others. Data from the National Health Survey suggest that the incidence of chronic illness among persons sixty-five years and over is likely to be about three times as high as in the general population.

While chronic illness increases with age, not every older person is afflicted. Many chronic diseases are the result of neglect and lack of early, effective treatment. Medical science in the future may discover new drugs and treatments for arresting chronic diseases. But even now much can be done to increase life expectancy and avert human suffering by suitable treatment when the infirmities are in their early stages.

Heart Disease. More than half of all the people who die each year in the United States die from diseases of the heart and circulation. People on the whole are living longer and escaping the diseases that formerly claimed many lives. Many fall prey to heart disease. The frequency with which "heart attack" is cited as the cause of death among executives almost gives it status as an occupational disease.

The types of heart disease afflicting adults over forty are arteriosclerotic, resulting from hardening or narrowing of the coronary arteries that supply blood to the heart muscle, or hypertensive, resulting from long-continued high blood pressure. It has not been determined how many deaths are due to coronary artery disease and how many to high blood pressure.

Most of the sudden deaths from heart attacks are caused by the narrowing and blocking of the coronary arteries. Just what causes the arteries to harden, putting too great a burden on the heart, is not yet known. Dr. H. M. Marvin, past president of the American Heart Association, points out in his book *You and Your Heart* that a heart attack is not necessarily fatal, nor does it mean a life of inactivity. About two-thirds of those having a coronary condition survive an initial coronary attack. Most of them recover to carry on normal business and social activities.

Hypertensive heart disease, resulting from high blood pressure, is not the result of too much blood. Medical research, however, has not yet found the complete explanation for high blood pressure. Emotional strain has something to do with it; so does heredity. High blood pressure may be caused by a number of factors which over a long time irritate or overstimulate the arterioles or little arteries which serve several purposes in the body, among them the control of the distribution of the blood. Considerable progress has been made in finding suitable agents to lower blood pressure. Over the last decade, the number of deaths from high blood pressure has decreased. A wide variety of new drugs have been tested and proved effective. Further progress in this direction may add to life expectancy.

One of the most important things to know about heart disease is that it can be controlled and its progress arrested. Recovery from some kinds of heart disease has to be natural. Other kinds can be treated medically. Others require surgery. The best way to keep from getting heart disease is to stop worrying about getting it; take good care of your general health; keep your weight down and watch your diet; get plenty of relaxation, exercise, and the sleep you need; get a good physical checkup once a year. An estimated three out of four persons who think they have heart disease haven't. If you have definite symptoms that might mean heart disease, go to your doctor for a thorough examination.

Cancer and Malignant Tumors are not part of the aging process. But since they are chronic diseases, the second leading killer, accounting for almost 17 percent of deaths, they should be mentioned. Dr. Clarence W. Lieb* tells us

Outwitting Your Years by Clarence W. Lieb, M.D., copyright 1949 by Prentice-Hall, Inc., Englewood Cliffs, New Jersey.

that cancer is almost a universal worry of older people.

Cancer is a cluster of body cells that somehow have gone wrong and begin to multiply. Thousands of people are alive today because their cancers were discovered and checked in time. Again the important thing about this disease is to see your doctor for a regular checkup each year. Early discovery is of the greatest importance in this disease.

Other Diseases. The slow and silent development of the degenerative diseases that occur with advancing years emphasizes the importance of thorough medical checkups, especially during the fifties and sixties. Again, early discovery is best assured by a regular physical examination every year.

A study of statistics on accidental deaths according to age and type shows that one-third of the deaths by accident are among people over sixty-five years of age. Falls and motor vehicles cause most of the deaths. Older people should give special attention to the prevention of accidents. Watch out for loose rugs, waxed floors, rickety and narrow stairways and walks. Avoid poorly lighted areas. Keep a night light burning in the bathroom.

Sickness and accidents are the enemies of long life and happiness. Don't wait until pain warns you that some ailment has progressed to the danger point. That is like waiting for your car to break down before you take the trouble to check the gas, oil, battery and spark plugs.

Periodic checkups are important at all ages. They are of the utmost importance in the later years. Don't run the risk of shortening your life by being your own doctor. The older we become, the more sensitive our bodies are to drugs. With approximately five thousand different cures for man's various ailments available in a modern drugstore, it is impossible for an individual to know what is safest and best for him to take. Self-medication is dangerous. Different people react differently to the same dosage of the same drug. See your doctor and follow through on his advice. Resorting to leftover medicines, health fads and old-fashioned remedies, without a doctor's advice, is unsafe.

There are organizations which specialize in such health examinations. The Life Extension Institute in New York City, for instance, is a medical group that has been specializing in preventive and diagnostic medicine for over sixty-four years. Its prominent director, Dr. John McCann, has advised thousands of people about how to live long and healthful lives.

The Institute provides several types of health examinations lasting from two to four hours. A week after the exam a conference is held with the person examined, at which time his questions are answered and preventive medicine suggestions are given.

Other Checkups. "See your dentist every six months" is good advice. Healthy teeth are one of your most valuable possessions. The kind of food you can eat may depend on how well you can chew. Keep your own teeth as long as you can.

Your eyes, too, need checking. A good plan is to have them examined every two years when you get past middle age.

If hearing is more difficult than it was in your younger years, you may need a hearing aid. Modern electronic hearing aids are easy to wear and have proved a great blessing to persons with hearing difficulties.

More health education, directed to the middle-aged and the older groups, is urgently needed. There is an abundance of knowledge now available in the fields of disease prevention, medical and vocational rehabilitation and mental hygiene which, if widely disseminated, could build a healthier and happier older population. Our senior citizens are entitled to a fair share of the community's educational and medical resources. The older generation has the right of access to available knowledge on how to make the harvest years of life the best years of all.

Medical care and facilities, geriatric clinics and visiting-nurse services for older people are inadequate in practically all sections of the country. The greatest opportunities for controlling chronic diseases among our aged, at the present time, are those that can be made at the local community level.

What an opportunity this problem of developing community health services for the elderly presents to retired educators and executives who wish to devote some time to public service! In this field the retiree will merely change jobs, putting in a great many working hours in a civic career. In some communities, groups of experienced citizens have formed committees to make the initial efforts to familiarize the community with the needs of older people.

Watch Your Diet for Longer, Happier Living

Many men and women in their sixties and seventies are not so healthy and happy as they might be because they don't make an ally of the food they eat. Some overeat. Others undereat because they are on some poorly considered reducing diet. Some have slim food budgets and don't observe nutritional needs. There are those whose diet is inadequate because they follow some food fad.

A chronically tired feeling, a gloomy outlook on life, anxiety over small things, loss of sleep—these result in many instances from being undernourished. The right food helps keep the body at its best. In the event of illness, a well-nourished body responds better to treatment than one in a rundown condition.

The number of older people in the population who suffer from malnutrition is appalling. This results not so much from not eating enough as it does from not eating a balanced diet, supplemented, if necessary, by vitamins.

It has been estimated that twenty-five million Americans are overweight. Overweight is America's number one health problem, according to the findings of public health officials. The solution of the overweight problem, it is declared, might increase the average life expectancy and greatly reduce deaths from heart disease, diabetes, high blood pressure and other major chronic diseases of the second half of life.

It is the kind of food you eat, not how much, that counts in your senior years. These four groups of nutrients are essential daily:

1. Protein—milk, eggs, meat, poultry, fish, cereals.
2. Vitamin C—citrus fruits, tomatoes, raw cabbage, peanuts.
3. B Vitamins—Enriched or unrefined cereals and bread, milk.
4. Calcium and Iron—milk, cheese, eggs, molasses, and vegetables of the cabbage family.

In our senior years when our physical activities are restricted, we do not need as many calories per day as we did during youth and pre-middle age. The average man or woman after reaching age sixty-five needs from 2,000 to 3,000 calories every day. After reaching the age of seventy many persons will require only from 1,500 to 1,800 calories daily.

Proteins have long been known as the "building blocks" of the human body because they are used by the body for the process of rebuilding itself by cell replacement. But since the body does not store protein as it does fat or carbohydrate, an adequate amount of good-quality protein should be included every day.

Since food plays such an important part in your life, you can never "retire" from the responsibility of eating the right kinds and amounts of food you need.

Acquire the Habit of Rest and Relaxation

Long periods of strenuous activity in work or play should not be engaged in after fifty. The older you are, the easier it is to overtax your heart. Laborious physical activities should be avoided when the temperature is above eighty-five degrees and relative humidity is over 70 percent. Employ labor-saving devices and shortcut methods wherever possible, especially for the heavy or tedious jobs. Let the younger folks do the heavy work. You do the planning and the supervising wherever possible.

Both bodily and mental fatigue can be reduced by scheduled periods of rest and relaxation. Break up physical and mental work with short rest periods. Don't continue when you feel tired. If you are driving a car on a business or pleasure trip, take at least a fifteen-minute rest after every two hours of driving. If you are doing fairly hard work, physical or mental, stop and rest for ten minutes every hour. When you quit for a rest, stop all over. Short periods of total rest and relaxation are one of nature's best tonics.

Relaxation is just as important as rest. To relax properly try to reduce worry and daily tensions. Tense nerves and muscles are the enemies of complete relaxation. Through observation and experiment you will find out the best conditions under which you can enjoy complete relaxation.

Keep Active as You Grow Old

The secret of longevity in retirement is to keep active both mentally and physically. If the mind and the body are allowed to remain inactive for any considerable period of time, the result is deterioration of their functions. The way to avoid or delay that process is to remain active throughout life.

The capabilities of the older age group to learn have been vastly underestimated. There is no truth in the adage, "You can't teach an old dog new tricks." Millions of persons past sixty-five who have the incentive to learn have acquired new skills and new techniques, are learning to live happily on reduced incomes, are learning to effectively use and enjoy increased leisure time. People can and do continue to learn at all ages. The lack of interest in learning rather than biological degeneration is responsible for the myth that older people are slow, or unable, to learn.

Leading psychologists have demonstrated by numerous tests that the ability to learn falls very slowly with the passage of years, after reaching its peak. The early twenties are said to be the peak years for learning, but the drop in the ability to learn is so gradual that at eighty we still have the learning ability we had at the age of twelve. One of the greatest obstructions to learning is self-satisfaction with the knowledge already acquired and the fear of competition in our youth-worshiping society. Given sufficient interest, motives and self-confidence, the old dog can learn new tricks and continue to perform them if he really wants to, irrespective of chronological age.

There is a group of older people who spend much of their time rebelling against the bodily process of aging. They attempt to camouflage, to keep up with the pleasures, stimulations and taboos of our youth-conscious culture. This they do in their manner of dress, use of beauty preparations, zealous approach to sports, following of diet fads and search for Fountain-of-Youth miracle drugs, so that they hope at sixty-five to look and act as if they were thirty-five. Persons of this group fall into a state of emotional depression and unhappiness when they are forced to face old age as an inevitable period of life. If there were nothing more to the matter of keeping one's youth than clothes, cosmetics and drugs, one would never grow old.

A wiser group of retired individuals live in the present and plan their personal happiness and security on a more stabilized program of intellectual growth and development. They are the rapidly increasing number of retired persons who are revamping conventional attitudes and thinking, and are evolving practical means for making the later years of life the best years of all.

Dr. Lillien J. Martin, a professor of psychology at Stanford University, retired at sixty-five, then went on to become a famous gerontologist and the founder of the San Francisco Old Age Counseling Clinic. She died at ninety-two, after devoting twenty-seven active years to aiding persons to salvage their old age. From over a quarter of a century of experience in rehabilitating the old, Dr. Martin* concludes:

> My picture of a fine, old person, one who by his later life gives proof of having lived well, is of the person who has learned much from his sorrows and built them into experiences useful to others, one who has continued his education all through life so that his mind is alive to changing conditions and is able to take on new views, one who has kept up in the race of progress and refuses to lag too far behind, who has outgrown the narrow needs and self-interest of youth, who has become impersonal but by no means indifferent, who can re-evaluate life after much experience, build up a philosophy and develop the spiritual side of his nature and who is willing to struggle for self-improvement and to live according to the highest ideals he has espoused.

Cicero, the ancient Roman orator and statesman, had a kindly eye on old age when, in his *De Senectute*, he wrote: "Old men retain their mental faculties, provided their in-

* *Salvaging Old Age* by Lillien J. Martin and Clare de Gruchy, Macmillan Co.

terest and application continue; and this is true, not only of men in exalted public stations, but also of those in the quiet of private life. Nature has only a single path and that path is run but once, and to each stage of existence has been allotted its own appropriate quality; so that the weakness of childhood, the impetuosity of youth, the seriousness of middle life, the maturity of old age—each bears some of Nature's fruit, which must be garnered in its season. You must become an old man in good time if you wish to be an old man long. As it is not every wine, so it is not every disposition that grows sour with age."

Here are a few examples that disprove the notion that individuals deteriorate in mental alertness and physical abilities when they reach sixty-five or seventy.

Dr. John Dewey, America's foremost philosopher of his day, retired from teaching at Columbia University when he was seventy. But he went on writing and lecturing, publishing more than three hundred books, essays and articles. When Dewey died at the age of ninety-two, his eyes were still keen, his mind was alert and he still typed his own manuscripts and letters. Winston Churchill, at the age of seventy-eight, once again became prime minister, leading his country in a great emergency. How did he do it? Churchill had a good philosophy of life, driving ambition, intense pride, a variety of interests, almost limitless enthusiasm for any task he undertook. The challenge of adversity only increased his vitality. Arturo Toscanini, at eighty-five, could memorize the complete score of an opera in a few days and, once having committed it to memory, never forgot it. Mr. Justice Holmes, at the age of ninety, took up the study of Greek. Titian painted the *Battle of Lepanto* at the age of ninety-eight. George Bernard Shaw wrote one of his best plays, *St. Joan,* when he was near seventy. Michelangelo was still painting his masterpieces at eighty-nine. Goethe completed *Faust* when he was eighty-two. Bernard Baruch, at ninety-one, and Herbert Hoover, at eighty-seven, are two examples of public figures who lived active lives. James W. Montee learned to fly an airplane at sixty and at eighty-nine was still flying. Adeline De Watt Reynolds, a grandmother, graduated from the University of California at sixty-eight and then took graduate dramatic courses. At eighty she began her movie career.

The Belgian psychologist, Dr. Jean Palus, told the Second International Gerontological Congress that he disputes the idea that intelligence and learning capacity reach their peak during youth and thereafter decline slowly. "I think any progress in maturation and motivation brings about, obligatorily, a corresponding gain in learning capacity and insight," he declared. Dr. Palus goes on to say:

> In youth, man is dominated by biological and physiological urges—the needs for acceptance and recognition, for possession and new adventures, sexual satisfaction and self-assertion. If these needs are not seriously checked in youth, then higher needs make themselves felt in maturity and old age.
>
> The forties and fifties and later years, when correctly entered, open the way for the well-balanced individual to discover new kinds of experience, meditations and accomplishments which are entirely beyond the possibilities of young persons. Many great men have done their best work in maturity. The average person, in his later years, can become more productive in many fields, such as professional work, community relationship, civic life and in many creative realms.

But a great number of persons fail to make their old age a success, Dr. Palus admitted. He pointed out that American society in particular puts great stress on youthful characteristics, such as physical vigor and quick adaptability, and that in many modern industries it is difficult for workers to maintain interest in their work, because of its machine-like nature.

Fixative behavior [Palus said], in which the individual clings to an earlier period of life—either because he missed the satisfactions normal to that period or because he got excessive gratification from them—is a major factor in unsuccessful old age. This explains the cravings for money and dominance in many older people. Here lies the explanation for the kind of pathetic regret immortalized in Goethe's "Faust."

People who keep young in spirit as they grow older are younger-looking for their age, more charming, more fun and probably live longer. When Solon, the Athenian statesman and one of the Seven Sages of Greece, was asked the secret of long life, his reply was "Learn some new thing every day."

Vocational Rehabilitation for Disabled Civilians

Not all persons living in retirement or semi-retirement do so because of voluntary or compulsory job retirement. Many are forced into a state of retirement because of disabilities through accident, illness or other causes. There are over a million men and women in this group in the United States today.

To enable the disabled civilian to be self-supporting, the Federal Government and the states have entered into a partnership for vocational rehabilitation. This Federal-state program of vocational rehabilitation is a public service in the same sense as the school systems, visiting-nurse service, health centers, libraries, water systems and police and fire departments. It is not charity. Vocational rehabilitation services are intended as a legal right. Many persons in early retirement because of disabilities can rehabilitate themselves and enter the employment market to work on a self-supporting basis.

Men and women of working age with substantial job

handicaps are eligible. The program is available to persons with unseen handicaps, such as tuberculosis, arthritis, heart disease, deafness and emotional disabilities, as well as for those with disabilities which are visible, such as amputees, paralytics, spastics and the blind.

Briefly, the following services are provided:

1. Medical examination in every case to determine the extent of the disability, to discover possible hidden, or secondary, disabilities, to determine work capacity and to help determine eligibility.
2. Individual counsel and guidance to help the disabled person to select and attain the right job objective.
3. Medical, surgical, psychiatric and hospital care, as needed, to remove the disability. Included are artificial appliances, such as limbs, hearing aids, braces and the like. These are paid for from public funds to the degree that the individual cannot meet the cost.
4. Training for the right job in schools, colleges or universities, on the job, in the plant, by tutor, through correspondence courses, to enable the individual to do the job well.
5. Occupational tools, equipment and licenses, as necessary, to give the disabled person a fair start. These may be paid for from public funds to the extent that the person is unable to do so.
6. Placement in the right job. Follow-up after placement to make sure the disabled person and his employer are satisfied with one another—at no cost to the individual.

Three conditions must exist before a person is eligible for these services: (1) He must be at an employable age; (2) He must have a disability which substantially interferes with employment; (3) There must be a reasonable chance of his becoming suitably employed. Those interested in further details should write to the State Vocational Rehabilitation Agency, or to the Department of Health, Education and

Welfare, Office of Vocational Rehabilitation, Washington, D.C., 20025.

Does Retirement Hasten Death?

Reports about some people dying shortly after retirement have created a suspicion that retired individuals die sooner than those who remain "in harness." While many people may have, the records of insurance companies show that persons retired and living on annuities actually live longer than those who do not have annuities.

To some people, separation from workday life comes as a shock accompanied by a serious emotional block. These people enter this new period of life as rebellious, confused and bitter adults. If this emotional pressure is not checked and released, it can lead to chaos. Unable or unwilling to adjust themselves to the new mode of living imposed by retirement, they wind up with high-tension emotional systems. Being totally unprepared for retirement, they lose all interest in living. Retirement, however, *usually* leads to an improvement in the health of the retiree.

It is the state of your health, your attitude and adjustment toward retirement, the preparations you have made for old age and your diet—not whether you are retired or employed—that are the governing factors in whether you live to a ripe old age. Your degree of contentment in retirement is often the key.

What Is the Best Age to Retire?

The best circumstances for retirement depend upon what your family responsibilities are, the state of your health, your age, your financial resources and probable retirement income, your general attitude toward retirement and a carefully prepared plan. Individual and family needs differ. Goals, ambitions, desires, standard of living—all are personal matters.

There is no natural law that says a person should retire solely on the turn of a calendar page. Retirement on the basis of age alone is socially wasteful.

But if you are employed by a company or organization that has a compulsory retirement program, the question of your retirement is arbitrarily determined for you in advance. The company sets the age when employees must retire. This is usually between the ages of sixty and seventy, most often at sixty-five.

Some organizations, on the other hand, do have retirement programs which allow employees to choose, within certain limits, the date on which they are to retire. If you are covered by this type of pension policy, you have some serious planning to do in the timing of your retirement.

Tapering-Off Retirement Process

Another approach to retirement is that of gradually cutting down in the hours spent working on the job and stretching out off-the-job time and vacation periods.

This sneaking-up, as it were, on retirement is becoming popular in the retirement programs of certain executives, professional men and women and individuals who have major control of small companies.

A sixty-year-old vice-president of a New York City business organization had a tapering-off plan approved by his company. It permitted him to retire from active participation in the company's business by degrees. Briefly, the plan is this. He works on the job in New York City all through January, February and March. During the remainder of the year he is alternately for two weeks at his New York office and two weeks away at his farm in Virginia. With his regular three weeks vacation he spends thirty weeks on the job and twenty-two on his retirement farm. While for nine months of the year the biweekly trips between the New York office and the Virginia farm are a bit strenuous, he enjoys the experience. Another part of the price of his tapering-off work plan is his reduced annual salary and bonus resulting from a shortened work year. The above plan has these advantages. The company benefits from this man's years of experience in developing and planning merchandising and promotional ideas. Younger men in this executive's department carry out the routine duties and details, while more of his time and experience are concentrated in over-all and long-range planning. While the plan reduces his job remuneration, it provides him with the opportunity and the time to make transitional adjustments to the conditions of full-time retirement.

The tapering-off program of one large organization requires all employees who work beyond the customary retirement age of sixty-five to take an extra month's vacation without pay for each year worked after reaching the time for retirement. That means an extra month for the first year, two months for the second year, and so forth, in addition to the regular vacation.

Transferring older employees to easier work assignments and reduced responsibilities at the same pay or at slightly reduced pay is another fairly common practice of management. This does not, however, solve the retirement problem. It is only a partial solution and merely postpones retirement to a later date on a fixed basis of age or retains employees on the payroll until they die.

Still another method of handling retirement is to retire an aging employee at his compulsory retirement date, and then rehire him as a consultant or for research, a staff job or other special assignment on a part-time, full-time or fee basis.

What About Early Retirement?

One good reason for early retirement is the opportunity it provides for getting a good start on establishing an income-producing business or a farm enterprise while you are still young enough to handle the details involved. Though many people in their sixties have established successful small businesses, getting started as early as possible has great advantages.

If your job means just making a living, drives you to nervous exhaustion, is a ball and chain that keeps you from doing the things you really want to do, offers little chance of future advancement in position and income, has a pension plan that is inadequate, adversely affects your mental, emotional or physical health—then you might as well look for a job offering better prospects, or retire right now.

Some people ought to retire when they are fifty or fifty-five, if for no better reason than to protect their health. Results of a survey among pensioners show that 25 percent retired because of poor health.

There is a small group of headstrong resisters who, because of their emotional temperaments, their refusal to give up power and authority, would never be happy in retirement. They might as well hold on to their current jobs as long as possible or until they die in harness.

Unexpected unemployment may force you into semi-retirement at a much younger age than you anticipated. Finding re-employment in business and industry is a serious problem for men over fifty and women over forty. An unemployed person in his or her early fifties should seriously consider establishing and operating a retirement business or a small farm enterprise.

You may have in the back of your mind the desire or urge to do something entirely different from what you are doing in your present employment. It might be the breeding of high-grade cattle, writing a book, the completion of some academic study or work. No matter what it is, retirement will give you the chance to fulfill your desire. Retire while you are young enough to enjoy and complete what you really want to do.

There comes a time in our business or professional lives when we reach the pinnacle of success in our fields. This crest of the wave may come to some in the middle years of life or to others in their late sixties. In any event, the years that follow do not bring forth any gain in income or advancement in professional recognition or reputation. Those who hang on too long may begin to fall behind and lose ground to younger colleagues with new techniques, new ideas and growing reputations. For their own physical, intellectual and moral well-being, those who have reached the peak of success would be much better off retiring early, and filling the remaining years with new, constructive, satisfying activities.

There is no one answer to the best age at which to start retirement. It depends entirely on what you need and want out of life. But, whatever your decision, bear in mind that retirement years can be the best years of your life. You owe it to yourself and your family to make them so.

Bibliography

BOOKS

Food and Health by James L. Mount (Halstead Press, N.Y.)
Exercise, Rest and Relaxation by Richard Mackey (Brown, Dubuque, Iowa)
Live Longer Workbook by Leonard Levinson (Bantam Books, N.Y.)
Live Longer Now: The First One Hundred Years of Your Life by John N. Leonard, J. L. Hofer, and Nathan Pritikin (Grosset & Dunlap, N.Y.)
Live or Die by Anne Sexton (Houghton Mifflin, Boston, Mass.)
Live Until You Die by Randolf Miller (United Church Press, Philadelphia, Pa.)

Live with Yourself and Like It by Don W. Hillis (Victor Books, Wheaton, Ill.)

Living Nutrition by Frederick J. Stare and Margaret McWilliams (Wiley, N.Y.)

Live Young as Long as You Live by Ira U. Cobleigh (Universal Publishing & Distributing, N.Y.)

Eat and Grow Younger by Lelord Kordel (Manor Books, N.Y.)

Live Longer, Control Your Blood Pressure by Max L. Feinman, (Coward, McCann & Geoghegan, N.Y.)

Live High on Low Fat by Silvia Rosenthal (Lippincott, Philadelphia, Pa.)

Live and Be Well by Harry Litchfield (Libra, N.Y.)

Live and Be Free through Psycho-Cybernetics by Charles Schreiber and Maxwell Maltz (Warner Books, N.Y.)

Live All Your Life by Reuel L. Howe (Word Books, Waco, Tex.)

U.S. GOVERNMENT PUBLICATIONS

Consumer Information—Family finances, recreation, gardening, health and safety, food, house and home. Send for free bibliography and price list of books and pamphlets on these subjects to Superintendent of Documents, Government Printing Office, Washington, D.C. 20402.

Also bibliography on Home Economics, Foods and Cooking.

Food Guide for Older Folks, Cat. No. A 1.77:17/6. 10 cents
Good Teeth, Cat. No. FS 2.50:83/2. 10 cents
Facts About Nutrition, Cat. No. FS 2.22:N95. 15 cents
Food and Your Weight, Cat. No. A 1.77:74/2. 15 cents
Food You Eat and Heart Disease, Cat. No. FS 2.50:89/2. 10 cents
Getting Enough Milk, Cat. No. A 1.77/57/2. 15 cents
Choosing a Hearing Aid, Cat. No. FS 14.118:55. 15 cents
Health Insurance for the Aged, a Brief Explanation of "Medicare," Cat. No. FS 3.25/2:965/2/rev. 10 cents

4

Income Planning for Financing Retirement Living

There are, as of now, approximately 21 million persons in the United States who are sixty-five years of age and over. Of these some 9 million are men and about 12 million are women.

According to the poverty index originally developed by the Social Security Administration, 3.3 million older people, or almost 16 percent of all older people lived in households with total incomes below the poverty line in 1974.

A 1968 report of the Social Security Administration shows that of all money income received by persons 65 or over:

29 percent came from earnings
34 percent came from OASDHI (Social Security)
7 percent came from other public pensions
5 percent came from private group pensions
15 percent came from assets
3 percent came from veterans benefits
4 percent came from public assistance

1 percent came from personal contributions
3 percent came from other sources

These figures are part of a survey taken every 10 years. The next survey will be published in 1978.

Benefits from public and private retirement programs combined thus represented almost one-half of the aggregate income for the aged.

Some are well off . . .

Almost 1.8 million older couples (27 percent) had incomes of $10,000 or more in 1974.

Over 2.8 million (41 percent) older couples had incomes from $5,000 to $10,000.

Many are not well off . . .

Over 2.2 million older couples (32 percent) had incomes under $5,000.

Over 5.5 million older persons (56 percent) living alone or with nonrelatives had incomes under $3,000.

From these statistics, it is obvious that our present retired population on the whole has to get by on rather slim budgets. This fact emphasizes how vital it is for individuals to plan ahead to obtain the income needed to finance the standard of living they desire for themselves in retirement.

A recent U.S. Senate report said that three out of ten Americans over sixty-five years old were living in poverty, yet "many of these aged people did not become poor until they became old."

Among the other economic pressures that compound the low-income problem of the aged are rising health-care costs and the fact that there are more years in retirement, putting a strain on resources they had when they left the work force.

"Even with the important protection of Medicare, many older people have mounting medical bills that must be paid out of pocket," the report said. It said that Medicare had met only 35 percent of all health-care expenditures for the aged in its first year, the 1967 fiscal year. Medicare in 1975 paid about 42 percent of health care expenses.

Americans are also retiring earlier and living longer. This developing trend "could seriously impede attempts to improve" the income of future aged populations, the report said.

It said that the "overwhelming proportion" of people retiring today received total pension income—from both public and private pensions—that was only 20 to 40 percent of their average earnings in the years before retirement.

How Much Will You Need for a Retirement Nest Egg?

You cannot tell exactly how much money you will require during the years you live in retirement. But you can make an estimate of the size of the reserve fund you will need to see you through.

The Bureau of Labor Statistics of the U.S. Department of Labor has prepared three hypothetical annual budgets for a retired couple. The budget costs represent the costs at autumn 1975 prices of three hypothetical lists of goods and services that were specified in the mid-1960's to portray three relative levels of living—simply termed lower, intermediate and higher—for a retired couple.

In the autumn of 1975, the estimated U.S. average annual cost of the lower level budget for an urban retired couple, excluding personal income taxes, amounted to approximately $4,500. At the intermediate and higher levels, the budget costs amounted to $6,500 and $9,600, respectively, as is shown in the following table.

Summary of Annual Budgets for a Retired Couple at Three Levels of Living, Urban United States, Autumn 1975

Component	Lower budget	Intermediate budget	Higher budget
Total budget* - - - - - - - - -	$4,501	$6,465	$9,598
Total family consumption	4,308	6,076	8,863
Food - - - - - - - - - - - - -	1,427	1,912	2,398
Housing - - - - - - - - - - -	1,514	2,192	3,430
Transportation - - - - - -	297	577	1,059
Clothing - - - - - - - - - - -	198	334	514
Personal care - - - - - - - -	128	188	275
Medical care - - - - - - - -	552 (P)	555 (P)	559 (P)
Other family consumption	191	317	628
- -			
Other items - - - - - - - - -	194	389	736

*For the autumn 1973, 1974, and 1975 updating of the budgets for a retired couple, the total budget is defined as the sum of "total family consumption" and "other items." Income taxes are not included in the total budgets.

(P) Preliminary estimate.

Note: Because of rounding, sums of individual items may not equal totals.

It is true that today the famed Townsend Movement is an insignificant force, its few remaining clubs isolated from the great body of the aged, and its proposals virtually unknown to the general population. While the Townsend Movement may never have achieved its goal, the imprint of the Townsend Movement is recognizable in features of our public policy, the configuration of public opinion and the techniques and forms of politics. As long as old age continues to pose difficult socio-economic problems for our society which becomes converted into issues of politics and public policy, the long-range effects of the Townsend Movement will be manifest.

Your Standard of Living Will Determine Your Requirements. People are disposed, as a rule, to regulate their standard of living as their incomes and savings increase or decline. Too great a decline in the habitual standard of life may bring about discouragement and unhappiness. While some downward adjustment of the standard of living may be necessary in retirement because of reduced income, the more nearly normal the standard maintained, the better are the opportunities for enjoying comfort and contentment.

You Will Probably Need Less Income in Retirement

1. Your living expenses will decrease, particularly if you decide on moving to the South or to a rural area, where the cost of housing, clothing, heating bills and food will be lower.

2. Work expenses will stop. You will eliminate costs of going to and from your place of employment. You will save the cost of work lunches. Expenses will stop in connection with business or association conventions, trips and clubs. Also with cost of books, equipment or tools.

3. You can cut down on "front" expenses. There is no good reason now for residing in an expensive neighborhood, belonging to expensive clubs, owning a costly automobile, wearing expensive clothes, giving parties to impress people.

4. Taxes will be lower. Your federal and state income taxes will be reduced; you may even be exempt. If you move into a lower tax-assessment community, your real estate taxes and personal taxes will be reduced.

5. Cost of supporting children in all probability will be reduced. In the majority of cases, children will have grown up and have finished school or college. They will probably be married and supporting families of their own.

6. Good pre-retirement planning will result in considerable savings. You will probably own your home outright. This will eliminate mortgage payments. However, this does not mean housing costs as a budget item can be dismissed from your mind. If you own a $50,000 home, clear, and can afford to enjoy it in retirement, then by all means you

should do so. If, however, your retirement income is less than $10,000 a year then, perhaps, you should do some arithmetic. For this same $50,000 reinvested in good common stocks, Treasury bonds or high-grade corporate bonds can bring in anywhere from $2,500 to $4,000 a year. This is based on the average yields on stock of 3 percent and on 6.5 percent on Treasury bonds and 8 percent on high-grade corporate bonds. If you add your current heat, real estate taxes, repairs and other maintenance costs to this $2,500–$4,000 figure, you will get a more realistic cost of what your retirement housing costs are. Perhaps you will still prefer to remain in your own home, and that is your privilege. But if you are living on a close budget, you ought at least to know what this privilege is costing you in order to compare the savings which could come from a rented apartment or smaller home.

The Best Years to Accumulate a Retirement Nest Egg

The years between the ages of forty and sixty-five, for the majority of individuals, are the fruitful years of income-earning power. These are the productive years when experience and vigor bring forth the biggest pay envelopes, salary checks or professional fees. They are also the years to plan wisely for retirement so that you may have adequate income in the harvest years of life.

If you desire financial security in retirement, you must first of all find out where you stand *now*. You must know where you are starting from, what you are currently worth, in order to plan successfully how to attain your financial goal.

What Is Your Net Worth Now?

Your net worth is a financial statement of what you own and the form in which it exists, together with what you owe and the nature of the obligations, and the surplus that exists between the two. Net worth is, therefore, a balance sheet showing how well off you are financially. An analysis of your personal financial balance statement discloses strength or weakness in the character of your financial program. Knowing where you stand now helps you to plan the steps necessary to guarantee your reaching the level of economic security you set for yourself.

Your net worth statement should look something like this:

Your Assets		*Your Liabilities*	
Cash on hand	$____	Accounts payable	$____
Cash surrender value of your insurance policies	____	Notes payable	____
Market value of stocks and bonds	____	Mortgages owed on real estate	____
Annuities and pensions	____	Debts and other money obligations	____
Market value of real estate owned	____	Claims against your estate	____
Mortgages owned	____	Unpaid taxes	____
Notes receivable	____		
Accounts receivable	____		
Cash value of business or other interests	____		
Cash value of furniture, automobile and other salable assets			
Total Assets	$____	Total Liabilities	$____

NET WORTH (excess of assets over liabilities) $____

Regular checks of your net worth statement every five years are a good safeguard against income deficiency. It is important that you be in good financial health as well as physical health to protect your interests today, and to assure yourself a comfortable retirement later on.

Obviously, these regular checkups must be frank and dispassionate. If you still hold 100 shares of a "dream" stock for which you paid $25 a share but which has now become a nightmare at $5, you are doing yourself a disservice if you still add this item in at $2,500, instead of $500. True, it may come back. Also, it may not. In any event, to be of any help, the net worth statement should not only give you a picture of what you own, but how these funds are invested and the annual year-to-year review should also give you an idea of whether you are moving in the right direction.

To come up with, let us say, a net worth figure of $75,000 is not the complete answer. In the first place, how does it compare with the net worth of last year, five years ago? Secondly, a balance sheet showing a $75,000 net worth figure for a man of thirty-five is a positive statement only if that $75,000 is successfully invested in aggressive, substantial growth-type investments: real estate, growth stocks or growth mutual funds. A young man's $75,000 net worth made up primarily of bank deposits reflects a commendable ability to save, but nevertheless is not correctly oriented if it is to be depended upon for retirement income twenty to thirty years hence. At age fifty, assets should be distributed more cautiously—sound commons, perhaps some bonds or preferreds (if convertible into common shares, all the better).

Basis for Financial Planning

The next step for you to take in making a plan for financial self-security is to decide how much money you can reasonably afford to put into various classes of estate-building investments and savings. The figure decided upon, of course, should be revised from time to time as your surplus income increases and your family circumstances vary.

Another factor to consider is the necessity for the family to enjoy a reasonably comfortable standard of living while building for the future. It is not wise to overdo things by employing a penny-pinching policy or an "austerity" existence now in the prospect of avoiding income deficiency after retirement. There should be a certain degree of thrift to accumulate savings, making the most of income-producing capabilities, and at the same time putting the savings to work to produce additional net worth, without interfering with the current standard of living.

For maximum retirement-income security, income sources should be diversified. Fixed income from Social Security benefits, employment pension plans, annuities and cash in the bank decrease in purchasing power as the value of the dollar shrinks in times of inflation. Persons are wise indeed who, during their greatest earning periods, buy future financial security by investing their money in a carefully planned, diversified portfolio.

As noted above, the emphasis in such investing should shift with the age of the retirement planner. During the years he is building capital, his main effort should be in that direction—literally, building capital through appreciation in the value of his investments. This is best done with the type of securities which over the years have proven an ability to gain in value because of the corporation's ability to grow at a faster rate than, say, the annual growth of corporate profits, which have been at the annual rate of 7.2 percent since 1945.

Naturally, the search for growth implies risk, because picking a growth company is synonymous with attempting to peer into the future. Losses must be expected, although —it is hoped—they will, over the long run, be more than balanced by profits.

As retirement age approaches, the prudent investor planning for retirement will naturally reduce his risk. Losing $1,000 on an unsuccessful venture at age forty can mean very little, since there are years during which the loss can be recouped. But a heavy loss a year or so before retirement day is far more serious and should be avoided even if it means a gradual shifting of one's investment portfolio from growth stocks to more conservative issues with long-term dividend records.

Forecast Your Retirement Income and Outgo

Now that you have found out where you stand, your net worth, it's time to estimate your retirement living needs— and then see what retirement income you can expect, to cover these needs.

Expenses	Now	After Retirement
Rent	$	$
Food	$	$
Clothing	$	$
Amusement	$	$
Doctor, dentist and hospital bills	$	$
Automobile	$	$
Telephone	$	$
Electricity, fuel oil, etc.	$	$
House repair	$	$
Furniture	$	$
Working expenses	$	$
Personal items	$	$

INCOME PLANNING FOR RETIREMENT **59**

Life insurance	$_____	$_____
Other insurance	$_____	$_____
Income taxes	$_____	$_____
Other taxes	$_____	$_____
Other items		
Total Monthly Expenses	$_____	$_____

Income	Now	After Retirement
Annuities, pensions	$_____	$_____
Retirement job	$_____	$_____
Social Security (65)	$_____	$_____
Spouse's income	$_____	$_____
Interest on savings accounts or government bonds	$_____	$_____
Dividends on stock	$_____	$_____
Real estate, sales or rentals	$_____	$_____
Income from other job	$_____	$_____
Profit from own business		
Total Monthly Income	$_____	$_____

Trends in Retirement

Most retirement plans are based on the concept of offering the employee some degree of security in his old age, as a reward for satisfactory service over a specified period of years. Retirement and pension plans are also conceived as a method of purchasing the employee's seniority rights so that the older employee will turn over the rights and duties of his job to a younger man.

The theory is that, in order to attract and retain ambitious younger men, opportunities need to be provided for them to move forward in their careers. Also, there is a feeling strong in many companies that one of the consequences of physical aging, after sixty-five, is a slowing down of vigor. This slowdown, employers say, can reduce efficiency at both the management and the production levels.

The trend toward compulsory retirement has been continuing. Some corporations are even encouraging early retirement at age fifty-five or sixty. Unless they prepare for it, many employees will find their many years of retirement to be a burden.

Emergency "Cushion" Fund

For a feeling of financial security, it is wise to have a cushion fund in which cash is available quickly. The minimum cash reserve you should maintain in the fund during your workday years should be equal to about three times your monthly average family living budget, or at least $2,000. For individuals living in retirement, a cushion fund equal to about the cost of living for two years should provide peace of mind financially. In other words, a retired couple whose living expenses are $300 a month should have between $7,500 to $10,000 in their emergency fund.

The best place to keep this fund is in a separate savings account in a bank or in a Savings and Loan Corporation whose savings deposits are guaranteed by the U.S. government. Here it will draw interest and is available quickly as emergencies arise.

The best way to build up a cushion fund is to make regular weekly or monthly deposits. The deposits should be supplemented by financial windfalls and other income additions such as legacies, bonuses, and so on. When the fund becomes larger than is required, the surplus over and above the minimum needed for the cushion can be withdrawn to pay off the mortgage on a home, or to purchase annuities or other investments to build capital.

A Few Things You Should Know About Social Security

The Federal Old-Age, Survivors, and Disability Insurance provides four different kinds of Social Security payments:

1. *Monthly Retirement Benefits* for workers who retire at or after age sixty-two or sixty-five, and for their families.
2. *Monthly Survivors' Insurance* for families of workers who die.
3. *Disability Payments* if you are totally disabled for work.
4. *Medicare,* including Hospital Insurance (Plan A) and Medical Insurance (Plan B, which helps cover physicians' charges.)

The level of Social Security benefits is adjusted from time to time by Congress.

Since Social Security benefits are so important to retired workers and their families, explanation of the law and how to figure total benefits are covered in Chapter 17.

The Pension Reform Act

The Comprehensive Pension Reform Act of 1974—officially designated as the "Employee Retirement Income Security Act of 1974"—adopted a sweeping overhaul of pension and employee benefit rules. The new rules have affected virtually every pension and employee benefit plan.

Mandatory rules for plan participation were established. The Act requires that all pension and profit sharing plans provide for vesting, which assures an employee of some income at his retirement even if he leaves a particular job before sixty-five. It also set up an insurance company (Pension Benefit Guaranty Corporation) to pay benefits to participants if the company plan went broke.

There is a three-way option for vesting of participant's rights, and the minimum funding standards became much more stringent. Self-employed persons, such as proprietors and partners, who are covered under plans (H.R. 10 plans) are entitled to increase their income tax deduction for contributions made on their behalf. The maximum annual deduction for taxable years which started in 1973 are geared to 15 percent of the self-employed person's earned income subject to a maximum deduction of $7,500 for the year.

An employee who is not a participant in a qualified or government plan is permitted to make contributions to his own private plan. He may deduct his contributions annually for income tax purposes to the extent to the lesser of $1,500 or 15 percent of his compensation for the year.

War Veterans' Benefits

Public laws provide a free indemnity payment to survivors of men and women who die while in the Armed Forces.

Veterans of military service may qualify for benefits under laws administered by the United States Veterans Administration. The VA may approve compensation payments for disabilities incurred in or aggravated by active military service ranging from $38 monthly for a 10 percent disability to $707 monthly for a 100 percent disability. These rates apply to the service-connected disabled veteran. Additional payments may be approved for the service-connected loss of certain parts of the body, such as arms, legs, hands, and eyes. Veterans having disabilities rated by VA at 50 percent or more are entitled to additional compensation for their dependents.

The VA also administers a non-service-connected pension program for disabilities not related to military service. These payments may be authorized in varying amounts, depending on the income from all sources of the former serviceman, provided he meets the service and disability requirements of the VA.

Survivors of deceased veterans may qualify for death pension and burial benefits administered by the VA.

Federal Civil Service Retirement System

The Federal Government's Retirement System for its civilian employees provides benefits based on length of service and highest average salary earned during any three consecutive years of service (the "High-three" average salary). Employees of the executive, judicial and legislative branches of the United States Government and municipal government of the District of Columbia are covered, except those that come under special retirement plans.

Seven percent is deducted from Federal employees' salaries for retirement purposes. Additional retirement benefits can be purchased through voluntary contributions to the fund of up to 10 percent of aggregate basic salary. To receive a retirement annuity a Federal employee must have at least five years of civilian service. If he retired voluntarily as early as age fifty-five he must have at least thirty years of service to his credit. An employee's annuity is reduced slightly if he provides for a survivor annuitant, or if he has a period of service for which no retirement deductions were made. If an employee retires for disability, his annuity is not reduced for age. There are also special provisions for retirement at lower ages with less service for employees who are separated involuntarily through no fault of their own.

The Federal Civil Service Retirement annuity consists partly of employee salary deductions and partly of government contributions. The yearly basic annuity will be (a) 1.5 percent of the "High-three" average salary times five years of service, plus (b) 1.75 percent of the "High-three" salary times years of service over five and up to ten, plus (c) 2 percent of the "High-three" salary times years of service over ten. The total annuity a retired employee receives cannot exceed 80 percent of his "High-three" average salary, unless the amount above 80 percent was produced by crediting unused sick leave.

Variable Annuity Plans

There has been an increase in variable annuity plans in an attempt to protect pensions against inflation. The plans have two units: a fixed-dollar fund and an equity fund. The fixed-dollar investments are in annuities, United States Bonds, and so forth. The equity fund is invested in good stocks. The goal is to insure the employee a variable return which may keep up with inflation.

That portion of the pension fund paid from this fund to the retired employee will vary with the value of his share of the fund. If the stock values are high, he draws a larger pension; if they are low, he gets a smaller pension. The theory is that this combination of a dollar fund and an equity fund will protect against dollar fluctuations. In time of deflation, the dollar funds provide a pension which will buy more. In time of inflation, payments from the equity fund hopefully will make up for the loss of purchasing power on that part of the pension coming from the dollar fund.

What You Can Do with Life and Health Insurance

The basic reason for buying life insurance is to protect the family by assuring them of an income in case death should take away the head of the family. No effective retirement planning can be developed unless the pre-retirement days are protected against financial loss from death and disability.

Many a widow today is living in comfortable circumstances as a result of her husband's planned insurance program. But, in addition to affording this protection, life insurance also has a cash-savings value that can be used directly for retirement income.

By the time you are ready to retire, your children will probably be grown and earning their own incomes, or married and establishing families of their own. In these later years, the protection value of your life insurance policy is not so important as in the earlier period of your life when the family was young and dependent upon you. Under these conditions you can often convert at least part of your insurance into life income. The rate of monthly cash income, of course, depends upon the cash value of the policy.

In the case of married persons with dependents to be provided for after the death of the insured, a retirement income on a joint annuity basis can be purchased by the cash value of the policy. This would continue the annuity payments after the death of the first annuitant.

For those who continue to need life insurance protection, it is often desirable, due to curtailment of income, to have a policy paid up at retirement age. This means it would be maintained in effect at its current value, without the payment of additional premiums. This relieves the drain of insurance premiums on the individual's retirement income.

Insurance that is not fully paid up at the time of retirement can be converted into a paid-up policy and continued in effect, although providing a smaller insurance benefit. This policy can later be converted to provide retirement income, if desired. The amount of the monthly annuity payment will depend upon the age and sex of the beneficiary and the cash value of the insurance policy.

Two insurance policies that are particularly valuable in planning toward a retirement program are the limited payment policy and the endowment policy. A widely used plan that combines both family protection and retirement income is the policy called the "Retirement Income Policy," which now is owned by hundreds of thousands of family heads.

A limited-payment policy calls for premiums during a specified number of years after which the policy becomes fully paid up. An endowment policy pays a specified sum of money at the end of a specified number of years—like $10,000 in twenty years. If an endowment policy were taken out at the age of forty, the money under a twenty-year endowment would be available at the age of sixty.

Insurance policies in many instances have a substantial loan value. Insurance companies will lend you money based on the cash surrender value of your policy; the longer you have paid premiums, the larger the amount you can borrow. It is necessary to keep in mind that such loans involve interest payments and unless repaid, must be paid out of any policy proceeds in case of death.

Investigate your job or group insurance plan, and check the features of the plan as they refer to your entire insurance program and especially any features that refer to retirement. Group insurance is usually term insurance and has no loan or cash surrender value. But an increasing number of plans now provide for extension of some portion at least, into the post-sixty-five years.

A large share of workers today have group life insurance in an amount equal to their annual income, with some plans running as large as two or three times their annual income. Also, a number of plans now use permanent types of insurance rather than term insurance. It is important to check periodically what your group plan is and how it can be used in retirement planning.

A veteran of World War I, or World War II carrying National Service Life Insurance has the cheapest of all forms of life insurance and should hold firmly to it. Present members of the armed forces have an economical group insurance plan written jointly with a large number of life insurance companies under a special act of Congress.

In your over-all insurance planning program, be sure you have hospitalization, and sickness and accident policies, in addition to life insurance. If you already have these policies, examine them to find out how they relate to your needs at older ages or how they relate to Medicare coverage, which begins at age sixty-five. Because older persons are more frequently ill than young people, the chances are that sickness, accident and hospital insurance will be of increasing importance to you.

A residence policy will protect you against fire and theft in your home and, usually, any liability hazard of a homeowner. If you, while driving your car, should be involved in an accident causing injury or death to others, or damage to another's property, your entire life savings could be wiped out, unless you are protected by automobile liability insurance. All of these types of insurance are important as part of your planning for both current and retirement needs.

Your insurance policies should be coordinated into a definite planned program. Life insurance offers a combination of protection and investment and is a practical way to create an estate. A reputable and conscientious insurance agent will help you work out a plan in detail. You will be much better off dealing with one agent in whom you have confidence than in buying insurance policies at random.

One friend of mine, preparing to take the plunge into retirement, took the proceeds of a twenty-year endowment insurance policy and bought a farm in North Carolina. He had some money left over from the endowment and used it for modernizing the old farm home. After estimating retirement living costs as carefully as possible and measuring them against his reduced income in retirement, he changed the provisions of his remaining insurance policies. These policies were converted into paid-up insurance as of his age sixty-three, so that he would have no more premiums to pay. Two of the policies were converted into retirement income policies to begin payments to him when he reached sixty-five.

Annuities Provide Protection Against Running Out of Money

An annuity guarantees a specified income for life, after you reach a specified age or date. You can buy an annuity by agreeing to pay a sum of money in monthly or yearly installments or in a lump sum. For this the life insurance company or certain religious and charitable institutions will pay you a specified income, to begin on a specified date and to continue as long as you live. It assures you freedom from investment worries while conserving savings. It assures you that, in retirement, your income will not be wiped out. Payment checks come in every month for life.

Annuities differ from insurance in that they are designed to give you an income as long as you live, while insurance, in addition to savings features, protects your dependents when you die. At 1977 rates, if a man pays the annuity company $20,000 in a lump sum at the age of sixty-five, the company guarantees to pay him a regular monthly income of around $175 as long as he lives. A woman of sixty-five would get around $154 a month for life for an investment of $20,000, because women on the average live longer than men.

The price of an annuity depends upon your age, sex and the kind of annuity you buy. There are several different types. A straight life annuity pays an income for life, but all payments stop at death. Joint and survivor annuities provide an income for life for two or more persons as long as either lives.

It must be noted that most annuities are set up with fixed dollars. If payments to build up an annuity kitty start years ahead of the time for pay-back, you will be getting back a depreciated dollar. You would likely be setting up your income in terms of present-day dollars which may turn out to be 10 or more than 20 percent less when you retire.

During earning years other investments could keep up with the dollar. Then, at R-day you could step up to the counter with X thousands of dollars and buy the best annuity policy you get on a no-worry guaranteed income of so many dollars a month for the rest of your life.

You might also consider a personal variable annuity plan which would return monthly amounts that would tend to keep up with inflation.

Current (1977) annuity rates are much better than those guaranteed in policy settlement options. Therefore it is better to take the cash out of the policy and buy an annuity on a current basis. Most insurance companies give a 3 percent discount if the annuity is bought with funds from a policy and no commission is paid on the transaction.

What About Stocks as an Investment?

Approximately thirty-two million persons own stocks in American corporations. They buy stocks because they believe the stocks will increase in value and provide additional dollars through capital growth. They buy stocks because of the income received from dividends. Some people buy stocks to build up an estate. Others buy stocks as a hedge against inflation. Generally speaking, there is not much chance that the average man will get rich overnight in the stock market.

Don't speculate in stocks to build up your estate. To trade in stocks successfully, which means buying well and selling well, you have to be right twice running.

Thousands of persons who have tried speculation with pet theories, formulas and hunches have had their fortunes wiped out. Investing in good stocks for long-term capital growth can be profitable. But, even the stock market experts and the professionals have widely divergent views as to the value of selected stocks and turning points in the stock market.

From an income standpoint, some stocks have given a 6–7 percent return on your money; some 1.5 percent; some have never paid a dividend; some have never missed one. However, the average stock since 1926 has shown an annual average compounded annual return of 9 percent plus. This, of course, is a combination of income (approximately 3 percent per annum) and appreciation (approximately 6 percent per annum). The average annual dividend rate today is about 3.5 to 4.0 percent (1977).

There are risks and rewards in investments in stocks, and in bonds too. Before you start buying stocks for income or capital growth, decide how stocks fit into your over-all plan. Any money you put into stocks should be over and above your cash reserve fund. For most people, it is wise to invest in life insurance and a few other stable investments, like a home, before buying stocks.

Managing a securities investment program is a serious business calling for a full measure of experience, judgment and objectivity. Good common stocks of reliable, leading and well-managed American companies bought for holding and not for speculation are a good investment. Stay away from new, small or local enterprises and the speculative stocks of large companies. Diversify your stock holdings. If you invest in stocks or bonds, the safest way to do it is on the basis of experienced technical advice. Don't play your own hunches. Be sure to pick a reputable brokerage house to handle your transactions. If you have over

$50,000, employ a professional investment counselor to ᴊandle your investments on a fee basis.

Income-building Opportunities of Mutual Funds— and a Regular Investment Plan

The charted record of one mutual fund dealing in common stocks shows the startling growth of $10,000 invested in shares of this fund. Had all the distributions from the fund, both net profits and income, been reinvested when received in more shares of the mutual fund, the asset value would have a total of $31,019 after ten years.

Of course this is past history. And there is no guarantee that the next ten years will bring the same results. Shares of mutual funds fluctuate in value with the changing market prices of the various stocks or bonds owned by the fund. Dividend income varies according to the income earned from the securities owned by the mutual fund.

A mutual fund is an investment company through which you and thousands of others pool money to obtain the diversity and safety you could not have buying stocks alone. You buy shares that represent a proportionate interest in the many diversified securities held by the mutual fund. Investment experts operate the fund and, based on their intimate knowledge of securities, select the stocks and bonds to be bought. Your investment is therefore spread over many companies and industries. Your money, instead of being all in one basket, is diversified.

There are about five hundred mutual funds, with widely differing investment objectives. Investors select their fund with various factors in mind, such as the degree of risk that should be assumed, the relative importance of current and future income and/or capital growth and the appropriate road to be taken toward any of these objectives.

One way to find the right fund is to study the long-term

performance of the various funds in the light of their stated objectives, comparing the results of funds in the same category. The prospectus issued by each fund reveals its management and their record, so it is a simple matter to check their ability and reputation.

It must be noted that all stock market and mutual fund history is *past* history. In the case of the small, speculative mutual funds this warning is even more important. A $2 million fund which "struck it lucky" with three new companies a few years ago may never repeat that performance. Unless you are well-advised on the matter, it's often safest to stick with the older, larger, more diversified mutual funds which have over the years established a record of solid, conservative growth.

Mutual funds are essentially a long-time investment program. They often take time to show a profit. If you began a fund program which has become too difficult to maintain, don't merely drop it. Consult the fund about revising it.

Many funds also offer declining balance term life insurance and a monthly withdrawal plan when you need income.

Most mutual funds are sold by brokers or fund salesmen. Commission, or "load," runs as high as 8.5 percent, so you should expect some high-pressure selling. There are also "no load" funds, funds which have no salesmen and therefore charge no selling commissions. A fund charging a "load" will be listed in your newspaper: "$12.00 bid, $13.12 asked." The $1.12 difference per share represents the commission. A "no load" fund will be listed "$23.25 bid, $23.25 asked."

One can make no judgment about a fund's performance merely on the basis of whether or not it charges a sales commission. The chief difference is that one fund is *sold,* the other you must *buy* on your own initiative. If you don't approach the fund, nothing will happen. You can get the address of most funds from the Investment Company Institute, 1775 K Street, N.W., Washington, D.C. 20006. Many specialize in certain industries like electronics, chemicals, utilities, etc.

If you have surplus cash to spare, say under $2,000, you would probably be better off buying shares in a mutual fund rather than buying stock directly in a company. You can set up a system of investing your surplus savings automatically by making regular monthly purchases of shares out of your current earnings. For maximum protection, divide your purchase of shares between investment funds that are old and reliable, with a good record of paying dividends. A mutual fund or trust composed largely of common stocks would be best for compounding income and the possibility of capital growth. Your reliable broker will tell you which are the best buys.

Regular Investment Plan. Another good way to invest your money deserves your investigation. Brokerage firms which are members of the New York Stock Exchange can enable you to develop a plan for conveniently investing small, regular sums and reinvesting dividends automatically. When you invest at regular intervals, regardless of market prices, you have the advantage of dollar-cost-averaging. Your fixed payment acquires more shares when prices are low than when they are high, and you continue to acquire stocks whether they are high or low, avoiding the worry of the occasional investor who feels he must buy low and sell high.

If you have to discontinue your payments, there is no penalty. You simply keep the shares you have bought, or ask the broker to sell them for you.

Real Estate Is a Good Field for Investment

Your first and most important investment in real estate is to buy and own your own home outright. Investment authorities say that the average family is justified in paying up to two times or at the most three times its annual income as the purchase price of a home. Many home buyers come to grief by taking on more than they can afford to carry financially when buying a home. You should be able to make a cash down payment of at least 25 percent of the total cost of the home. So start your home-buying program as early in life as possible. Pay off the mortgage as soon as you can. When the mortgage is paid off, you can use your surplus cash for other investments.

If you're getting near retirement age and want to buy a home for your take-it-easy years, you had better have an assured cash income, or some large insurance policies for mortgage security. It is considerably harder for a person nearing sixty-five to borrow on a mortgage than it is for a family head in his forties. Prospective home buyers in the aging group will have to make bigger down payments than are required of younger borrowers. Mortgage lenders generally want the payment schedules worked out so that the mortgage will be largely paid off by the time the borrower reaches the age of seventy.

The best time to buy real estate for investment purposes is when real estate buying activity is low. Income-producing properties bought at such times can usually be sold later at substantial profit. The real estate market operates in a cycle of prosperity and recession generally following the lines of the business cycle. Real estate cycles, however, usually have longer intervals between the top and the bottom of cycle swings.

Most profits in real estate are made by those who buy and sell income-producing properties in growing sections of prosperous cities, towns and communities. It takes keen observation to spot localities that are ripe for increased real estate values—to know what and when to buy and sell. The values of real estate depend on the use made of it and the nature of useful improvements placed on it. Question the common practice of buying a lot in Florida or Arizona twenty-five years ahead for your retirement home. In the first place, in that period of time many things can happen. Second, the same amount of money put into good stocks might well do better and not tie you down as to where to retire.

The greatest values for investment purposes are not in lots for residential dwellings but in property that develops into income-producing units such as business districts, sites for gasoline stations, and so forth. However, in many cities alert operators buy large old homes, and remodel and modernize them into small apartment units. These properties are sold at advanced prices, or kept and rented for income.

Another way people make money in real estate is to buy a lot and erect a new home on it, furnish the home, live in it for a time and then sell it completely finished. This method is popular in Florida and California. Houses of this character may also be rented furnished or unfurnished for income. Building two-, three- or more family dwelling units on the same lot, living in one unit and collecting rentals from tenants for the other units is also a popular way of securing retirement income from real estate. Still another popular type of real estate investment is a building with stores occupying the ground floor and with offices or living units above.

Don't attempt to act as your own broker when buying or selling real estate. The expert, practical advice of a reliable and competent realtor should be sought by those not familiar with local real estate development conditions. A good realtor knows the values and potentialities of real estate in the locality which he serves. If you do not know a competent realtor, ask your banker or the local real estate board to recommend the names of accredited realtors with reputations for honest and fair dealings.

Income from Personal Savings

A savings bank is a safe place to keep money. Your account is protected up to $40,000 by the Federal Deposit Insurance Corporation. Money deposited in a savings bank earns 5.25 percent interest. An interest account at compound interest is a growing investment. However, it takes a large principal to provide enough income from interest alone to provide for an adequate standard of living. For $100 a month, you would need a principal of $25,000 earning 5 percent. Or 7.5 percent bonds could pay you a still greater, safe return.

A good way to accumulate savings is to take at least one-tenth of what you earn each pay day and deposit it in your savings account. Soon you will see your wealth growing like a tree. A safe return, even though a small one, is more desirable than a risky one for retirement purposes.

United States Savings Bonds

This is another safe place for your savings. The United States Government would have to become bankrupt for you to lose your principal. Series E Bonds which mature in five years and ten months pay 6 percent interest if held until maturity. If you buy a Series E Bond for $75, you get $100 for it at maturity. No interest checks are paid on E Bonds so long as they are held by their owners. If the bonds are held until maturity, interest is paid in a lump sum. If they are cashed in before maturity, proportionate interest is paid. E Bonds are ideal for laying away money you don't want to spend but which can be instantly available if needed. You pay no income tax until such time as you can cash them. If that time doesn't come until you've retired, your lower tax bracket represents an important plus for your E Bond funds. United States Saving Bonds can be had in denominations of $25, $50, $70, $100, $200, $500, $1,000.

Investigate Before You Invest

Here is some counsel that experienced investors give: Don't speculate with money you need for insurance, home payments or emergencies. Keep that separate. There is a certain amount of risk in managing money. Even if you bury money in your own back yard, you're still taking a risk—the risk that your money won't buy as much if prices rise and inflation sets in. When investing your money stay away from tips of well-meaning friends. Get advice from an unbiased specialist—a reliable banker or investment counsel on how to protect your capital and at the same time put it to work to earn a return on investments.

Supplemental Security Income

Supplemental Security Income (SSI), which replaced State-operated programs for the needy aged, blind, and disabled in January 1974, is a federally administered program for financially needy people who are at least 65 years of age, or needy people of any age who are blind or disabled. Although SSI is administered by the Social Security Administration, it is not Social Security and is not financed from Social Security trust funds. It is possible for a person to be eligible for payments under both programs.

Since SSI is based on financial need, only persons with little or no income and limited assets—such as stocks, bonds and jewelry—can be eligible. An individual is permitted to have assets of up to $1,500, while a couple may have $2,250 and still be eligible for benefits. A home, personal effects and household goods do not count toward this amount.

People may have other income of $20 per month and still receive full benefits. Income above this amount—such as from Social Security or Veterans Compensation—reduces the amount of the SSI payment. Those who work while getting SSI may earn up to $65 a month with no reduction in benefits. Above this amount, the SSI payment is reduced $1 for every $2 earned.

Eligibility based on blindness or disability requires a medical determination. Blindness is defined as central visual acuity of 20/200 or less in the better eye with the use of a corrective lens, or visual field restriction of 20 degrees or less. To be considered disabled, a person must be unable to engage in substantial gainful activity because of a physical or mental impairment which has lasted, or is expected to last, for at least 12 months or is expected to result in death.

A total of 4.3 million persons received SSI payments in September 1976, as follows:

Category	Number (Millions)
Aged	2.2
Blind and disabled	2.1

Most states supplement the Federal SSI payment to provide added income to recipients. Total Federal and State SSI payments amounted to $6 billion in fiscal 1976.

Winding Up Business Interests

Disposing of personally held business interests at a fair value can be a critical factor when the time to retire comes. That is why persons who own controlling interest or a large capital investment in business organizations should plan in advance how to dispose of their holdings. The owner of a retail establishment, wholesale business or small factory, for example, may face worry and financial loss if he tries to dispose of his business under unfavorable conditions. Finding a suitable buyer can be a serious problem. Other factors that should be considered are taxes, proper timing, the transfer of franchise deals with suppliers and customers from present owner to new owner, patent ownership and arrangements, real estate and leases and other conditions peculiar to the type and size of the business.

Winding up a business is no easy matter. Many a man's life work has been sold at fifty cents on the dollar because little or no planning had been given to this problem. If you are a sole proprietor you should ask yourself this question: "What plans have I to dispose of my business at a fair value when I reach the time to retire?"

Stretching Retirement Income to Cover Both Husband and Wife

When planning retirement income, special consideration should be given to the various sources of payment. This is particularly true in cases where the income is planned to cover both the husband and the wife.

Suppose retirement income sources are from Social Security benefits, employment pension plan, life insurance converted to regular annuity, and income derived from rents, investments, or other interests. The monthly income statement might look like the following for a worker retiring at age sixty-five who had median earnings all his life.

Social Security (husband's benefit)	$395
Company pension (husband for life)	120
Annuity (husband for life)	100
Investment and other income	100
	$715

But if the wife becomes widowed at age sixty-five some of the sources might cease, or be reduced. The full amount of the husband's pension and annuity may no longer be payable. The widow's income statement could now read:

Social Security (widow's benefit)	$395
Company pension (widow's share)	60
Annuity	none
Investments and other income	100
	$555

Most retired couples need to plan a financial program that provides adequate retirement income not only while both are living but also for the surviving spouse. Fortunately for the wife in this case, the Pension Reform Act of 1974 requires that a Joint and Survivor Annuity be provided for employees. The surviving spouse's annuity must be at least 50 percent of the amount the couple was receiving. (However, the participant may elect not to take the J and S Annuity if he files such a request.) Payments can be stretched not to just one person for life but to two persons as long as either of them shall live. This is called the joint-and-survivor method of payment. Not every pension plan or annuity has this method of payment. You should check your pension plan or annuity policy and see whether you could take advantage of this method of payment.

The exact amount of income received under the joint-and-survivor provision depends largely upon a combination of the ages of the husband and wife. It would be different in cases where the husband and wife are both sixty-five, the husband sixty-five and the wife fifty-five, or some other age combination. In the case where the husband and wife are both age sixty-five, instead of the husband alone receiving $120 a month as long as he lives from his company pension plan, it might be possible to arrange that $90 a month be paid as long as either one lives. In the case of the annuity, it might be possible to receive $75 a month as long as either one lives, instead of $100 a month during the life of the husband.

Based on the above assumptions, while both the husband and wife are alive, their monthly retirement income statement might show the following:

Social Security (husband and wife)*	$395
Company pension (husband and wife)	90
Annuity (husband and wife)	75
Investment and other income	100
	$660

*For wife without benefits of her own

After the death of the husband, the wife's retirement monthly income would now remain the same as before his death.

Under the revised income plan the husband and wife are assured an adequate retirement income while both are alive and yet the widow is protected against a substantial loss of income at the death of her husband.

Importance of Making a Will

After having made provision for security by building up the net worth of your estate, the next most important duty in your financial program is provision for the disposition of these assets in the case of your death. Only about 50 percent of husbands who die before their wives bother to make a will. This is a careless way of protecting an estate. It can be very costly for the wife and dependents.

Many people fail to make a will because they mistakenly believe that, in the absence of a will, the property will automatically go to the wife or to the children as they would wish it to go. This is not necessarily so. If there is no will providing for the disposition of an estate, then upon the owner's death it will be divided among heirs according to the laws of descent of the state. In some states, the wife would get only one-third of the estate, the remaining two-thirds being divided among all the children on an equal basis. If property is located in two or more states and there is no will, real estate is usually disposed of according to the laws of descent of the state in which it is located.

Under these circumstances, serious problems sometimes arise and hard feelings develop among the heirs. The home where the wife lives might conceivably have to be sold to settle the estate. Property you originally intended for your wife or some particular member of the family could easily get dissipated in court actions and lawyers' fees while heirs fight a family feud to determine their rights.

Mortgage insurance is important if you want to leave the full value of your home to your heirs. However, it usually expires without value when the house is sold. Some insurance companies now offer mortgage insurance plans that will provide security for several homes.

So many people spend a lifetime of effort building an estate, only to have it torn apart by the tax collectors who want cash, and plenty of it. Most estates do not have enough cash, so in come the auctioneers and the bargain hunters, while the family watches in dismay as their inheritance is chopped to bits.

These taxes must be paid, so smart people plan ahead to avoid as much depletion of their estates as they can. Here's where life insurance can come to the fore to allow you to pay these necessary amounts at a discount, by a carefully worked-out plan to take care of estate taxes.

See a competent lawyer for expert advice before making a will. Do this while you are in good health and have plenty of time to study the will. This reduces the risk of your will being contested and assures disposition of your assets according to your wishes. If you have a large estate you may want to make certain dispositions of the estate while you are living to avoid high estate and inheritance taxes that otherwise would drain off a substantial part of your assets.

It is also important to keep up-to-date records of the status and location of important papers relating to personal property. Such information might include:

RECORD OF VALUABLES

Life Insurance Policies

Company	Policy No.	Amount	Agent	Address

Health Insurance Policies

Company	Policy No.	Agent	Address

Automobile Insurance

Company	Policy No.	Agent	Address

Property Insurance
(If house and household goods separate, list each)

Company	Policy No.	Agent	Address

Real Estate Owned

		DEED		MORTGAGE	
Kind	Location	Names		Location	Holder

Cemetery and Location

Deed Location

Bank Accounts (type)
        Bank Name/Address   Location of Book

_____   _____
_____   _____
_____   _____

Stocks and Bonds

			Date	
Company	Description	Cost	Purchased	Listed Owner
_____	_____	___	_____	_____
_____	_____	___	_____	_____

Savings Bonds

		Date	
Maturity Value	Serial No.	Purchased	Listed Owner
_____	_____	_____	_____
_____	_____	_____	_____

Where are these located:

Birth Certificate _____
Marriage Certificate _____
Will _____
Social Security Card _____
Safe Deposit Box _____
Key to Box _____
Federal Tax Records _____
State Tax _____
Veteran's Papers _____
School Records _____
Car Title _____

List previous employment under Social Security:

Firm name: _____from _____ to _____
Firm name: _____from _____ to _____
Firm name: _____from _____ to _____
Firm name: _____from _____ to _____

Notes Payable, Other Debts:

Amount	Creditor	How and when payable
_____	_____	_____
_____	_____	_____

Notes and Loans Receivable:
  Amount   *Debtor*   *How and when payable*

  ———————————— ———————————— ————————————————

  ———————————— ———————————— ————————————————

Other Important Information:

——

——

Planning Your Personal Estate

In today's world more and more wives are working, during and after their role of mother and homemaker. Along with their career lives, they should join their husbands and play a role in planning their mutual estates.

Life-expectancy records show that women live longer than men. Most family fortunes eventually are inherited by women. Wives should therefore be equipped to handle money and property lest they mismanage or dissipate the estates left to them by their husbands.

Husbands can help their wives to learn by taking them into partnership on all financial matters which have a bearing on the future of the family. Many wives have no idea, until after the husband has died, of the extent and nature of the family's financial resources. They are often unprepared to handle many critical situations that arise when the family estate falls into their hands.

One way for wives to secure training in the investment and management of family finances is to take up a selective reading or study course. They can also enroll in adult education courses on estate planning and management. A number of wives and husbands are using part of their retirement leisure to do this very thing.

Still another plan is for the husband to make a gift of money or property to the wife while he is alive. The husband guides the wife in her investments and management of the fund or property. This gives her the practical experience she will need in administering the entire estate when the husband is not there as an active protector-provider. The same idea can be followed in training children to take over estate management.

Recently, many more women have proved their ability to handle business and financial matters by their successful records of achievement in many occupations in the office, factory, government and professions previously reserved for men. Women are fully capable of making a success of estate management if they are properly trained for it.

To make things easy for a wife to carry on the original estate planning, keep detailed records or memoranda of the entire contents of your estate among your personal papers. Go over the entire estate program periodically with your spouse, or the executor of your estate. Let them know where all your personal papers can be easily and quickly found. This may save time, trouble and expensive legal proceedings.

If your wife has not been interested in your investments then she should at least have the name of the broker or financial adviser you trust. Too many women, suddenly widowed, have fallen prey to dishonest brokers and to swindlers who read the obituary columns solely to seek out the names of new widows.

The old saying has it that the time to teach a woman to be a financially protected widow is when she is still a wife.

You can dispose of your personal estate in these ways:

1. Through your will you can make outright disposition of your assets.

2. You can make outright gifts of parcels of your estate during your lifetime.
3. You can create a "living trust" by transferring your estate or part of it to a trustee. The income from the estate is paid to you during your lifetime or to a specified person or persons for life, other persons to get the principal later. Some retired persons have established a living trust so that they can live a free life and not be bothered by the responsibilities of managing property and investments, yet be assured that they will have income protection against old age.
4. You can protect your spouse or other dependents by assuring them an income for life by use of a "testamentary trust." This is done through a trust established by your will. The reason for creating a testamentary trust instead of giving the assets outright is to protect the beneficiary against his or her inexperience or folly in the management of the estate you created, and for substantial tax benefits.

The disposition of an estate if you are wealthy is by no means a simple matter. Most states have their own estate or inheritance taxes. In many instances a large part of an estate has to be disposed of to pay these taxes.

The Tax Reform Act of 1976 makes the most extensive changes in our estate and gift tax structure, certainly within the past thirty years and, perhaps, going back as far as 1916, when estate and gift taxes appeared on the scene. The Act contains completely new concepts, new approaches and layer upon layer of added complexities to challenge the estate planner.

Most of the changes increase the amount of property you can give away or leave to your heirs without incurring estate or gift taxes. The new law generally applies to estates of decedents dying after 1976.

The estate and gift tax rates are now integrated into a single schedule that applies to all transfers, whether made by will or lifetime gift.

Married persons can now leave their spouses up to $250,000 or one-half the value of their adjusted gross estates, whichever is larger, without incurring any estate tax. In 1977, for example, an individual with an estate worth $370,000 could leave the entire amount to his or her spouse and pay no tax at all. In 1981, the amount would be $425,000. Also new is an unlimited marital deduction for the first $100,000 of gifts from one spouse to another.

Retirement Planning Schedule

Your retirement can mark the beginning of a rich new life free from the financial cares, the rigid time demands, the confining influences of the workday world—a life in which you can devote your talents and abilities to the pursuits that interest and excite you. As so many others have done, you can make your retirement years the happiest, most productive years of your life.

To make them so, however, you must plan ahead. The following suggestions are meant to guide you in organizing your planning schedule for a carefree, happy retirement.

Thirty-five to Forty-five: This is an ideal age to make plans to meet your financial requirements in retirement, to adopt a program of living that will equip you spiritually, mentally and physically for a purposeful life during your harvest years.

The attitudes, hobbies, talents and skills you develop during your middle years, your savings program, the diet you follow, the care you give your health, your philosophy of life—all will greatly determine your well-being after retirement. Retirement should not be a complete break with the past. It should be merely an extension of your plan for better living, conceived and developed during your pre-retirement years. If you make life worth living before retirement, you won't have difficult adjustments to make to enjoy retirement.

Keep a checking account balance equal to two months' income, reinforced by an emergency cushion fund sufficient to cover three months' living expenses. Be sure you have adequate life, health and hospital insurance. When you have attained these goals, the next step is to buy your own home.

Now, if you still have a cash surplus, consider investing it in E bonds, since all the time it is lying there acting as a cushion it is earning 6 percent and not costing you anything in taxes. After you have built a cushion in E bonds which makes you comfortable, the surplus funds should—in the age bracket thirty-five to forty-five—be directed at capital building via growth common stocks.

Before deciding where to invest your surplus, determine first what your long-term debt situation is. A younger man with a surplus need not rush to pay off his mortgage if his money can earn more than the rate he's paying on his mortgage. This would certainly be so if he had assumed an old 5.5 to 6 percent mortgage. Should you, on the other hand, be in a liquid cash position, with only modest long-term debt obligations, you can afford to invest a larger share of your surplus savings in more speculative investments. Next, decide the objective of your investing. Do you want to get the largest possible income from your capital? Do you want to increase the size of your capital? Do you want to protect your capital at a higher income than you would get from fixed assets? After you have decided your objective, talk to your banker or reputable broker, and ask for advice.

One suggested method for investing your surplus is to put one-third into buying bonds, one-third into buying high-grade common stocks or mutual funds and the other one-third into "growth" company stock. Be sure to diversify your holdings.

Now also is the time to devote some of your spare time to developing new interests. Perhaps you would enjoy being a weekend painter like Winston Churchill. You might choose to devote your spare time to public service as Bernard M. Baruch did as a young man. Or you might prefer to take up gardening, photography, amateur radio, and so forth. Time invested in these creative activities will be rich assets when you retire.

Observe the rules for healthful living. Overeating and poor diet can result in shortening your life. Rest and relax; avoid emotional tensions. Begin to formulate a positive philosophy of life. Regular attendance at church or synagogue, spiritual reading and a genuine interest in life will enrich your outlook and fortify you for retirement.

If you plan to change jobs to increase your income, now is probably your best time. After forty-five, it is often difficult to make new employment connections, especially with the larger organizations.

As to vacations, try going to a different place each year. Use your vacation time as an opportunity for a personal investigation of retirement locations that might appeal to you and your spouse.

At Age Fifty-five. You are probably at or near the peak of your business or professional responsibilities and earning power, with possible retirement ten years away or less. With your children grown and educated and on their own, you face decreased family responsibilities. Consider starting an individual tax saving retirement account. See subsequent explanation of "Individual Retirement Plans."

If you are still five, ten or more years from retirement, your investing should be directed toward building capital via growth stocks.

If you already hold growth-type securities, you should continue to hold them right up to retirement—planning, however, to take any losses on them in time to reduce your income taxes in your last years of employment. Profits on low-yield growth stocks are ideally taken *after* you retire, when your tax bracket will normally be lower. Proceeds from either type of sale should go into income securities.

Begin to clean up your fixed, long-term debts and get your financial structure into a more liquid position. While still maintaining a respectable checking account and cushion fund, you can afford to take a little more risk in investing. Continue to save, but don't begrudge yourself and family the right to some of the fruits of life that can be enjoyed now.

Confine yourself to easy-to-digest foods. Give up eating heavy meals and watch for overweight. Cut down on sweets, drink more milk and fewer alcoholic beverages. Build up health reserves against chronic illness.

Develop the kind of hobbies that appeal to you now and which potentially could be your bread and butter in retirement. Collect all the information and assistance you can to develop the hobbies of your choice.

Use vacation time to make a more serious survey of the states to which you would like to retire. Look over possible locations with an eye to low-cost living, climate and health advantages, facilities for leisure-time activities, opportunities to establish a part-time activities, opportunities to establish a part-time business or farm. You might use a vacation or two to get practical experience in your retirement avocation.

At Age Sixty. You may have five more years in which to build up your financial resources. Make an analysis of your financial net worth. Review your entire estate program in the light of retirement income needs and income sources as you see them.

You can still do something about increasing your retirement income, if you have not done so already. But you will have to take greater risks. First, clean up mortgage and other long-term debts and don't contract for any additional ones. Work toward financial solvency. Use about half of

your surplus cash in growth stocks, always remembering
you have little time to recoup any losses. A good mutual
fund is an alternate way of spreading the risk. Don't put all
your money in this type of investment or all in just one
stock.

Be sure you carry enough accident, health and hospital
insurance. The need for these increases as you get older.
Also investigate your coverage of fire, automobile and per-
sonal-liability insurance. Your retirement estate could easily shrink if you are not protected against possible property
loss and court damage awards.

If you plan to retire early it's wise to check with your
company's personnel officer or union welfare official to see
if your on-the-job health insurance can be converted to an
individual policy without having to go through a physical
examination. Some company health benefits even continue
after you reach the age of sixty-five, as a supplement for
Medicare.

You should know by now the kind of part-time employment, small business or farming activity you plan to follow
after retirement. Become more active in your hobby and
other interests. Now is the time to bring them into full
bloom.

Consider adult educational courses offered in your community. One or two evenings a week devoted to a course
in arts, crafts, trade or business training, agriculture, retirement preparation, and so on, will reward you well for the
time spent. You will discover that you can learn how to do
new things and enjoy doing them.

Look upon your vacations as a period of semi-retirement.
Spend the time getting personally acquainted with a few
families who have settled permanently in the area where
you plan to retire. You will then not be a total stranger in
the community when you take up retirement residence.
Investigate real estate possibilities with an eye to buying a

lot, and building, buying or renting a house.

At Age Sixty-two or Sixty-five and Over. Welcome retirement as the beginning of a new career. Accept retirement and make the most of it.

Get a complete geriatric checkup and follow your doctor's advice on living in the late years. If you are only a year or two from retirement and own no securities but realize that you should, for protection against inflation, you might as well now begin accumulating income stocks, since a switch from growth to income securities in the short period of a year or two may prove costly.

If you have already retired, you should consider selling any low-yield securities (those yielding less than 5 percent, figured on *current* market price—*not* your original cost) and putting the proceeds into higher yield issues, including both common shares and bonds. The older you are the more high-income bonds may be included in your portfolio since you need relatively less protection against inflation.

E bonds should be redeemed and the proceeds reinvested, or switched into H bonds for current income. Here again your tax position should be the determinant.

Consider selling some of your stock and properties and converting some of your insurance into an annuity.

Increase your emergency cushion fund to the amount needed to cover your cost of living for at least two years.

Make application for Social Security and Medicare. As payments are not automatic, you must apply for your retirement benefits.

Put your hobby and leisure-time program into effect within a reasonable time. Too long a period of idleness invites despondency and robs you of the contentment and satisfaction you should enjoy in retirement.

Work out a budget of expenditures that will keep you within your retirement income. Stay out of debt. Avoid time-payment or installment buying. Buy only needed items in economical quantities during sales as often as possible.

Preferential Tax Advantages for Older People

The level of living achieved by retired persons depends not only on their money but also on other provisions that affect their total income situation. Preferential treatment for tax purposes results in additional money for the purchase of more goods and services.

Federal income tax provisions recognize the income problems of the aged in a variety of ways. Persons sixty-five and over are allowed double personal exemptions amounting to $1,500. This exemption, together with the minimum standard deduction, means that no federal tax need be paid by a retired couple, both sixty-five and over, with an income as high as $5,100. Social Security payments, railroad retirement benefits, veterans' pensions and life insurance proceeds are excluded from gross income for tax purposes. A "credit for the elderly" makes allowance for such sources as annuities, interest, dividends and rents.

The new law eliminates the work experience requirement and increases the maximum base for the 15 percent credit to $2,500 for a single person and to $3,750 for a married couple. The maximum amount of the credit base is reduced by (1) one-half of adjusted gross income in excess of $7,500 for a single person and $10,000 for a married couple filing jointly, and (2) exempt Social Security and exempt retirement income. For taxpayers under 65 receiving a public retirement system pension, the new rules are comparable to the old.

Costs for drugs, medical expenses and health insurance premiums are deductible. In some instances, the aged receive preferential tax treatment on certain state and local taxes. Generally, the greatest tax burdens on the retired are sales taxes on food and other essentials which form a large part of their expenditures.

Taxpayers over 65 can now sell a home worth $35,000 without incurring any capital gains tax. The old limit was $20,000. If a home sells for more than $35,000, a portion of any gain realized will still escape tax.

Much More to Be Done

Watch the newspapers for items on bills and public hearings on possible legislation to reduce taxes for older persons, at state and local levels. Attend hearings, write to state representatives or city councilmen, voice your support of such legislation. Respond to preferential benefits for the aged with an affirmative ballot when the question comes up for voting.

The fact that many older persons, including some with very low incomes, are burdened with heavy real estate and property taxes on large outmoded houses in which they live has given rise to many new regulations for special real estate tax relief for retired homeowners.

Retired individuals planning to move their residence to another community should check into the state and local tax situation before moving from their present home location.

Recommendations of the White House Conference on Aging

The Section on Income Maintenance of a White House Conference on Aging reported the following policy statement and recommendations:

The income security of older people is an important objective of American society.

The security of older people, like the security of all Americans, depends upon a strong, sound and secure economy capable of providing a high level of goods and services. The first principle of a constructive approach to the income maintenance needs of the aged, therefore, is that the measures taken to promote old-age security be in harmony with broad economic objectives.

The second principle of a constructive approach to the needs of the aged is that there should be the opportunity for productive employment for those who are able and want to work. Employment is frequently more satisfactory for the individual than retirement on a pension, and such employment contributes to the economy and reduces the cost of pensions. We urge a re-examination of policies of compulsory retirement and also urge that industry and Government plan for both full-time and part-time use of an increasing number of older persons.

Although there is agreement that, to the extent possible, the aged should have a chance to work, it is recognized that on the most optimistic assumptions the number of nonearners among the aged will not only remain very large . . . but will grow as the number of aged grows. Employment is largely out of the question for the very old, the severely disabled, and for many of the older women who spent their younger years as homemakers. Increasing opportunities for employment of the aged cannot, therefore, be a substitute for income maintenance for those who retire.

In providing income for the retired aged we believe that the pluralistic approach we have established in this country, with the individual saving on his own, the individual and his employer joining in private pension arrangements, and the individual and his Government joining in social insurance and assistance programs is the best approach.

We believe that the establishment and development of private pensions should be encouraged and that individuals should be encouraged to save on their own.

Our goal should be, insofar as possible, to prevent dependency. It is recognized, however, that there will continue to be persons whose needs are not met in any other way and will continue to need help through the public assistance program.

This program, therefore, should be improved with the view of assuring all aged persons a reasonable minimum level of living under conditions which preserve their dignity and self-respect.

Individual Retirement Plans

If you are not covered by a qualified retirement plan you could consider one of several individual retirement accounts.

The IRA (Individual Retirement Account) gives you a tax break for the money you put into it. Those who qualify can put in as much as 15 percent of their salary, up to a maximum of $1,500 a year.

The money set aside is invested in a government-approved retirement plan. The interest earned while the money is left on deposit is not taxable until withdrawn by you.

Working couples who qualify can open up separate accounts. If neither spouse is covered by a qualified retirement plan, each can open a separate IRA. In this way they can together set aside up to $3,000 each year with the same tax advantages.

Individuals can transfer the benefits of their employer's plan to their own individual Retirement Account. These dollars then become tax sheltered in an IRA account until retirement.

The retirement fund, which includes your contributions plus earned interest, can be withdrawn in a lump sum on retirement. Or, the fund can be paid out periodically. Either way, you will probably be in a lower tax bracket than you are now, so tax savings can be considerable.

The Federal law specifies that withdrawals, without penalty, can begin as early as the age of 59½, but not later than age 70½.

In similar vein the Keogh plan also allows tax grace periods for self-employed people. Under this plan the ceiling on both contributions to the plan and deductions are $7,500 annually or 15 percent of earned income, whichever is less.

In general "earned income" is that derived from personal services. Where both capital and services contribute importantly to earnings, the entire net profit will be treated as earned income.

For both of these plans the place to go for details is your bank.

Bibliography

The Intelligent Investor by Benjamin Graham (Harper, N.Y.)

Investing for Your Future by Sam Shulsky (Simon & Schuster, N.Y.)

Private Pensions and Individual Saving by George Katon (University of Michigan Social Research, Ann Arbor, Mich.)

Employment Income and Retirement Problems of the Aged by Juanita Kreps (Duke University Press, Durham, N.C.)

How to Start a Profitable Retirement Business by Arthur Liebers (Pilot Books, N.Y.)

Income in Retirement by Carter Osterbind (Institute of Gerontology, University of Florida Press, Gainesville, Fla.)

Retirement Dollars for the Self-Employed (Dun and Bradstreet, N.Y.)

Investors Information Kit—Includes booklets entitled "Understanding Financial Statements," "Growth Leaders on the Big Board," "Glossary of the Language of Investing," "Understanding Bonds and Preferred Stocks," "Understanding Convertible Securities." Publication Section, N.Y. Stock Exchange, 11 Wall Street, New York N.Y. 10005 Kit of above booklets, $2.00.

U.S. GOVERNMENT PUBLICATIONS

Finance—National Economy accounting, insurance, securities. Send for free bibliography and price list of books and pamphlets on these subjects to Superintendent of Documents, Government Printing Office, Washington, D.C. 20402.

5

Housing for the Retired

To move or not to move. This is the question more and more people face as their retirement days become imminent. It's not an easy decision to make because so many factors are involved. It certainly should not be a hasty one, because contentment in the later years has very much to do with how well the decision is made. One of the most important decisions you will ever make may well be your choice of a new home and place to live after retirement. It is worth every bit of advance thought and study you can give the subject.

The majority of people should think twice before considering the glowing stories of life in the sun countries. They usually have deep roots in their present soil. If they're lucky, their married children live nearby. Here too are their friends and relatives. Here they have their contacts with former business associates. Here are the local stores, churches, libraries and other familiar landmarks that have long given meaning to their lives.

On the other hand, many of these familiar props to one's life may have disappeared and the seeking of a new location may offer the answer to better recreation, more social engagement, more adequate community facilities. For those considering the move to a new locale, the choices are many. There has been a gathering momentum of activity in the development of all types of housing for the elderly in recent years.

Moving to a different area may bring a freshness into the lives of many retired people. In many regions of the country there are colonies of older folks, all with the same aspirations and desires. Here retired persons find substitutes for old neighborhoods, for old friends who have moved away or passed away, for former family relationships.

In community-sponsored recreation and handicraft centers, in social clubs and church groups, they meet and make new friends, and avoid loneliness. Many times these new companionships made in later life, at new retirement locations, are more satisfying than earlier friendships formed with people associated with regular workday life. With fast transportation by airplane, modern streamlined trains, and with the telephone always handy, the old hometown does not seem as distant as it did originally. A vacation visit from or to family and friends is something to be appreciated on all sides. Somehow the new location substitutes values and virtues that more than replace those of the old neighborhood. Life again offers a challenge full of new and interesting things to accomplish.

You Have Many Choices

Before trying to decide what type of accommodation would satisfy you most, you should first be thinking through the question of *where to live*. Find out in what region you and your spouse might find most contentment. You should be considering such matters as whether to:

Remain in your present hometown
After you have weighed its virtues for retirement living.
Move out on the fringe of town
Where the homes may fit your pocketbook better.
Where you may have a garden.
Move to a nearby town
Where it is quieter.
Where taxes are lower.
Live on a farm
Because you have long dreamed of doing so.
You want to produce for your own sustenance or sell some of your produce.
Move nearer friends, relatives, contemporaries
Seasonal migration
Rent a small house or apartment in southlands in winter and a resort cottage in the north in summer.
This plan offers variety of friends, climate.
Buy a house in a retirement community
For built-in sociability
Health facilities available.
Move to
Florida, California, Arizona, other states.
Neighboring countries: Mexico, Canada, etc.
The islands: Bahamas, Virgin Islands, etc. Or Europe.

Types and Qualities of a New Location

Having thought through the foregoing broader potentials open to you of *where and how to live* and perhaps reduced your choices to a few, then you and your spouse should get more specific in your thinking and do some on-location research of possible locations.

Your soul-searching and investigations should bring up questions like the following to ask yourselves:

1. What kind of climate are we looking for?
2. What physical capacities and limitations do we have?
3. How much isolation do we want?
4. How close is the proposed area to our family and friends?
5. In the proposed community, will we be able to find congenial friends?
6. Are there neighbors who might share our interests?
7. Is there a community spirit to which we can contribute?
8. Where can we find recreational activities that we enjoy?
9. Is there handy transportation?
10. Is the house near a shopping center, church, recreational facilities?
11. Is the neighborhood zoned so that it won't deteriorate with the building of undesirable structures?
12. Are there any nuisance operations nearby—a factory, busy highway, railroad?
13. To what extent do living costs set limits as to where we can live?
14. What about taxes? Find out what they are from the owner or tax collector. Will new schools or roads make them rise?
15. If we need to supplement our retirement income, will this be possible in the proposed community?
16. If we need help from the community or the state with social, economic, health or other problems, how difficult will it be to get it, as compared to where we live now?

This is not a complete questionnaire but rather a starting point. You can make up your checklist of all the things that are important to you and your happiness. With such a master list in hand you can first see if your present home town measures up. You can also use this same list to size up any new community you may want to consider. Vacation days offer a good opportunity to do this type of research.

Housing Facilities for the Elderly

Housing facilities for the elderly have increased to such a degree that there are now several national directories giving the facts on every conceivable type of living facility you can consider. (See bibliography at the end of this chapter.)

Everyone should realize how important the choice of housing is for people of retirement age. It's wise to spell out all the questions you should ask yourself before making decisions such as: whether to move, where to move, type of housing to select, specifications this housing should include. There's no room for hasty decisions.

Many retired persons live in houses or apartments originally constructed for the living patterns of younger people. They live in big houses built for the period when they were raising a family—houses that become burdensome to maintain when strength and income decline. Or they live in apartments booby-trapped by slippery floors and bathtubs, dangerous equipment, poorly lighted rooms, or stairways that take a toll of the heart.

In their attitudes toward housing, today's retirees differ considerably from their counterparts of twenty years ago. They are more active, more healthy, more vigorous and are rapidly becoming more accustomed to the idea of changing living arrangements as their age requirements change. Most retired persons want a smaller house on a smaller lot than they now have. Apartment dwellers also want smaller quarters. Whether in a house or in an apartment, they want dwelling units that are easier to maintain and modern housekeeping conveniences that their own homes lack.

Experts who have made detailed studies in the field of housing for the aged say: "There is no single solution to the housing needs of senior citizens. Housing requirements of the elderly vary widely, and the needs of a given family or individual change with time." Some retired families can afford to pay the full going costs of good suitable housing; others can only meet the low rentals of public housing.

Types of Housing to Consider

The next area to think through is the specific type of living accommodations you would prefer. The following checklist of considerations should help you come to some tentative conclusions. But of course *where to live* and *how to live* are inextricably interrelated because you may not find the type of accommodations you seek in the areas of your choice.

In the ever-widening choices available for retirement living, consider the following and try to decide whether to:

Remain in your present home
> If it still fits your needs for your shrunken family— doesn't cost too much—is not too difficult to maintain.

Seek a smaller home
> Fewer rooms to maintain. More snug and comfortable for two. Easier on the budget.

Get a duplex or multi-unit home
> Rent some of the apartments and let this income maintain you.

Build a house to fit your needs
> A special design to fit your needs.
> A precut house which you help to build, and finish off the interior.

Buy a vacation home, or use one you have
> Convert it to a permanent home or use it part of the year while you live the balance of the year in the southlands.

Convert part of your home into an apartment
> And rent the balance.

Renovate barn or cottage on your grounds
> Live in it and rent your house.

Rent a regular apartment
With its easy upkeep.
With its freedom from exterior maintenance.

Live in a special apartment for seniors
With its many special features for retirement living: safety, health features, communal dining, recreation, and sports facilities. These may be on a cooperative or a condominium arrangement of ownership.

Live in a hotel for seniors
With its simplicity of living, its great recreational potential.

Move into a mobile home
The extreme in easy upkeep both inside and out. And with its mobility, you can live in the north in summer and the south in winter.

Own two homes
Many have a summer and a winter home, and find that the two combined cost less than their former suburban home. Some rent one while they live in the other.

A rented house
Some people live abroad in a rented villa, palazzo or Swiss chalet and find it costs no more than at home —sometimes less.

Build or Buy an Independent House

If you are in reasonably good health, are able to take care of yourself and have the assured minimum income for retirement living—the best way to live is probably in a home of your own. This may be owned outright or rented.

The chances of a mutually satisfactory arrangement in living with a son or daughter are slim. The average American household today provides little accommodation for the privacy and personal living arrangements needed for the heads of a family, growing children and grandparents all living under the same roof. "Keep your own independent household as long as possible," is the advice of many who have tried living the other way.

You will probably never be as happy any place else as in your own home. As much as you enjoy visits to your children's homes, you probably would find it difficult to make the adjustments necessary to live with them for the rest of your life. You may find it difficult to resist the impulse to boss your children, in-laws and grandchildren. Or, even worse, you may find that they want to boss you. On the other hand, a type of arrangement that works out well for some calls for a separate wing built onto the home of the children. In this little home of their own, the older folks can maintain personal and private living quarters independent of their children's living quarters. A similar solution that has worked is the building of a separate, small guest-type of house on the children's property.

Yes, first choice of accommodations of the younger, well, able, active retirees is usually an individual house, but with dimensions suitable to their new needs.

Commercial builders in many sections of the nation have taken the challenge and built homes designed for the size, type of facility and price that the average retiree can afford. Some of them are in communities of houses catering to retirees, while others are in mixed-age communities.

They are most frequently located in the more popular retirement areas of the South, Southwest and West, but some builders are catering to the stay-at-home retirees offering homes on the fringe of Northern communities or in rural areas.

A Good Home Is a Good Hedge against Inflation and Insecurity

Houses and farms are bought by many as a hedge against inflation. A dollar used to purchase bonds may be worth only 50 cents when the bonds mature. Houses and land, though, tend to keep pace with economic conditions. Their value may fluctuate but they will still be there when they are needed. As long as it is paid for or the mortgage payments are kept up, no one can take your house or land away from you. A good house, a well-bought farm, will care for you in your old age, and do the job all over again for your children. If you own it outright by the time you retire, it is one of the best safeguards for security you can have.

A number of retired couples in Florida have small apartments built over their two-car garages. They move into these apartments during the winter season and rent their houses to tourists. From four months' rent they get the income needed to pay the taxes plus enough to live on comfortably all year.

The executive of an oil company who prefers alpine sports bought fifty acres on a Vermont hillside. His retirement home is being constructed bit by bit during his summer vacations. When it is eventually finished, the entire upper floor will be rented to ski lodgers. With additional ski lodges he is planning and some farming in season, he expects to have fun as well as make money when he retires.

The Compact Home for Active Retirement

For those making advance plans for retirement, for those ready to retire or retired, for builders and developers interested in providing retirement housing—the American Plywood Association of 1119A Street, Tacoma, Washington, and the American Association of Retired Persons co-sponsored and planned a house for comfortable, safe and easy living. Such a house—the "House of Freedom" was built and displayed at the time of the White House Conference on Aging.

Here are special features of the house that make it good for active, useful retirement living:

The one-level design is compact (880 square feet of interior space) and can be adapted to modern, ranch or traditional architectural style. Materials require a minimum of maintenance.

The roof overhangs to protect walks, walls and windows. Extra-wide doors and halls are easy to get through. Big windows add light, spaciousness, pleasant views to all rooms. No steps at entry. Nonskid floors prevent slipping. Light switches and doorknobs 36 inches above floor level, and electrical outlets 18 inches above floor level are easy to reach. Three-way switches and master controls at entry, in garage, and in master bedroom. Dressing seat next to bathtub. Strategically located grab bars in bathroom for safety. Well-planned storage easy to get at. Low kitchen counters with knee space permit sit-down meal preparation and dishwashing. Pull-down lighting fixtures make bulb replacement easy. Perimeter heat for warm floors. Extra space and hobby workshop in garage. The basic plan provides for two bedrooms, bathroom, living room, dining room, kitchen, garage and a garden court.

Safety, Health and Recreation Features to Include

If you plan on building a new home for retirement living, or buying or renting one, here are a few check-list guides to follow:

House:

One story with no high steps, steep thresholds or stairs. Ground-level entrances. Nonskid floors. Wide doors. Good view from windows. Adequate electrical outlets. Good heating system. Good ventilation. Good lighting. As thorough fireproofing as possible. Building materials well suited to climatic conditions and easy to maintain.

Bedroom:

Close to bathroom. Good light for reading. Plenty of storage space. Large enough to take twin beds. Windows low enough to see out when sitting or lying in bed but not so low that they cause fright. Have wide, water-impervious sills installed; they give a feeling of safety and provide for window gardens.

Bathroom:

Safe step-in type bathtub with grab bars in the wall, also can be put on floor and secured at ceiling; nonslip stripping in bottom of tub; all fixtures such as soap dishes, towel racks, etc. should also be installed with weight considerations for use as aids in bathing. Why not showers with a seat? Far safer. Ample size medicine chest. Light switch outside the door. Night light between bedroom and bathroom.

Kitchen:

Labor-saving and step-saving type. Electric range should have controls at front. Electric water heater. Good ventilation. Easy-to-reach shelves and cabinets. Adequate storage space. Dining corner.

Faucets:

Single mixing to avoid scalds.

Electrical Outlets:

At least 18″ from floor to prevent unnecessary stooping.

Door Knobs:

Big, easy-to-grip knobs of lever-type or hexagonal or octagonal shape. Sliding doors are preferable on closets.

Windows:

Double-glazed insulating window panes save on heating and cooling costs, no storm windows to hang, only two glass surfaces to clean.

Living Room:
Picture window if desired. Raised fireplace.
Cellar, if there is one:
Dry. Well lighted. Stair handrail.
Heating System:
Automatic oil burner. Electric or gas heating (if rates are low).
Garage:
Near to street. Easy lift-up doors. Wind- and rain-proof passageway to house.
Workroom or Hobby Shop:
Good heating and ventilation. Good lighting. Non-skid floor. Ample storage space.
Patio or Outdoor Recreation Area:
Private for some open-air living. Outdoor fireplace.
Septic system:
Large. In good working order.
General Information:
Deal with a reliable and experienced real estate agent. Don't sign or pay anything without checking with a lawyer. Don't be in a hurry to close the deal. Don't plunge into mortgage debt over your head. Remember this purchase of a house is likely to be the most important investment of your retirement life. If you plan to build a house, consult an architect for advice on design and materials. If you plan to buy, experienced local appraisers and builders can help you select a retirement house in the community where you plan to settle.

Retirement Housing for Rural Areas

Rural living is the choice of many a couple who have had former experience with this way of life. Others have harbored the yen for rural living for many a year, and retirement can satisfy their desire.

A good plan for older people to consider is a housing arrangement which groups houses in a cluster, to allow a

sharing of land and facilities. It can allow several benefits. Less expensive construction is one. Built-in social factors is another, provided by the presence of near neighbors.

A useful booklet (Agriculture Information Bulletin 297)
put out by the U.S. Department of Agriculture, Washington, D.C., can aid your thinking, if the idea appeals to you.
It is called Multi-Unit Retirement Housing for Rural Areas.
It offers plans for one-and-two-bedroom units which could
be combined into multi-unit clusters.

The philosophy behind the design is given: "Each design
must reflect the philosophy that shelter alone is not sufficient, but that consideration has been given to creating a
healthful, safe and stimulating environment without over-
emphasizing features that may remind the occupant of his
age or possible infirmities."

Financing the Retirement Home

There are a great many persons already retired or ap-
proaching retirement who own their homes mortgage free
or have a large equity in their present homes. These homeowners can finance a retirement home by selling their present homes. Some new home builders report that many of
their sales to senior citizens are for cash. Many retired
families with small incomes can afford comfortable housing
as easily as young people earning more.

Financing a retirement home can be accomplished under
a conventional mortgage or a mortgage insured under one
of the programs of the Federal Government. Both types are
available to senior citizens.

Mobile Home Communities on Upgrade

The mobile home way of life has become increasingly popular with older people who like its simplicity and the sociability allowed by a tightly populated community. Some of these facilities have been well planned to accommodate all the amenities of life.

One man's meat may be another man's poison—for instance, with regard to the proximity of other mobile homes. It's an easier way of life but one may lose his house pride in the lack of need for grounds care, and house upkeep which otherwise keeps many a retiree well occupied and content.

Many of the mobile home parks offer additional facilities, such as laundries, food stores, private baths, recreational areas and motion picture entertainment. Some of them can accommodate as many as two thousand mobile homes. Charges are usually about $50 a month, including all facilities. Deluxe parks may charge several times this figure.

Today's mobile homes average 60–75 feet in length; they have a spacious living room, a kitchen-dinette, one or two bathrooms and one, two or more bedrooms. Custom-designed cabinetry and closets are frequently included. The kitchens are equipped with brand-name appliances, and feature the most up-to-the-minute functional floor plans.

Mobile-home living has come a long way. For most people a mobile home is a permanent home for living a normal enjoyable and economical life. The price of a new, modern mobile home varies from $10,000 to $17,000, depending on size and furnishings. The average price is around $12,250.

A Compact Home Afloat

You can live a life afloat, enjoy a "dash of salt" and the leisurely pleasure of cruising without chartering a liner or owning a palatial yacht. You can do this in the same comfort as those who live ashore in house trailers.

You can spend many interesting days around yacht yards and basins looking for a bargain buy in a thirty- to forty-foot pleasure cruiser, or for a commercial fishing craft that has outlived its usefulness for deep-sea runs but is still good for use in protected waters.

I know of a man who lived this way for many years in Florida. He earned enough income from writing and doing publicity jobs ashore not only to support himself but also to pay for his son's college education.

Here are a few of the many advantages of living on a boat. You can cruise up to Maine in the summer and down to Florida in the winter. You can pick interesting spots along the coast for short stays or choose a location for a permanent home afloat. Berth space can be found in protected harbors, at private or public docks offering electricity, drinking water, telephone, ice, gas, showers, laundromat and recreation rooms. A boat can be used as an economical home afloat while you are engaged in pleasure-seeking activities, or as temporary living quarters while looking for a permanent house or apartment ashore.

Many Seek Apartment Living

Apartment living for retirees has been on the increase steadily as community after community makes this available, either via public housing or with private facilities. They vary too, in size, shape and form. Some are in the motel style with one story, adjoined units; others are of the garden-type of two-story apartments and many more are being offered in the high-rise apartment category. Every community has, or will soon have choices for you among these several types.

Many of the apartments are in the downtown sections of cities, and residents can blend right into the fabric of the community. The buildings appear very similar to regular apartments. The features that give them their special suitability to older people are barely visible. While they do have their own recreational, social, medical facilities, these are also available in the neighborhood, so residents can feel a part of the regular stream of the life of the community.

As one study on housing for older people points out, some of the advantages of apartments are:

a. Freedom from maintenance and heavy cleaning.

b. Freedom to come and go as you please without worry about leaving a house uncared for.

c. Freedom from the emergency expenses of home ownership.

d. The ability to move easily, if you want to for one reason or another, without the trouble of negotiating for refund of down payments or other fees, since there is no involvement of capital outlay.

Payments for these facilities vary. Some are rental facilities with extra charges for special services; some are purchased as cooperative apartments; others are purchased as condominiums.

In a few areas, cooperatives—particularly management cooperatives—serve to improve the situation of financially secure elderly householders. The cooperative apartment type of dwelling unit offers essentially all the advantages of home ownership while transferring many burdensome responsibilities to management for a fee.

The buyer of a cooperative apartment does not purchase

his own particular apartment. Rather, he purchases a share in the entire project. The buyer may deduct from his income tax his share of the real estate tax paid by the entire project and his share of the interest on the mortgage paid by the entire project.

Condominiums offer a new kind of ownership and financing of apartments or homes. Each resident in a condominium carries his own mortgage, owns his own dwelling unit and shares in the ownership of some common facilities.

Some types of cooperatives offer special services. The residents pay a founders' fee. These fees usually range from around $5,000 to $25,000, depending upon the amount of luxury involved, and monthly charges of $200 to $500 and more per person per month, depending upon the size of the apartment unit. The founders' fee entitles the individual to a life-lease on a particular dwelling unit or it purchases a long-term interest in the project. The monthly charge covers food, heat, laundry, maid service and short-term infirmary stays.

For example, Willamette View Manor, a Methodist-sponsored project in Portland, Oregon, offers apartment-hotel-type quarters, with kitchenettes in almost all units. The project provides life care for its residents, including nursing home care. Residents are obliged to pay a founders' fee ranging from $7,725 for a one-room efficiency to $20,950 for a corner unit with a view of the Willamette River. The cost of life care, which includes meals, maid service, laundry and infirmary care, is from $267 a month per person, to $522 for a couple.

Casa de Manana Hotel, operated by the Methodists, and White Sands Hotel, operated by the Presbyterians, both located in La Jolla, California, offer life-care programs similar to those at Willamette View Manor.

Federal Assistance Programs for Housing the Elderly

The U.S. Department of Housing and Urban Development (HUD) administers the Federal Government's programs to aid local communities with development of housing for the elderly and handicapped. The Federal investment in housing for the elderly is in the billions of dollars and provides dwellings for around a half million senior citizens. In addition to helping to finance the housing, HUD has made special efforts to develop housing design to fit the needs of elderly or handicapped persons.

HUD programs provide assistance for the development of housing for the elderly through a variety of financing methods, including direct loans, subsidies, annual contributions, mortgage insurance, and "seed money."

Direct Loans Program (Section 202)

Under this program to provide housing and related facilities for the elderly or handicapped, HUD makes long-term direct loans to eligible, private, nonprofit sponsors to finance rental or cooperative housing facilities for elderly or handicapped persons. The current interest rate is based on the average rate paid on Federal obligations during the preceding fiscal year. (Until the program was revised in 1974, the statutory rate was 3 percent.) Maximum mortgage limit is $50 million.

Private, nonprofit sponsors of multifamily structures may qualify for loans. Households of one or more persons, the head of which is at least sixty-two years old or is handicapped, are eligible to live in the structures.

FHA Mortgage Insurance

Federal mortgage insurance facilitates financing of rental housing for the elderly or handicapped. To assure a supply of rental housing suited to the needs of the elderly or handicapped, the Federal Housing Administration (FHA) insures mortgages to build or rehabilitate multifamily projects consisting of eight or more units. Maximum mortgage limit for private developers is $12,500,000; for public sponsors, $50,000,000.

Investors, builders, developers, public bodies, and nonprofit sponsors may qualify for mortgage insurance. Persons at least sixty-two years old are eligible to rent such units.

Low-Income Public Housing

Local public housing agencies develop and operate low-rent public housing projects, financing them through the sale of bonds and notes. HUD furnishes technical and professional assistance in planning, developing and managing the projects and gives two kinds of financial assistance: 1) preliminary loans for planning; and 2) annual contributions to pay off the bonds and notes, assure low rents and maintain adequate services and reserve funds. Rents that are based on the residents' ability to pay contribute to the costs of managing and operating the housing.

Several different methods are used to produce housing. Under the "Turnkey" program, the PHA invites private developers to submit proposals, select the best bid, and agrees to purchase the project on completion. Under conventional-bid construction, the PHA acts as its own developer, acquiring the site(s), preparing its own architectural plans, and advertising for competitive bids for construction. The PHA may also acquire existing housing, with or without rehabilitation, from the private market.

Assistance to Nonprofit Sponsors
of Low- and Moderate-Income Housing

Technical assistance and loans are provided to some sponsors of certain HUD-assisted housing. To stimulate the production of housing for low- and moderate-income families, HUD provides information and technical advice to nonprofit organizations that sponsor such multifamily housing.

HUD also makes interest-free "seed money" loans to nonprofit sponsors or public housing agencies to cover 80 percent of the preliminary development costs. Current HUD regulations limit these loans to nonprofit sponsors of Section 202 housing for the elderly or handicapped. Loans may be used to meet typical project development costs, such as surveys and market analysis, site engineering, architectural fees, site acquisition, and application and loan commitment fees. Loans are made from a revolving Low- and Moderate-Income Sponsor Fund.

Nursing Homes and Intermediate
Care Facilities (Section 232)

The Federal Housing Administration (FHA) insures mortgages to finance construction or renovation of facilities to accommodate twenty or more patients requiring skilled nursing care and related medical services, or those in need of minimum but continuous care provided by licensed or trained personnel. Nursing home and intermediate care services may be combined in the same facility covered by an insured mortgage or may be separate facilities. Major equipment needed to operate the facility may be included in the mortgage.

Investors, builders, developers, and private nonprofit corporations or associations, which are licensed or regulated by the State to accommodate convalescents and persons requiring skilled nursing care or intermediate care, may qualify for mortgage insurance. Patients requiring skilled nursing or intermediate care are eligible to live in these facilities.

HUD's housing programs are operated under a philosophy that the proper housing environment for the elderly— wherever they live—is one rich in social and cultural opportunities, security, and complete freedom to participate in activities of their own choice. This philosophy also extols a continuing role for the elderly in the total life of the community.

The Farmers Home Administration administers housing for the elderly in rural areas. The Senior Citizens Housing Act of 1962 gave the authority to the FHA which has two types of programs: one provides loans for purchase or repair of individual homes; the other provides for multifamily rental housing in rural areas.

Hotels and Residence Clubs

Hotels and residence clubs have long been the residence of wealthy retired people. Offering the ultimate in service, freedom from responsibility and a location in the heart of the city, the hotel has appealed in recent years to an increasing number of older people.

Some of these hotel-type facilities are especially built to serve the needs of older people, while others are merely commercial hotels converted with varying degrees of success for this type of living. It is advisable for anyone considering these facilities to give it a trial first, perhaps several months, before giving up one's old pattern of living. Any move to a new, untried pattern of life should be tested, because once the step has been taken, it is often irrevocable.

In a residence club you have complete freedom from housekeeping. You also have the sociability of a common dining room. The better ones have many cultural and recreational activities, as well as health facilities.

Many of these facilities provide two and sometimes three meals a day as part of the monthly charges. Linen, maid service and other special attention available in hotel-type living is offered and welcomed by those who no longer wish to cook, or are unable to cook and keep house.

The advantages to be considered in this type of residence, according to the National Council on the Aging are:

a. Assurance of regular meals and diversified food.

b. Sociability at the dining hour.

c. Complete freedom from housekeeping.

d. Someone on call, twenty-four hours a day, in case of emergency.

e. A doctor in residence and a small infirmary on an as-needed basis in some clubs.

f. A carefully thought-out health insurance program as offered in some places.

g. Cultural and recreational activities in many clubs.

h. Furnished units in most facilities; in some the management permits residents to furnish their own quarters in part or entirely.

The charges for residence-club living may vary from $150 to $500 per month depending on facilities and services.

Retirement Villages Are Developing Everywhere

You have undoubtedly also witnessed the growth of retirement villages which cater to older people of different ages but most usually from age fifty. In many clusters of small homes you also often find small duplexes, triplexes or multi-unit buildings. In some cases these are sold as condominiums and in some cases as cooperatives.

Thoughtfully planned communities usually include individual houses, apartments or hotel-like rooms and suites in residence clubs, all of them designed and constructed to insure maximum enjoyment for the individual in retirement.

In quite a number of such communities there are extra facilities available such as clubhouses, activity programs, marinas, golf and all manner of sports facilities. Often there are resident doctors available and other health facilities. Communal dining is sometimes offered as is transportation to nearby shopping areas.

One development in this type of housing for older people combines many of the elements of the different types of housing discussed. It is a life-care plan which offers all types of housing in a campus-like setting. This plan most nearly serves the unfolding needs of residents, from independent housekeeping to hotel-like facilities, to nursing-home care, and to hospitals. It gives a resident a sense of security for the rest of his life.

The operations of the General Development Corporation specialize in home building and community development, and are on a gigantic scale. While its housing is for all ages, the majority of the buyers are retirees.

General Development Corporation tackles the task of putting together a whole new metropolis from the ground up—the streets, houses, stores, office buildings, public structures, parks and playgrounds and recreational centers, even the utility systems.

Within a month of opening 80 percent of the first group of 400 houses at Palm City, California, had been sold. In this retirement community, the houses, coop apartments and all facilities are geared to healthy, active people. Retirees as young as forty-five years are eligible to live in Palm City. It is located 16 miles from Palm Springs, which offers city shopping and other facilities. At inception the developers offered both individual homes and coop apartments in a 30 million-dollar, 560-acre community. Both FHA and conventional financing are offered. Conventional mortgages are available for five to twenty years with down payment.

Community Concept of Rossmoor Leisure Worlds

Rossmoor Leisure Worlds is a chain of planned, cooperative, all-adult communities. They are among the largest communities now in operation for people fifty-two years of age and over.

Originally conceived by Ross W. Cortese, president of the Rossmoor Corporation, the first Leisure World at Seal Beach, California opened in 1961 near Long Beach. Today it has a population of 11,000 and is valued at $85 million.

In addition to providing attractive housing at economical costs, many other benefits are derived by residents. Monthly payments are made after an initial down payment ranging between $2,000 and $4,200. Leisure Worlds offers unlimited use of golf courses, fare-free intracommunity transportation, several clubhouses equipped with heated swimming pools, shuffleboard courts, ballrooms, kitchen-equipped classrooms, sewing, lapidary and billiard rooms, as well as art galleries, tennis courts and riding stables. Monthly payments include principal, interest, insurance, taxes, exterior maintenance and security protection twenty-four hours per day. All-electric kitchens with built-in range, refrigerator and disposal are offered in a wide variety of floor plans.

A second Leisure World community is located at Laguna Hills, California, halfway between Los Angeles and San Diego.

It also serves as headquarters for all Leisure Worlds. Eventually, it will be a $375 million community of twelve thousand manors, with a projected population of twenty thousand residents. The third Leisure World at Walnut Creek, California, now known as Rossmoor, in the San Francisco Bay area, will reach an ultimate valuation of $250 million, housing for thousands of residents in share-ownership manors built on 2,200 acres of rolling hillside land on the former Stanley Dollar ranch. A fourth Leisure World at Olney, Maryland is located near Washington, D.C. Its ultimate value will be $250 million. The fifth Leisure World opened at Cranbury, New Jersey, near New York City. Both eastern communities are also now known as Rossmoor.

Nursing Homes for the Aged

The residence clubs and hotels with non-housekeeping living arrangements should *not* be confused with homes for the aged, which provide vital services for infirm and ill older persons who require a protective setting and personal care. Such care includes, when necessary, help with bathing, dressing, walking and eating, and skilled medical, nursing, and rehabilitation services.

The nursing-home field has burgeoned in the last few years. There has been a vast increase in facilities, both in adapted buildings and in multi-million-dollar new facilities of all sizes and shapes.

Along with this, there has been a continual stiffening of

required specifications and of regulations concerning the management of nursing homes. This greater stringency is now exercised at federal, as well as state, level—for the federal government is entering the control area also. It is aiding in financing of construction and it is also financing patient care via the Medicare program.

Services offered in the modern nursing home have also been improving. The traditional custodial care has been expanded to include many therapeutic and recreational facilities and services.

Age is a prime factor in considering any special type of housing facility. The independent living arrangements of a house or an apartment are of primary appeal to those in their fifties and sixties. Those who seek the hotel-type accommodations include a variety of people, usually over sixty, career women and widowers who have long shunned housekeeping. The homes for the aged and nursing homes are usually populated with men and women over eighty, those who need custodial care.

The housing horizon for men and women in their fifties through their eighties is becoming ever brighter. The choices are increasing, but the selection of what's best for each individual or couple must still be made with great care and understanding of true needs.

Bibliography

Housing for the Elderly: The Development and Design Process by Isaac Green et al (Van Nostrand Reinhold, N.Y.)

National Directory of Retirement Residences, Best Places to Live When You Retire by Noverre Musson (Frederick Fell, N.Y.)

For Adults Only, Retirement Communities (Transaction Books, New Brunswick, N.J.)

Retirement in the West by Morie Morrison (Chronicle Books, San Francisco, Calif.)

Foreign Retirement Edens by Martha L. Smith, (Naylor, San Antonio, Tex.)

Woodall's Mobile Homes, Parks and Retirement Communities (Woodall, Highland Park, Ill.)

Successful Retirement in Florida by Carroll L. Scott (Sun Rise House, Longwood, Fla.)

How to Retire in Mexico on Two Dollars and Forty Cents a Day by Eugene Woods, (Robert R. Knapp, San Diego, Calif.)

U.S. GOVERNMENT PUBLICATIONS

Homes—Construction, maintenance and community development. Send for free bibliography and price list of books and pamphlets on these subjects to Superintendent of Documents, Government Printing Office, Washington, D.C. 20402.

6

Leisure-Time Activities with a Retirement Perspective

Everyone Should Have a Hobby

There comes a time in middle life, around the forties and fifties, when children are grown, when the confining responsibilities of fatherhood and motherhood slacken somewhat. This presents a good opportunity to use the leisure time available to re-awaken some interest which captured you during your earlier years, and to begin to develop new hobbies in fields of special interest which can be carried over into retirement.

If you dig down beneath the surface and get to the root of the problem of those who say they are unhappy in retirement, you will find that the majority have no satisfying leisure-time activities. These people need to stimulate their thinking, to help them accomplish something positive with their skills and abilities.

Develop serious interests outside of your job early in life and you will probably not have to search for something enjoyable or satisfying to do when you retire. Doctors and psychiatrists agree that a man or woman with stimulating interests can find retirement one of the happiest times of life.

If you have several occupations of interest, you will be on safer ground. By keeping several hobbies going, you can switch from one to another whenever you find that your interest in one of them seems to be waning.

Some investigators, when making a field survey among retired workers, found that reference to the word "hobby" did not always bring favorable answers to questions. Hobbies were considered by these retired persons to be "sissy" activities or beneath their dignity. When the words "out-side-of-work interests" or "leisure-time activities" were substituted for "hobbies," the responses to the questions showed more positive interest. It makes little difference whether you call them spare-time activities or outside-of-work interests. The important thing is to have them. In retirement you can hardly have too many.

Everyone should be encouraged to develop leisure projects that appeal to him. Many wives are obsessed with the notion that, because their husbands have an absorbing outside interest, they have lost interest in their families. Such thinking is largely selfish on the part of the wife. Instead of criticizing, these wives would be better off developing positive interests of their own. This would provide the couple with new opportunities for exciting topics of conversation. The wise and understanding will encourage their mates to develop new interests. Also, many creative hobbies can be carried on by husband and wife together.

There seems to be no end to the list of possible creative pursuits. You can have outdoor hobbies and indoor projects, summer as well as winter ones. There are occupations which involve making things, collecting things, learning things and doing things.

A hobby or special interest is one of the best conversation stimulators in the world. It encourages cooperation with like-minded folks and has been the basis for many lifelong friendships. The rewards sought and the satisfactions derived from these activities have nothing to do with monetary returns. In fact, many hobbies have no financial merit in themselves. They serve mainly as an insurance against boredom, contribute to cultural development, are activities leading to personal happiness.

On the other hand, there are hobbies which, if carried over into retirement, can open the door to income potentialities. They can be developed to the point where they become a profitable business.

Grandma Moses, who died at the age of 101, was able to provide excitement for living in her senior years through her famous primitive-style paintings. This charming, tiny, lively, self-taught artist whose paintings hang in many museums in the United States, and in Vienna and Paris, painted her first picture when she was seventy-six years old. Grandma Moses took up painting because arthritis had crippled her hands so that she could no longer embroider. She painted more than a thousand pictures, twenty-five of them after she had passed her one-hundredth birthday. Her paintings have increased in value from $3 and $5 price tags to $8,000 or $10,000 for a large picture. In *My Life's History*, her autobiography, published by Harper & Row, Grandma Moses expressed her philosophy: "I look back on my life like a good day's work; it was done and I feel satisfied with it. I was happy and contented. I knew nothing better and made the best out of what life offered. And life is what we make it, always has been, always will be."

Popular Hobbies

There are some three million stamp collectors in the United States. Some people have large sums of money tied up in stamps as a long-term investment or as a form of savings. World-famous stamp collectors were the late King George VI of Great Britain and President Franklin D. Roosevelt.

Almost four hundred thousand women collect handmade glass. Other popular collectors' items are coins, old prints, buttons, antique furniture, dolls, phonograph records, china, books, jokes, autographs, shells, miniature objects of all kinds—the list of items for collection is endless. Collecting is a fascinating and stimulating hobby. Some collectors have correspondents all over the United States and in many foreign countries.

The popular creative hobbies include such diverse activities as gardening, oil painting, ham radio, model railroading, home craftwork, photography and workshop projects.

A retired New York City banker has a hobby of building cradles. He has built almost a hundred to date. It takes this retired banker a day to make a cradle. He gives them away to small girls in the Connecticut town where he lives and to little girls in hospitals all over the East. Since retirement he finds himself busier than ever.

As a contrast to the retired banker with his cradle-making hobby, there is a retired vice-president, reported in *Fortune,* who commutes almost daily to New York City on the same train he took before he retired. He does this just to meet and talk with his old cronies. After killing most of the day going to movie theaters, he joins the crowd on the five-twenty back to the suburbs for the ride and talk. He has been doing this for seven years. He refused to accept or to make adjustments to his retirement. This retired vice-president would be much more contented, if, like the retired banker, he had an absorbing and active interest. He could, of course, as so many retired executives have done, engage in a small money-making enterprise or give his time and talents to one of his town's community or welfare boards.

An ex-newspaper man in Jackson, Mississippi, who retired and took up flowers as a hobby, planted a garden of one thousand rose bushes.

Home gardening has always been a popular leisure-time hobby. You will find in your public library more books on the various branches of gardening than on any other hobby classification. It is a hobby you can enjoy with a patch of ground around the house or with a formal garden complete with greenhouse. Poets and philosophers have written much about it. Physicians and psychiatrists recommend gardening to many of their patients. There's nothing like getting your hands into Mother Earth to forget the cares and problems of the world.

A vegetable or herb garden, if large enough, can provide you with relaxation and a source of income. A vegetable garden will certainly keep down expenses by providing food for the table. And flowers, in addition to their beauty and decorative value, have provided many a person with supplementary income from the sale of cut flowers or the selling of novelty potted plants or flats of seedlings. One woman who makes a good living from gardening has a three-acre plot. She divides this into three gardens— spring, summer and fall. She sells cut flowers and plenty of white ones for weddings.

"Uncle Charlie" is a seventy-seven-year-old amateur gardener who for forty years has boarded the Staten Island Ferry to Manhattan every weekday morning at nine-fifteen with an armful of fresh-cut flowers. These he distributes to his fellow passengers as he walks down the aisle. What price does "Uncle Charlie" ask for his flowers? Just a "thank you" or a smile. Gardening as a hobby has a spiritual virtue as well as a practical one.

You can, in retirement, cash in on your practical gardening experience by establishing a custom landscape service, offering your knowledge and time for hire in pruning, care of shrubs and hedges, lawn maintenance and mowing, seeding lawns, rock-garden work, installation of flagstone walks, and so on.

Carl J. P. of Toronto, Canada, started his hobby of sculpturing at the age of seventy-five, and he is still going strong at ninety-nine. "Every day brings new pleasures," he said. "Life is never dull, but richer with the years." For ten years he has been studying sculpture in night classes at the Northern Vocational School in Toronto, where he still refuses to use the elevator to reach the third-floor studio. Carl is a retired consul for Norway who found time for sculpture and happiness in his senior years.

Here are some hobbies with profit-making possibilities and a few items you can make to bring in supplementary retirement income:

CERAMICS—Vases, ash trays, mugs, novelty salt-and-pepper shakers, jugs, bowls, figurines, lamps, tiles, pottery, floral containers.

WOOD—

Carving. Statuettes, animals, birds, figurines, plaques, picture frames.

Cabinetwork. Reproduction of antique furniture, lawn furniture and ornaments, end tables, tea wagons, colonial, period or modern furniture, coffee tables, pinup lamps, children's furniture, benches, stools, cupboards, kitchen cabinets, picket fences.

Small Articles. Flower stakes, trays, boxes, colonial kitchenware, lamps, knickknacks, hanging shelves, serving plates, bookends, salad bowls, toys, novelties, rustic birdhouses and feeders, forks and spoons.

METAL—

Copper. Giftware, trays, teapots, decorative plates with fused-enamel finishes.

Gold or Silver. Jewelry, such as bracelets, earrings, pins, brooches.

Pewter. Plates, jugs, candlesticks, ash trays.

Iron. Hand-forged fireplace sets, hand-forged lanterns, colonial hardware, candlesticks.

LEATHER—Pocketbooks, billfolds, belts, wallets, original-design tooled leather goods.

PLASTICS—Novelties and fashion accessories.

TEXTILES—Needlework, crocheting, knitting, tatting, embroidering, sewing, quilting, braided rugs, woven rugs, stuffed toys, hand-woven place mats, bags, gloves, fabric-painted blouses, aprons, scarfs, ties, coverlets, draperies, luncheon sets, baby robes.

CONCRETE—Birdbaths, pedestals, garden urns, inlaid flagstone sidewalks, garden pools and ornamental objects, pottery, flower boxes.

MISCELLANEOUS—Handmade greeting and Christmas cards, hand-painted trays, shellcraft, perfume, food products, repair work of all kinds, restoration of old houses, writing, painting, composing music and songs.

Your local public library will have reference books on arts and crafts. Some states have state-wide extension services, usually under the Department of Education, to promote and develop arts and crafts in their states. A good list of over two thousand references to hobby and recreational subjects is *How-to-Do-It-Books* (Bowker, N.Y.).

In home workshops, men and women are turning their hobbies into a source of supplementary retirement income. With modern power-driven bench tools and attachments, jigs and fixtures, new materials and finishes, some become experts in the quantity production of distinctive and original items, novelties and gadgets of every shape and form. In basements, attached garages and sheds many a retired person finds relaxation and a source of income.

These products are usually sold directly by the craftsman, through city and resort gift and curio shops, by mail order or through novelty and gift jobbers located in the leading merchandise-buying centers. In selling through stores it may be necessary to place the items with the store owners on consignment. This means that after the item is sold the shop owner takes a commission for selling it. Commissions usually are from 20 to 40 percent of the purchase price. When establishing the purchase price, be sure you have figured in the cost of materials, packaging, if any, and the value per hour you place on your time and artistic ability.

Illustrative Cases of What Others Have Done

A man who lives in Maine was ordered by his doctor fifteen years ago to give up his regular job and retire because of his health. After overcoming his health problem, he started a small sign-painting business, lettering advertising cards for local merchants. Eventually he drifted into making small wooden novelty items commonly sold at resort spots. He conceived the idea of painting original saucy sayings on rustic wood plaques. These sold like hot cakes at $1.00 to $1.50 each. A silk-screen printing process was developed to turn out the sign plaques in large quantity. One of the largest toy distributors in New York City has ordered thousands of his novelties and souvenirs. They are now sold at novelty and souvenir counters all over the country. Over the years the business has been built up to what it is now—a $100,000-a-year-enterprise.

A New Hampshire hobbyist developed her own formula and method of making realistic-looking flowers. For an orchid corsage of her own creation, her prices range upward from $3.50 for a single large orchid. She handles her own sales and exhibits at New England fairs and exhibitions. In the three years since she started, this hobbyist has sold over a thousand orchids. In addition, she makes ten other types of flowers from lilies to pansies.

An advertising agency man had a hobby of mixing salad dressings. For a while he made a hobby of supplying his friends with his original salad dressing mix. Still producing from his apartment kitchen, he tried selling by mail. In less than a year he had over one thousand mail-order customers. With the mail-order business rolling under its own steam, he decided to try direct mail to grocers from names submitted by his steady customers. Five hundred grocers stocked his product. By this time, production was too big for the kitchen and it was farmed out. At this point the bulk of the business is now handled by food brokers. What started five years ago as a hobby has now grown into a business valued at $150,000, with four new items added to the line.

A couple in California spent their last dollar to buy a ranch house. They used improvised nail kegs and boxes as furniture for a while. Finally they decided that if they were going to have furniture, it would have to be home built. The husband and wife laid out a pattern for a chair, drawing it on wrapping paper, and set to work to make it. It turned out fine. Eventually, they built a lot of furniture for the ranch home, each piece drawn to full size on wrapping paper. Neighbors saw their handiwork, liked it and asked for copies of the homemade drawings. Word spread and the demand for the pattern drawings became so great that eventually the drawings had to be printed. Today, these printed furniture patterns, covering more than sixty articles, are sold by mail order all over the world.

In Florida, a seventy-one-year-old retired white-collar worker who had no special skill in craft work, looking for something to occupy his time, began making novelties out of bamboo. After a little experience, he got courage enough to put some of his items in a gift shop run by a relative. Among popular items sold in the gift shop were tiny Guatemalan dolls made up as earrings. This retired man got an idea that bamboo poles cut into narrow slices at an extreme angle would make good, tiny frames for the dolls. As a result he turned out attractive earring frames into which he fits the one-inch dolls. The frames are sanded smooth, lacquered and fitted with ear screws. He now turns out several dozen pairs of bamboo earrings daily which he sells to gift shops at $10.50 for a dozen pairs. Gift shops retail them for $1.50 to $2.00 per pair. Selling the earrings at retail prices, he makes a net profit of $50 on three dozen pairs. By selling to gift shops he makes enough money to pay himself several dollars an hour for his work. This man's hobby provides him with supplemental income which, added to his inadequate pension and Social Security benefits, enables him and his wife to enjoy a decent living standard.

Handicraft is a big business in some communities. Within one hundred miles of Asheville, North Carolina, some six thousand families are engaged in making hooked rugs. Families earn from a few dollars to more than $3,000 a year. The work is almost exclusively spare time, sandwiched between farm and household duties.

Many a hobbyist has found a happy adventure in rejuvenating and selling antique furniture, after mastering the techniques of the trade.

One man's hobby recently saved the United States Army 28 million dollars in practice ammunition. The man, a civilian who lives in Columbus, Georgia, has a hobby of inventing. His invention is a subcaliber device for the Army's recoilless rifles which enables the rifles to fire a smaller shell than is regularly used.

An Ohioan of seventy-five enrolled in a correspondence law course. After graduating he took his bar examination, passed it and practiced for several years. A beauty-culture school tells of successfully training several retired persons who, after graduating, opened their own businesses. Similar reports come from a professional weaving school about teaching persons up to age seventy who then went into business for themselves.

In Los Angeles, a woman turned her hobby of making medallions into profit by selling her work to fashionable select shops in Beverly Hills and Pasadena. In three months she made $1,300.

A fifty-cent investment in United States Government publications on the federal income tax started a Virginia woman on a career as a tax consultant. She renders a personal tax service which yields her $1,000 for seventy-five days' work.

Over a twenty-one-year period a Lancaster, Pennsylvania, Amish housewife has sold more than twenty-five thousand eggs, dressed up to resemble human and animal faces and figures. The eggs are sold at stalls in Lancaster's farmers' markets.

A garment cutter retired at the age of sixty-eight, after fifty years in New York City's garment center, and turned his leisure into developing his talent for painting. Within ten years he was giving one-man showings at important art galleries.

Forced to give up his regular line of work because of a heart attack, a Vermont resident, while ill, began making old-fashioned wooden toys for his grandchildren. They and their friends liked the toys so well that he soon found himself designing toys for mass production. After two years, having recovered his health, he has established "Grandad's Toy Shop" across the road from his home. He doesn't make many toys himself. Instead, his projects keep a woodworking mill busy making and assembling parts. Grandad paints them.

When the Hamptons of Gering, Nebraska, toured the United States in 1939, they decided to get only one kind of souvenir—pitchers. They got a pitcher at nearly every stop they made. And so developed a hobby for pitcher-collecting that now numbers over fifteen hundred. From collecting, Mrs. Hampton developed an interest in ceramics and now sells much of her own work.

An old sailor in Vancouver, British Columbia, spends his days feeding birds. At night he works in a steel foundry to make more money to feed more birds. Aviaries now cover almost the whole acre of his property. The bird count is in the hundreds. It's impossible, he says, to keep an exact count.

You would never think offhand of New York City as good territory for an archaeology hobby. But there's a dentist living in the Bronx who has dug out more than forty-five hundred Indian artifacts in New York's five boroughs. His cottage and dentist's office is an Indian museum. Reading newspaper real estate pages and news columns, he gets tips on where the bulldozers are about to begin foundation excavation. These yield collection items. From New York City's soil he retrieves all manner of minerals—garnets, tourmalines, jasper, flint and several kinds of quartz—which he fashions into lovely polished ornaments.

After learning the technique of fabric painting, a Brooklyn, New York, woman began painting designs on handkerchiefs and blouses for herself and her friends. Today she buys blouses, scarfs and aprons from wholesalers in dozen or more lots and hand-paints the garments with fabric paint in floral effects and designs of her own. These she sells at good profit to a number of New York retail outlets.

Retired from the Navy, a cabinet-making hobbyist acquired an old schoolhouse near his Virginia residence and converted it into a workshop. Here the hobbyist faithfully duplicates, with modern tools, the construction details and quality standards of craftsmanship of eighteenth-century antique furniture. The mahogany tea caddies and trays, cherry mirrors and other articles he reproduces are duplicates of antiques two hundred years old. So great is the demand for his antique reproductions that he is swamped with orders. The Reproduction Program of Colonial Williamsburg is his best customer.

If you don't have a hobby now, you will do well to consider developing one. Select a hobby you would really like, not a hobby someone else likes, or one somebody forces you into or one that happens to have profit possibilities. Most people follow their hobbies for the pure enjoyment they get out of them. Your hobby has to be something that is fun for you, otherwise it won't provide the stimulation, recreation and satisfaction you are looking for. Start to develop your hobby slowly, as a part-time project, to see whether you are on the right track. Keep up to date on new techniques and materials, since improved processes can sometimes save you time and money.

There is joy in turning one's mind and hand to the development of one's own style and quality in design and workmanship. The development of intellectual and creative talent and skill in the hobby field of your choice will lead you to read many books and magazines, to attend instructive exhibitions, to compare your work with that of the masters, and to enjoy friendly visits with professionals and amateurs who will help you develop into a finer artist or craftsman.

Should you be undecided as to which hobbies to cultivate and develop, attend local hobby and handicraft shows, exhibits and lectures. Local art supply stores, YMCA, YWCA, community workshops, adult education centers or the public library can direct you to local hobby groups, craft guilds or other hobbyists who are glad to assist you in getting started.

Bibliography

PERIODICALS DEVOTED TO VARIOUS HOBBY ACTIVITIES

Popular Crafts, 7950 Deering Ave, Canoga Park, Cal., 91304
Popular Handicraft and Hobbies, Box 425, Seabrook, N.H., 03874
Rockhound, Box 328, Conroe, Tex., 77301
Treasure Hunting, Unlimited, Truth or Consequences, N.M., 87901
Antiques, 551 Fifth Avenue, New York, N.Y. 10017
Antiques Journal, Box 1046, Dubuque, Iowa 52001
Collectors World, 536 S. Popular, Kermit, Texas, 79745
Model Railroader, 1027 N. Seventh St., Milwaukee, Wis., 53233
American Aircraft Models, 733 15th St., Washington, D.C. 20005
Auto Modeler, 7950 Deering Ave., Canoga Pk., Cal. 91304
Better Homes & Gardens Do it Yourself Ideas, 1716 Locust St., Des Moines, Iowa 50336
Collectors Weekly, Drawer C., Kermit, Tex. 79745
Creative Crafts, Box 700, Newton, N.J. 07860
Gems and Minerals, Box 687, Mentone, Cal. 92359
Hobbies, Magazine for Collectors, 1606 S. Michigan Ave., Chicago, Ill. 60605
Lapidary Journal, Box 80937, San Diego, Cal. 92138
Ceramic Arts and Crafts, 30595 W. Eight Mile Rd., Livonia, Mich. 48152
Popular Photography, 1 Park Ave., New York N.Y. 10016
Art News, 750 Third Ave., New York N.Y., 10017
Flower Grower and Gardener, 4251 Pennsylvania Ave., Kansas City, Mo. 64111
Ladies Home Journal, Needle & Craft, 641 Lexington Ave., New York, N.Y. 10023
McCall's Needlework & Crafts, 230 Park Ave., New York, N.Y. 10017
Workbasket, 4251 Pennsylvania Ave., Kansas City, Mo. 64111
Coin World, Sidney, Ohio 45365
Numismatics News Weekly, Iola, Wis. 54945
American Philatelist, Box 800, State College, Pa. 16801

7

How to Enjoy Leisure

When I asked a number of people, "What are you going to do when you retire?" the majority answered: "Take it easy." No one can dispute their right to relax as they enjoy the fruits of a life well spent. Unfortunately, though, most of them had not given any special thought to what they meant by "take it easy."

Taking it easy should not mean merely eating, sleeping, reading the newspaper, listening to the radio or watching television, chatting with neighbors and sitting on a park bench. These passive activities, if engaged in for prolonged periods, can lead to boredom and frustration.

Writing about leisure, Dr. Edward J. Stieglitz, in *The Second Forty Years* (J. B. Lippincott Company) concluded: "Success or failure in the second forty years, measured in terms of happiness, is determined more by how we use or abuse our leisure than by any other factor." Stieglitz goes on to say that a "superabundance of leisure, or the abuse thereof has marked and initiated the decadence of cultures throughout history."

A planned program of leisure-time activities will help you formulate a positive attitude toward retirement. Such a program will insure that you make and keep desirable social contacts; develop and express creative talent; keep from becoming a burden to yourself, your spouse and family, as well as the community; and achieve a status of usefulness. In planning leisure time, however, don't feel that you must have a rigid time schedule for everything you do. It is not desirable that every minute be assigned to a prearranged activity. Don't be a slave to a program. Attempting too much is just as bad as having no program of spare-time activities at all. In arranging your program, be guided by your tastes, and natural inclinations. Live one day at a time, but live a full, active day. You will find that your schedule will become a habit. That is good if the habit is basically right for you. You should not work too much, play too much, loaf too much—but do a little of each to some satisfying degree.

The hours between 9:00 A.M. to 5:00 P.M. are usually the most troublesome ones for the retiree. These are the hours formerly filled with job or housework routines. Unless these hours are planned wisely they are likely to turn into periods of loneliness and boredom, a threat to emotional security. Planned wisely, they can be the richest, happiest hours of your life.

Group Activities

"All who would win joy, must share it; happiness was born a twin," says Byron. Group activities provide a means of doing worthwhile things and an opportunity to enjoy the companionship of congenial people. Group activities provide a focal point where retired persons can receive recognition for personal accomplishments. They are a meeting place for collaboration with others on useful activities. They provide retirees with an opportunity to belong to a socially desirable group in the community.

Most communities have, or are making provisions for, community facilities for the recreational and cultural needs of older people. These facilities provide for a wide range of activities, such as shuffleboard, horseshoe pitching, card and checker games, hobby workshops, sports, amateur dramatics, concerts, picnics—in fact almost any kind of recreational activity.

Other group activities include social and service clubs and organizations, such as the American Legion, Red Cross, Wednesday Afternoon Music Club, Garden Club, Camera Club, University Club, the Old Guard, Senior Citizens, Golden Age Club, fraternal lodges, as well as many other cultural, political and church groups.

Those who have been too busy earning a living to devote time to social activities will find wonderful opportunities in these group activities. Here they can enjoy pleasant, stimulating friendships with persons who have interests and backgrounds common to their own.

Find out what social, civic and other groups are active in your locality. Visit several of them until you locate those in which you feel at home. Join groups which you think would benefit you. Take the initiative in making known your desire for membership. Sharing companionship with people of similar interests and outlooks is one of the best ways of enjoying a contented retirement.

I know a man who had the reputation of being a successful sales manager. A few years ago he retired to a place he bought in New Hampshire. When I met him in New York City recently, he said: "None of that retirement for me. I just sat around on the porch for months, with a drink always handy, and nothing in particular to do. I like to meet new people. I just couldn't stand being isolated. So I'm back selling again." Had this man planned his retirement to include some kind of group activity, he would probably have found plenty of opportunities to meet new people and to channel his talents into worthwhile activities.

Clubs for the Retired

Dr. Allen G. Brailey, a Boston physician, stated in an address that there exists a large group of retired people who, while they make no complaint and seem satisfied with life, "taste only a fraction of the zest of life which might be theirs." Dr. Brailey said he advises his patients who have held positions of responsibility: "Do *not* retire from work; retire to more congenial work—for the Community Fund, for the Red Cross, for the church or the schools, for the Scouts."

Too many of his patients, contends Dr. Brailey, are satisfied with edging the lawn, shopping with the wife and visiting with the grandchildren. While these people keep busy enough to escape boredom, "they are too willing to dally away their days, to let their special talents and abilities, perfected by long years of experience, gradually rust away from sheer disuse."

Like so many centers the San Francisco Senior Recreation Center was planned exclusively for older people. The Center is maintained by a private agency. It is open five afternoons and two evenings a week. Some of the Center's activities include classes in folk dancing, dramatics, crafts and painting, personality and charm demonstrations, millinery and group singing. A poetry group meets each week. Weekly luncheon forums are held with able speakers on subjects of interest to senior citizens. There are service projects such as making quilts for veterans' hospitals. Members enjoy regular programs of music and dancing. Picnics, outings and trips to historic landmarks are scheduled during the year. The ratio is approximately one man to three women, with members coming from all walks of life.

The Little House at Menlo Park, California, sponsored and maintained by Peninsula Volunteers, Inc., a woman's organization devoted to community service, is nationally famous for its broad range of activity programs for senior citizens. It serves a number of nearby communities. Members' handcrafts are sold at a bazaar three times yearly. The art, craft and hobby show is an eagerly awaited annual event. More than twelve hundred retired men and women are members of Little House.

Golden Age and Senior Citizens' Clubs are on the increase in every state of the Union. If there is no Golden Age or Sixty Plus or Senior Citizens or other appropriate club in your locality you can be instrumental in founding one. Many such social groups have been formed by enterprising people who wrote "letters to the editor" or inserted advertisements in the newspapers. All you need say is: "Persons over sixty, of good character, interested in forming a club to scotch loneliness and cultivate fun come to (street address)." An advertisement such as this was the seed from which sprang an active and flourishing club in a Pacific Coast community.

The Old Guard

The Old Guard is a nonsectarian and nonpolitical organization which started over thirty years ago with the founding of the first group in Summit, New Jersey. It is a social club for retired men, usually sixty and older. Some chapters have women's auxiliaries.

The purpose of the Old Guard is to cultivate good fellowship, to renew old friendships and to form new ones; to preserve mental alertness; to foster deeper interests in the community; and to devise ways and means to be more helpful. The members are retired men from all walks of life, retired bankers, chemists, editors, engineers, lawyers, manufacturers, merchants, clergymen, physicians, teachers, blue collar workers and men in other business and professional occupations. The wealth of diverse experiences represented by these retired men assures stimulating friendships and provides the opportunity for useful community service.

The motto of the Summit chapter is a quotation from Dr. Samuel Johnson: *"If a man does not make new acquaintances as he advances through life he will soon find himself alone. A man, sir, must keep his friendship in constant repair."*

Meetings of the Old Guard are conducted in such a manner as to provide the maximum of informal good fellowship. Dues are seven dollars a year. Meetings are held in YMCA buildings once a week in the forenoon. The members do not feel out of place in the YMCA, for many of them have contributed substantially to it.

There is no professional promotion or propaganda of any sort for the Old Guard. There are twenty-five chapters in New Jersey and the movement has spread of its own momentum to other chapters in such states as West Virginia, Minnesota, Connecticut, Massachusetts, Ohio, Pennsylvania, New York and Texas. There is no intention to make the Old Guard national in scope. Each group remains an independent unit, formulating its own regulations. The Summit chapter has about 400 members from all stations in life. The Old Guard Chapter at Princeton, New Jersey, includes many famous retired members of the Princeton faculty among its members. Those desiring more information should communicate with the parent chapter—The Old Guard, c/o YMCA, Summit, New Jersey 07928.

Senior Citizens Service Corps Recommendation

Dr. Donald P. Kent, former Special Assistant on Aging to the Secretary of Health, Education and Welfare, in a statement before the United States Senate Special Committee on Aging said: "There will be a tremendous net gain if we can create a situation which frees and makes available to the nation the vast potentials of skill, knowledge, and wisdom of our almost 23 million older Americans. If we make it possible for our senior citizens to heed the admonition of the President to ask what they can do for our country, we must think boldly and constructively. Why shouldn't we make it possible for older persons to take more active roles in community, civic and political activities?"

Additional Ways to Occupy Your Leisure Time

National and State Forests and Parks. There are thousands of lakes and ponds, miles of flowing streams in national and state forests and parks for fresh-water fishing and hunting. Thousands of miles of leafy roads and trails await the hiker, horseback rider and picnicker. Mushrooms, berries and edible roots can be gathered in these public playgrounds. You can enjoy camping out in a trailer or tent. You can stay in cabins or other accommodations from deluxe hotels to motor courts located in or near many of these national and state recreational areas.

Adult Educational Courses. Don't overlook the opportunity to add to your education by taking advantage of courses offered by colleges, high schools, trade and vocational schools, both public and private. You are never too old to learn. Many retired people are getting a lot of fun out of retirement living by going back to school or college. Some take up a second career. Others continue their education in order to keep up with cultural and scientific developments of the day.

The Institute for Human Adjustment at the University of Michigan provides a ten-week program in pre-retirement education. In organized group discussion with others like themselves, people compare their ideas about retirement. Reading materials, films, and still pictures stimulate ideas and help participants make satisfactory decisions regarding their future.

Several other universities, including New York, Chicago, Purdue, Wisconsin and Cornell, are offering special "package programs" on retirement education and pre-retirement planning.

Consult the department of adult education of the public school system in your locality for a listing of courses available. You will be surprised at the range of subjects covered, in classes that meet one or two nights a week, in demonstration laboratories, workshops, forums and informal discussion groups. Lecture courses and forums on the preparation for aging and retirement living, designed for middle-aged people, are offered in many communities. Your interest in the subject is usually all that is required for registration. Going back to school can be one of your most satisfying retirement activities.

⧊ *The Public Library* is said to be the poor man's university. It is the answer to many a retired person's prayer. Here you can find books, magazines and bulletins covering many fields. The range of subject matter is wide, from how-to-do-it books to classics, earning a living, personal finance, biographies, mysteries, arts and crafts, personal growth counsel, fiction, technical subjects, travel, adventure, and reference information on practically any subject you can think of. No matter what your tastes may be, your public library can provide provocative reading material. One of the pleasant aspects of retirement is the time and opportunity it affords to catch up on one's reading. It is a good time to increase your knowledge of subjects that fascinated you when you did not have time to pursue them.

Community and Civic Organization Jobs offer opportunities for channeling spare-time energy and abilities. A large number of these agencies operate at a community, state or national level. They welcome volunteer workers even on a part-time basis. Here you will find a chance to be useful. Your help will be appreciated. You will enjoy the rewarding satisfaction of helping in a noble and worthy cause. The chamber of commerce or community social service agency should be able to help you line up worthwhile civic jobs.

Museums and Art Centers are another source of pleasure and education worth looking into, providing opportunities for further cultural and educational development. Find out whether or not the museum and art centers offer special lectures, classes and discussion groups. One of the richest experiences of living is the development of an appreciation of nature's beauties. Have your name placed on the mailing list announcing new activities.

Local Politics offers opportunities to use training and experience, to engage in activities that are interesting and exciting. Many retired men are doing useful and constructive civic work in city and town elective offices, as well as in state legislatures.

Music is a good medium for recreation and a tonic for the heavy heart. "Music is the fourth great material want of our nature—first, food, raiment, shelter, then music" *(Bovee)*.

You can enjoy music as a listener at concerts and recitals, on the radio and on television or by playing recordings. You can enjoy music as a participant by joining community singing groups and choruses or glee clubs, or by playing an instrument alone or in instrumental groups.

Local Pageants and Festivals. Don't overlook the recreation and pleasure afforded by the many colorful and historic dramas, pageants, exhibitions, musical festivals, summer and winter theater groups presented in season in many communities. Also, watch for symphony and band concerts, lectures, forums and conventions that may be offered locally.

A university or college town is usually a good location for retirement because of the variety of recreational and cultural activities that are available to local residents.

Travel Trips. In retirement you have plenty of time to travel and see for yourself those far-off places you have daydreamed about. You can do your traveling by plane, train, ship, pleasure craft, bus, trailer or automobile—whichever appeals to you most.

It is possible to enjoy travel trips on a slim pocketbook and not miss any of the high spots in the places you visit. The trick is to know as much about the pleasure potential of the places on your trip as possible. You probably know where to find the best local fun, the best scenic spots and the good eating places in your home town. The same sort of knowledge about the places in your travel trips can make a small budget work wonders.

In your local library you will find many travel and historical books about the areas you plan to visit. They will give you a good background on the growth and life of the area. For descriptive and illustrative information write to the chambers of commerce at the places you plan to visit. Ask specific questions about cities or towns. Make notes of the scenic, historical, cultural, artistic and eating places that appeal to you. Plan to make your travel trips when the tourist crowds have gone. Accommodations then are easier to get and prices are often lower. Your travel budget will take you a long way, if you plan in advance.

Letter Writing. Retirement is a good time to take up letter writing seriously. Writing a conversational letters to relatives and friends is a happy way to use up some of your leisure time. You can visit your friends by mail, exchanging letters that express thoughts as naturally as you would talk to them if you were visiting them. You like to receive letters. So do other people. So keep letters flowing back and forth to friends, relatives and pen pals.

Fishing and Hunting enthusiasts will find numerous opportunities to engage in their favorite sport for recreation or as a means of supplementing the food basket. In many of the retirement locations covered later in this book, fishing may be enjoyed at all seasons of the year. For those who enjoy hunting, the open seasons permit plenty of excitement hunting big game, wild fowl, ducks and game birds.

Golf. Innumerable golf courses at country clubs, resorts and public or municipal links invite devotees of the game. Don't play too hard. Don't try to defeat every other member in the club. Try to get pleasure, exercise and relaxation out of your game whether you shoot eighty or one hundred and twenty.

Additional Outdoor Sports and Activities. Joseph Lee, the father of the playground movement in this country, said, "We do not cease playing because we are old; we grow old because we cease playing." All of us need a certain amount of physical exercise to keep our bodies in good shape. During retirement we should see to it that we get the kind of physical exercise which is beneficial to body structures and to our muscular and nervous systems. As long as they are not against doctor's orders, not carried out too vigorously or to excess, the following activities are highly desirable:

Archery	Horseback riding
Boating	Horseshoes
Bocci	Nature study trips
Bowling	Picnics

Camping	Quoits
Croquet	Roque
Excursions	Shuffleboard
Gardening	Softball
Geology trips	Swimming
Hikes	Trips

Commercial Entertainment. There are times when a certain amount of relaxation and enjoyment is to be had by watching others perform for your pleasure and amusement. Some of these activities like attending the theater, symphony concerts, selected radio broadcasts and television programs stimulate creative thinking or provide genuine entertainment. Others are just plain time killers and provide little in the way of satisfaction. A great many amusements and entertainments are built around thrills, sensations and stunts for the purpose of increasing the "box-office take" or the "gate." Avoid these.

Your Own Back Yard. Don't overlook the opportunities in your own back yard to provide recreation, not only for yourself but for neighbors and friends. Outdoor play space can be used for lawn games, outdoor fireplaces for preparing lunches and suppers. The back yard provides space for a variety of leisure-time activities and a place to meet and entertain friends. And don't forget the pleasures derived from home gardening and attracting birds.

Religious Activities. For many, a rich full life does not have a meaning without some form of religious belief. Each individual comes to an understanding of God in his own way. Men may not agree as to the precise needs and goals of the human spirit. But one important thing for each individual to realize is that he has spiritual needs which he can define and fulfill through study, discussion and participation in religious activities. It may be through the path of adherence to the creed of a particular church. Or he may develop his own personal and private approach. The important thing is that man is, by his constitution, a religious creature. He needs spiritual reliance in a power greater than his own, an inspiring force around which to build a philosophy of life.

Religious interest often increases with age. Those who were too preoccupied with earning a living and making a place for themselves in society during their younger years seem to derive increasing satisfaction from religious experience as they grow older. Churches and synagogues are beginning to recognize the special needs of the rapidly increasing number of older folks in their congregations. They are planning to meet these needs with programs of adult activities. Several religious groups maintain assemblies as well as camps and conferences. These activities attract thousands annually. In making up your schedule for your leisure time, include attendance at church or synagogue services, committees, bazaars or other activities, especially those designed for senior members.

Another Aspect of Leisure

This chapter has attempted to show how leisure activities fit into the retirement program. It has explained how time invested in planned leisure activities, not in idleness, can pay big dividends in helping retirees get more out of life.

Physicians and psychiatrists tell us, "Illness is often the result of maladjustments rather than organic disease." Writers in gerontology strongly emphasize that the rest cure for retirement ills has been condemned by medical science in favor of stimulating, invigorating recreational or leisure-time activities.

A distinguished specialist in geriatrics, as well as a renowned writer on the subject, Dr. Martin Gumpert had this to say: "The chief bar today to happiness in old age is our defective understanding of retirement—with its bleak connotations of enforced leisure and idleness. Leisure should never be more than the passive counterpart of active work."

Bibliography

BOOKS

Leisure, The Basis of Culture by Josef Pieper (New American Library, New York)

Leisure and Mental Health by P. A. Martin, (American Psychiatric Association, Washington, D.C.)

Leisure and Recreation Places by Neil Cheek (Ann Arbor Science, Ann Arbor, Mich.)

Leisure and the Quality of Life (American Alliance for Health, Physical Education and Recreation, Washington, D.C.)

Leisure in the Modern World by Cecil D. Burns (Consortium Press, Washington, D.C.)

U.S. GOVERNMENT PUBLICATIONS

National Parks, Historic Sites and National Monuments. Send for free bibliography and price list of books and pamphlets on these subjects to Superintendent of Documents, Government Printing Office, Washington, D.C., 20402.

8

A Small Business of Your Own

Select the Right Field

So you think you would like to own and operate a small business! Many others have done it. Perhaps you can too. In fact, if you plan on retiring in your fifties or sixties, you may even develop a small business into something more profitable than anything you've done before.

You must realize, however, that small business, like large business, gets more complex each year; but for those who have the dream and the energy and ample resources to fall back upon—a small retirement business can offer many rewards.

When you operate an individual enterprise you are not faced with automatic retirement at age sixty-five. You can go as far as your talents and energy allow. It can bring you a sense of independence, an opportunity to use your ideas. It may mean a chance for higher income because you can collect a salary plus a profit as a return on your investment. You will experience a pride of ownership. You will not be bored by having nothing to do. As a matter of fact you may be working longer hours than you ever have before.

What business should you choose? Technical or professional training, previous experience in business, special skills and talents, hobby interests or a deep-seated longing to engage in a specific type of business—these are the motivating factors that should influence you in the choice of a business to own and operate.

Naturally, it is smartest to pick a field you know something about. Skill, experience and adaptability are essential for success.

Managerial experience is a "must." The best way to obtain operating knowledge for a specific type of business is through actual experience. Some of this experience can be acquired before you retire, by part-time work on weekends or during vacations.

You should have sufficient capital to solidly establish the business, and to provide for your own living expenses for the first year or two. In many cases, the necessary equipment, tools or furnishings to operate the business can be acquired well in advance of your retirement. It is best not to start your retirement business by contracting large obligations, thereby running too great a risk with your money, your time and your future.

While the success stories that can be told about small businesses are legion, another side of the picture must be given serious consideration. Studies indicate that approximately one-fourth of new business do not survive the first year, and over half operate less than three years. The success or failure of a business venture is determined by many factors. The most important single factor is the ability of the owner-manager to apply sound principles of business management and promotion in the operation of his business. If you do not know how to run a business, you had better work first for someone who is successful and learn his methods. Many persons fail because they pick a business that is not suited to their temperament and past experience. Lack of working capital to equip and operate the business adequately causes many a businessman to go broke. Failure to keep records, slipshod service and too liberal credit policies are also roads that lead to failure.

Keep away from fields calling for physical strength, long hours and a daily grind of close attention to many small details. This is of importance to retired folks. Stay away from the usual crowded fields, like gasoline stations, corner groceries and dry-cleaning establishments where competition is likely to be intense. Make or sell specialty items whose volume is not great enough to interest the larger stores or factories. Operate a service type of business in which your skill, talent and specialized equipment are too personalized for competition by large organizations.

Keep the operation small enough so that you can always run the business and so that the business does not run you ragged. Don't try to compete with others organized for large-scale volume.

You will find much helpful information in the many good books in your public library on the subject of organizing and operating various types of small business enterprises. The Small Business Administration of the United States Government and other U.S. Departments have a great interest in the welfare of small businesses and publish many bulletins which can be profitably applied to small business procedures.

Some Businesses Don't Need a Lot of Money to Launch

If you have a specialty that your friends rave about—whether it is a food specialty, like party or gift cookies, a home-recipe salad that is out of this world or unusual handwoven rugs or mittens—you may have the makings of a good small business. And you don't need a barrel of money to get it started on the road to producing an income for you.

There is a woman in Connecticut who has an enviable reputation among her neighbors and church associates for baking excellent and unusual cookies. Friends always called on her to bake cookies for parties and special events. When the friends of friends sampled these fancy cookies, the demand for them snowballed.

Two years ago this woman and a church friend decided they would go into business together—one to bake the cookies, the other to sell them. A local department store with a lunchroom was lined up as a customer. When patrons of the lunchroom asked to buy some of the cookies to take home, the cookie baker knew that she was off to a good start. The country club was the next large customer. This was followed by several wayside inns noted for their fine foods. In each instance, patrons of the establishments inquired about buying cookies to take home. By word-of-mouth this homemaker became famous locally for her tasty cookie specialties. At this stage, the baking of the cookies was a home-kitchen operation. But the mixing, baking, packaging and storage of ingredients soon outgrew the kitchen. To keep up with the demand, they moved the growing cookie business to a small, low-rent neighborhood store, and fitted it out with the necessary equipment for greater production.

With business thriving, sights were set for retail distribution in the quality grocery stores. A local concern bought one hundred one-pound boxes of cookies to be used as Christmas gifts. Some customers wanted cookies sent by mail to friends in distant cities and to relatives in the military services overseas. A couple of food brokers dropped in, asking for the line to sell to retail stores.

How a Musical Recital Started a
Strudel-Baking Business

Amazing circumstances sometimes lead directly to one's establishing a small business. Take the case of a young concert pianist in New York City who planned a Sunday afternoon musicale at her home. Her mother, as a contribution to the success of the musicale, decided to bake and serve Viennese strudel made from a family heirloom recipe. "What's this?" the guests asked. "It's one of mother's homemade strudels," the pianist replied. "Do you think she would make some to sell?" Mother said she would be glad to bake each guest one of her strudels. The guests protested. They wanted to buy several to serve as refreshments at their own parties. The mother and daughter talked it over in the kitchen—and decided it might be a good idea for pin money. A few orders were taken right then and there. For over a year, the mother has baked Viennese strudels to order. She now has two kinds: the sweet to serve with tea or coffee, the unsweet to go with cocktails. From morning until night the kitchen oven is kept busy baking strudels to fill special orders. This is just another example of how a special home-baking skill was turned into a profit-making opportunity.

Here's another case history of how a woman's baking talents were turned to profitable use. A retired schoolteacher, looking around for something to keep her busy, decided to try her luck at baking homemade coconut and angel food cakes. She offered them for sale at a farm market near Washington, D.C. Today, her cakes, named "Della Cakes" after her daughter, are famous in the capital district. So successful is this retired woman's business, she had to build a bakery with two large bake ovens and employ five full-time bakers.

Whether it's cookies, cakes, jellies, jams, bread, or a host of hand goods, there are thousands of these personalized proprietor-operated small businesses in the United States. The success of these small enterprises depends on having a good idea and an outstanding quality product, and sticking to it enthusiastically, continuously through a period of years.

There's Money in Personal-Service Businesses

You can prepare in your spare time for a retirement career in a service business of your own. There are a number of personal-service businesses that offer opportunities for financial security, independence and working hours regulated to your own desires. Many of these service businesses can be run from a home workshop, garage shed or basement. Age or minor physical handicap is no barrier. The work is light, pleasant and profitable.

It doesn't matter whether you have had previous experience. Very little capital is required to start them. You can learn the how-to-do-it techniques from practical, down-to-earth home-study courses offered by reliable and accredited correspondence schools. In many of the larger cities, private trade schools and vocational and technical high schools offer classes in some of these occupations.

A retired post-office worker took up the study of law and began practice as a lawyer after passing his bar examination at age of sixty-seven. A Newburgh, New York, woman at age sixty-five completed a course in beauty culture and became a successful owner of a beauty salon employing three other beauty operators. Mrs. J. of Denver, Colorado, completed a one-year practical-nurse training program, entered the private duty field and has more cases offered to her than she can handle.

Television and Radio Servicing is a field which employs

many technicians. About three-fourths of all service technicians work in service shops or in stores that sell and service
television receivers, radios and other electronic products.
Most of the remaining technicians are employed by government agencies and manufacturers.

Employment of television and radio service technicians
is expected to increase continually. In addition, many job
openings annually are expected to result from the need to
replace experienced workers who retire or die.

Electrical Appliance Repairing is another field offering opportunities for you to start your own business. There are
millions of electrical equipment units in daily use in homes,
office buildings and farms. Skilled technicians are needed
to keep this equipment in good running condition. If you
are mechanically inclined, you can learn by correspondence how to repair vacuum cleaners, washing machines,
motors, refrigerators, and so forth. I know a man who quit
his job as a bank teller over twelve years ago and has made
a good living ever since, working from his home, as an
electrical repair specialist.

Automatic Saw Filing and Lawn-mower Sharpening. With only
a small investment you can start a general repair shop specializing in saw filing. This is another one of those personal
service businesses you can start at home in your spare time,
and build up to a full-time business assuring you an income
to cover your living expenses. Overhead and operating
expenses are low. Prospective customers include furniture
and other factories, newspapers and printers (they use circular saws to trim printing plates), building contractors,
carpenters, manual-training departments of schools, farmers and home owners. Between April and September, lawn-
mower sharpening is a profitable business. You can add
other services like key making, knife and tool sharpening.

Oil-burner and air-conditioning installation, repairing and
servicing also offer good opportunities for retired men.

Other types of service businesses are *venetian blind laundry, farm machinery repairing, rug and upholstery washing.* Manufacturers who sell special equipment to do these specialized jobs assert that many men have built profitable businesses with their equipment. You can obtain their names and addresses from advertisements in popular and crafts magazines. It is advisable to investigate these service propositions thoroughly before devoting time to them and investing money in special equipment.

A Sewing Shop Can Be Profitable

In the custom-made field there are opportunities for making-to-order bridal costumes, clothes for handicapped people, party and regular dresses and costumes, children's dresses, infants' wear and sportswear. Innumerable opportunities exist for sewing slipcovers, draperies, smocks, coveralls, aprons, embroidery, gloves, quilting, unusual toys, handbags and novelties.

Some enterprising, creative dressmakers have pyramided their original custom-made creations into a line that finds ready sale in local specialty dress shops. Unusually good design or style, good materials and high-quality workmanship are the essentials for success in operating a custom-dressmaking or sewing shop. The finished product should look handmade, not homemade. Original styling and attractive design gives the product talking points over factory-made products. Concentrate on high-profit items. Stay clear of the low-profit, highly competitive market, especially fashion items on the way out.

There is also a growing market for mending and alterations. One woman has a successful business based on the yearly refurbishing of draperies in a nearby college. Some women are successfully conducting sewing classes. The scarcity of competent seamstresses is so great that a woman skilled with the needle can unually find plenty of work doing alterations for specialty dress shops, department stores, and men's shops.

A sewing shop is a small business you can establish and operate from your home. List your shop in the yellow pages of the local telephone book. Send postal cards to specialty shops and women's clubs. Have business cards made up. If you live near a boarding school, college or hospital, send postal cards to students and nurses who are usually too busy to do their own wardrobe repairs.

If zoning laws permit, display an attractive sign in the front of your home. You should be sure to price your products or time according to your skill and efficiency. Older people cannot usually compete with younger, skilled craftsmen producing at a higher rate of speed.

Additional Personal-Service Activities

Here are a few other activities that can be operated on a part-time or full-time basis from the home: addressing envelopes for mail-order businesses and businessmen, telephone answering and soliciting for local business concerns or professional men, typing manuscripts for authors, taking care of children during the day (children called for and returned, balanced meals provided), laundering curtains, pick-up and delivery service, hand-ironing dresses and blouses, cooking special diet meals, teaching auto driving with dual-controlled car, refinishing furniture, sanding and refinishing floors, cleaning attics, cellars and yards, repairing sewing machines, writing articles for professional or trade magazines, providing convalescent care, renting furnished or unfurnished rooms, operating photographic studios, developing and photo printing.

How About Establishing a Small Retail Business?

Gift Shop. Here is an opportunity for men and women with an appreciation of art and craft values to cash in on their knowledge. To be a successful operator of a gift and art shop, you should specialize in items that are unusual and unique. If you can get the exclusive rights for a number of these items in the city or county where your store is located, so much the better. Your best chance to obtain an exclusive is to act as the sales outlet of experienced craftsmen. They might be individual craftsmen who work alone. They could be members of an organized homecraft or art group. You might be able to arrange to be the exclusive representative in your locality for the many products of a regular state or local homecraft industry or association. Many gift shops are also workshops where original items are produced on the premises.

You probably will not be able to obtain enough products from individual craftsmen alone to profitably operate a gift and art shop, so you will be dependent also upon manufacturers who produce in volume for the national gift shop market. Even in this type of merchandise, many gift shop operators can and do obtain exclusive items.

While there are many gift shops that do a large volume of business, the smaller gift shops do an average business from $30,000 to $50,000 a year. Gift shops do best in college towns, towns with a historical background, recreational and resort centers, and the local shopping center of towns where the standard of living is high. Many gift shops are associated with roadside tearooms and fine restaurants. Others operate on highways where tourist traffic is heavy. The important ingredients for success are location, capitalization, adequate and unique stock-in-trade, credit facilities, merchandising ability, modern methods of management, display of merchandise and accounting and the friendly personality of the owner and assistants.

Bookstore. Bookselling is a business which will have special appeal to booklovers. You may have to spend a good many hours on your feet, so you should be in good health. In a small store the owner is obliged to open all shipments and handle returns, shift stock, etc. Energy and patience are important qualities due to the infinite detail work punctuated steadily with interruptions. Profits are low.

The over-all profit figures for bookstores are not high. They indicate that $25,000 in sales will probably be necessary to provide you with a $3,500 annual salary.

Woodworking Shop. An almost unlimited number of articles can be made and sold or repaired in a well-equipped woodworking shop operated by a skilled craftsman. Here are some of the things that can be done: furniture and cabinet-making and repair, repairing and restoring antiques, upholstery and repair, novelty toy and bric-a-brac manufacture, hobby products. To succeed, you should be a skilled craftsman.

It is impossible to say with any degree of accuracy how much capital is required to open a shop of this kind, because there are too many variables. With good business judgment, shrewd management and rigid economy, you might be able to begin business with as little as $1,000 or $2,000. However, experience shows that more than half of the ventures set up within too narrow capital margins fail within the first year. If you attempt to set up shop on $1,000, your equipment will have to be bought on the installment plan. This is a bad way for a retired person to start business. It is safer to start with sufficient capital to cover all initial expenses. This should include cost of equipment and materials and rent if you lease a shop or building, and a capital checking account to cover six months to two years of living expenses.

Some of the articles that can be made in a small wood-working shop are garden and lawn furniture, doghouses, bird-feeders and birdhouses, driveway arches, gates, lattice fences and trellises, covered sandboxes, ironing boards, folding seats, poultry nests, clothes-drying racks, workbenches, bookcases, breakfast tables and benches, wall bookracks and many similar items. These articles may be sold completely assembled or knocked down. Knock-down kits containing all the material cut to size will appeal to customers who prefer to assemble and paint the articles. Wooden articles can be sold to roadside- stand proprietors, mail-order houses, hardware and paint stores and other retail stores that can be induced to take on a line of articles made from wood.

Metal-working Shop. A skilled machinist or craftsman in metal can handle a great variety of jobs operating his own shop. With a little ingenuity in adapting attachments and special tricks with tools, he needs comparatively little equipment. He can do general repair work and service work on machinery, household equipment and farm implements.

Those who have an artistic sense can add ornamental iron-fabrication equipment for making handmade products such as lighting fixtures, wrought-iron lamps, hinges, latches and hardware, stair rails, gates and the like. Architects and builders, antique dealers, garden shops and lighting fixtures stores are prospects for ornamental metalwork.

In rural communities the proprietor can operate a traveling (truck-mounted) shop with a power take-off from the engine of the truck.

A Letter Shop. Retired advertising men, reporters, printers, office managers, stenographers and salesmen might consider establishing and operating their own letter shop. A small shop with one or two persons in addition to the proprietor, which offers typewriting, duplicating, addressing and mail service, could provide income for a fair living for the owner.

In order to start a small but well-equipped letter shop offering these services, you would need about $5,000 capital. This would provide for new equipment, supplies, shop furnishings, working capital, personal reserve and miscellaneous expenses. A great deal of this equipment can be bought in the working years before you retire. Successful letter shops can be established in both large and small communities.

Sporting-goods Store. Experienced fishermen and hunters, former athletes and coaches, and handymen who can repair rods, reels and guns, restring tennis rackets, fix bicycles and do hundreds of little jobs can start a small sporting-goods store and make a fair living doing something they really enjoy.

This type of business can be operated successfully in a small town, especially in resort and vacation areas. A sporting-goods store has the best chance of success in an area that is active, progressive, likes sports and has a good recreational program. The area should permit the operation of some kind of sports activity twelve months of the year. In some small towns, the line of sporting goods is combined with phonograph and radio equipment, flashlights, books and other items. Repair service on sporting items is a good source of revenue.

Bookkeeping, Accounting and Tax Service. This might consist of only one individual and an assistant. This type of business can be located either in a large city or a small community. Clients may be small businessmen, professional men or private individuals with income tax problems.

The increasing need for records and reports, because of tax laws, and the growing awareness of the value of accurate record-keeping for good business management, all point to a long-term demand for small bookkeeping and tax firms. Obviously, a person interested in starting a small bookkeeping firm needs to have a technical background and training in accounting and related subjects. He should also have some knowledge of finance and insurance. In this business you can work at home and either do your own typing or have it done on a part-time basis. Or you may rent desk space in an office. It is not necessary to be a C.P.A., but it helps. Some state laws require an annual registration and license fee before you can practice public accounting. You should investigate the matter thoroughly before taking up residence in a state. New York State, for instance, no longer allows accountants to be registered, so that only C.P.A.'s are permitted to practice. The size of the city or town will affect your dollar income. Since living and business expenses are higher in the larger cities, a greater dollar income may not be worth more in terms of real income than a somewhat lesser income in a smaller community.

In rural communities you can operate a traveling (truck-mounted) office, with farmers and rural businessmen as clients.

Mail Order Is a Good Business if You Have a Good Item

The mail-order business offers income-making opportunities for many retired persons who are looking forward to an independent business of their own. It appeals to people who have a keen desire to pursue a hobby, craft or avocation.

Broad experience is not a prime essential for success in the mail-order business. Much of the success depends on your product, the market in which it is sold, the method of presentation. You can pick up knowledge and experience as you go along. Of course, to be successful, some know-how is essential. You can secure much of the specialized information you need from several how-to-do-it books now on the market.

The type of mail-order business referred to here is not the large, general mail-order house carrying a complete line of consumer goods. What we have in mind is a small specialty mail-order operation carrying one good article or a narrow line of goods for sale by mail.

To get an idea of the scope of specialty mail-order houses, look through the advertising sections of popular and craft magazines and farm magazines, and the mail-order sections of large metropolitan Sunday newspapers. Notice the variety of mail-order propositions offered. Some of the advertisers are manufacturers, growers or distributors. Others are one-man mail-order specialty businesses. Some are operated only during seasonal periods. A number never get beyond the part-time stage.

Stock propositions, consisting of a supply of merchandise and imprinted literature offered by some manufacturers are, as a rule, not good money-making propositions. Staple merchandise that is commonly sold in stores will not be highly profitable when sold by mail. Specialty items, home gadgets, household specialties, novelties, curios, unusual jewelry, craft items, handwoven rugs, garden furniture, fruit-and-nut gift baskets and packages, unusual articles made at home or in a small workshop—these are the types of articles that offer the best prospects for a profitable mail-order business.

How-to-do-it books, "information" instruction and correspondence courses, equipment and supplies for home craftsmen, are also good items for mail-order selling. Many mail-order operators do not have the facilities or equipment to make the products they sell. They have the items manufactured for them on a contract basis.

A small mail-order project can be started in your spare time without interfering with your regular work. It is the type of business that can be started and developed before you retire. In fact, to build a good mail-order business you should start small and proceed slowly while you test your proposition. When you're convinced you have a profitable product, you can strike out with more capital.

According to research surveys, 30 percent of all mail-order businesses were started with a capital of less than $500, while another 30 percent began with $500 to $3,000. Much depends upon the individual, his manner of working and the cost of the products he sells by mail.

Here are four elements usually present in successful direct-by-mail selling: (1) a letter that sells; (2) a circular that supplements the letter, describes and illustrates the product and contains testimonials; (3) an easy-to-order business-reply card, order form or self-addressed envelope; (4) a good mailing list. Seventy-five percent of the success or failure of direct mail campaigns is said to depend on the type and quality of the mailing list.

The mailing list can be built up from replies to advertising placed in newspapers and magazines, and from radio and television advertising. Or you can buy or rent a specific mailing list from a list broker or list compiler.

The mail-order beginner should check the legal aspects that might apply to his operation. Foods, drugs, drug devices and cosmetics are subject to regulation by the Federal Food, Drug and Cosmetic Act.

Developing New Products

Retired engineers, mechanics, draftsmen, professional men, salesmen—almost anybody with a fertile imagination and a gift for recognizing practical possibilities might use some of their retirement time for the development of new products.

An executive's wife had an idea that started a meat packer

in the canned onion soup business; a salesman thought up an idea for a canned chicken product; the president of a company had the idea for a golf bag "toter"; the list of government-owned patents available for sale was the idea source for a kitchen gadget and for an insecticide; a food broker thought up the idea for canned apple juice; a museum exhibit resulted in a new vase for a pottery manufacturer; a doctor's hobby of experimenting with wheat germs resulted in his bringing out a new line of health foods; a mechanic watching his wife having difficulties holding material while sewing got the idea for a simple clamp device.

There are so many possibilities in new products that no hard-and-fast rule can be laid down about the types of products to look for. Manufacturing companies are always on the lookout for new products that can be made by their present labor force with existing equipment and sold by the sales force to their customers.

Large companies generally use their own research-and-development laboratories and market-research personnel to develop new products. Smaller firms not in a position to organize for large-scale new-product development are good prospects for privately developed new products. Some new product developers start their own small businesses to manufacture and sell practical new products that have profitable market potentials. Others have the products made for them on contract and do their own selling by mail order, or to jobbers and retail outlets or through manufacturers' representatives.

Before investing money in the development of a new product, it is wise to assemble and compare several good ideas and select the best. You should make a market-and-consumer survey to avoid putting too many dollars and too much time into an item that has limited profit possibilities. Design and develop a product fitted to consumer needs and desires—not just something *you* like. Test the product carefully under actual use conditions before placing it on the market. Have a patent search made before making your final design and tooling up for production.

Other important factors in marketing, in addition to selling, are price, package design, a good product name (be careful not to infringe on registered trademarks), advertising and sales promotion. Keep a precise record-history of the inception and development of a new product. You might need it for patent application or protection in case of being cited for patent infringement. Be sure to read the United States Department of Commerce publication, *Developing and Selling New Products*.

Opportunities in Selling

The opportunities and possibilities in selling are vast. You can adapt your talents and skills to that branch of salesmanship which gives you the most working pleasure.

You can sell a product or a line of products to substantially the same people. The route salesman who calls at the home selling milk, eggs and butter is in this classification. So is the salesman who calls regularly on an established list of dealers, wholesalers or manufacturers in a selected city, county or state.

You can sell popular consumer products like clothing or apparel, technical products like electronic devices or intangible services like insurance or advertising space. There are salesmen who specialize in selling to manufacturers, others who sell to distributors and dealers and still others who sell to ultimate consumers. Further breakdowns in the specialization of selling are manufacturers' salesmen, sales engineers, manufacturers' representatives, wholesale salesmen, retail-store salesmen and clerks, and house-to-house salesmen. Some salesmen are paid a straight salary. Others work on a straight commission basis. There are many variations and combinations of these two basic compensation plans.

Retired salesmen and sales managers, advertising men and women, business people, engineers and others with qualifications for making a success at selling should consider some type of selling as an opportunity to supplement retirement income. Try to pick a product you like. Your regular workday experience will probably help in making a choice. Be sure the physical demands of selling are not greater than you should undertake and that you are well fitted for the task.

A good salesman is always needed. The man or woman who knows what kind of merchandise he or she would like to sell and the type of selling he or she would like to engage in has an excellent opportunity to secure profitable, satisfying work. No hard-and-fast figures can be given on earnings in so variable an occupation as selling.

The Real Estate Business

This covers selling or leasing property, placing mortgages, collecting rents and performing other services. It is such a popular retirement occupation that it is overcrowded in many localities.

In the real estate business, your time is a primary asset. You must be willing to serve customers at all times, including at night and over weekends. Also educational requirements become more demanding as the real estate market becomes more complex.

In handling any type of a real estate transaction, the broker or sales person is involved in probably the largest financial transaction of any given family, and consequently should be thoroughly grounded in such subjects as zoning, financing, tax laws, market trends, and simple legal procedures, just to mention a few.

When one enters commercial or industrial real estate,

property management, or appraising, educational background and experience become even more demanding. A broker's income depends on the number and the size of the transactions he closes. This is governed by his energy, ability and initiative. The real estate boards in key cities have set up schedules of minimum commission rates which board members are requested to observe. This is usually 6 percent of the base amount of the sale price for city property. The commission rate specified by some real estate boards for the sale of farm and land property is 10 percent of the sale price.

To protect the public as well as the honest and competent brokers, states have license laws which regulate real estate brokerage. Almost every city has a local real estate board which is interested in promoting and protecting local business. Local boards are affiliated with the National Association of Realtors. Many individual firms, many of the local real estate boards, and most state associations conduct courses to train both newcomers and experienced personnel in the many facets of the field.

If you would like to know more about preparing yourself for a career in real estate, write to The National Association of Realtors, 430 N. Michigan Ave., Chicago, Illinois 60611.

Property Management

Managing income property for the owner is a specialized business. You can hardly expect the owner of important property, such as an apartment house or office building, to allow you to operate it until you have experience in this type of business. If you have no experience, you might start by managing a small property which yields fees too small to interest seasoned managers of larger properties. You might, also, take care of vacation cottages for owners during the months they are empty. You could act as renting

agent, too. In this way you can acquire property-manage-
ment experience.

There is a good deal more to managing income-producing property than collecting rents and attending to tenant
complaints. Duties fall into three classifications—those pertaining to tenants, such as service and rent collecting; operating duties, such as inspection and maintenance of the
building; managerial duties, such as keeping records, providing statements to owner, tax and financial problems and
budgeting expenses. While practical experience is necessary, knowledge may be acquired from special courses offered by the Institute of Real Estate Management, 155 E.
Superior St., Chicago, Illinois 60611. Local real estate
boards in a great many cities have set fees for managing
properties. These fees vary among communities.

The Motel Business

The growth in the number of motels and motor courts
along the highways is evidence of their popularity and of
their profit-making possibilities. For the most part, big operators have become an increasingly significant part of this
growth. While operating a successful motel is not so easy
as it looks, there are many opportunities for retirees with
plenty of energy, initiative, business ability and a willing-
ness to tackle a variety of odd jobs.

The average motel has approximately twenty-five units
to a court. Authorities in the motor-court industry advise
that it is impractical to start a motor court with less than
twenty units or rooms. The larger motels or motor courts
have from sixty to several hundred units.

If you have the idea you can run a motel on a semi-retired
basis without hired help, you are mistaken. If you and your
wife try to do most of the work yourselves, you will find that
you are working harder than ever. More difficult than the

work is the confinement. If a husband and wife run the motel, one or the other must be on hand throughout the day and night. Should the court have less than ten units, it cannot afford more than the services of one maid.

Success or failure in the motel business depends upon the owner's own efforts and abilities, routing or re-routing of the main traffic highway, legislation affecting roadside businesses, change of neighborhood, competition, economic conditions of prosperity or depression, sufficient capital invested in the business. Florida State University and others offer courses in the operation and management of motels.

Other Types of Businesses in the Same General Classification

Vacation cabins and trailer parks in resort areas are rented by the week or month. You can rent out rooms in a large house to tourists or vacationists. With a little remodeling, a large house can be converted into an attractive tourist home. Location, parking and garage facilities are important factors in the successful operation of a tourist home. If located in a college town, you can rent rooms to students.

Brains and Experience Advisory Services

Here are a few case histories of management men who, retired from business, have formed groups, offer their pooled talents for consultation and seasoned advice.

Retired engineers and draftsmen from the General Electric Company and American Locomotive Works, Schenectady, New York, formed the Mohawk Development Service. Here for some years more than a dozen men, from sixty-six to seventy-four years of age, have provided engineering, drafting service and consultation on electrical and mechanical problems of all kinds.

A group of thirty retired executives of large and small industries in Wilmington, Delaware, offered business advice free to small businessmen in the area.

This idea can be expanded. A movement in this direction is the formation of Senior Achievement Groups, similar to the popular Junior Achievement programs. Retired persons organize themselves into groups. They establish their own managerial, supervisory and production groups, and market their own products.

The Senior Achievement movement also could expand in another direction. A local association could be formed for the purpose of making members self-sufficient by applying the homely principles of the early New England colonists. This would take the form of pooling the knowledge, skills and labor of each of the membership for the benefit of all.

The plan in a modified form would cover swapping work projects among members. Each member would file a list of his skills in such jobs as house painting, paper hanging, carpentry and alterations, reconditioning furniture, landscape gardening and similar work. The skills of the womenfolk could be catalogued for homemaking specialties. At regular get-togethers, assignments would be made on a group project. The member most experienced in, say, house painting, could act as supervisor on projects calling for this type of work. In this way what one member could not do alone, the group could.

If the group should run out of projects for the association membership, it could take on community projects like constructing a shuffleboard court or building and installing picnic tables or fireplaces in the community park or recreational area. While every community wants things like this done, the community somehow seldom finds the time or the manpower.

There is a wide variety of useful and cooperative jobs that such a Senior Achievement group could do in its spare time. By helping themselves and others intelligently they would create active and worthwhile careers.

Baby- or Invalid-Sitting Service

This is an ideal way for a retired woman to earn a supplementary income. It also provides a means of combating loneliness. You can engage in baby-sitting or invalid-sitting by offering your own services. Or you can establish and manage a group of sitters by setting yourself up as a sitting-agency service.

To operate as an agency you need a group of older women or men or teen-agers on whom you can absolutely depend, a telephone and a system for keeping records of sitters and clients. You can operate the service from your home. You will need to advertise your service by inserting a small advertisement in local newspapers and mailing postal cards to a list of neighborhood parents, church groups and clubs, listing your service in the yellow pages of the local telephone book. Consult the town clerk to learn whether you need a license to operate a sitting-agency service in your locality.

The owner of one agency once told us that the bulk of her paying business came from supplying "substitute mothers"—housekeepers who take the place of a mother in times of illness, unexpected absence from home or during vacation periods. For this reason she had on her list the names of about a dozen or more women in their late forties through their early sixties who were completely trustworthy to take over the running of a household for a period of from three days to two weeks.

Rates vary from area to area. For baby-sitting after midnight, rates go up; $125 or better would be paid to someone who comes in or takes over for a week as a household manager. As the operator-manager of the agency service you should collect 20 to 30 percent of the fee.

There's Money in Worms

A Californian does an annual business of $50,000 raising and selling earthworms. A woman in the earthworm business started with $10 invested in worms and in three years had her earthworm sales up to $4,000. A poultry farmer started raising earthworms as a sideline and in four years made more money from the sale of worms than from his poultry hatchery.

The principal uses for earthworms are for soil building of farms and gardens; for fish bait; for zoos, laboratories, aquariums and game breeders; for breeding stock sold to earthworm raisers.

With as little as $10 to $20 you can get started on an earthworm breeding project. For about $100 you can buy ten thousand fine breeding earthworm stock. In about a year you should have enough worms to start selling on a regular businesslike scale. Earthworm raising offers good prospects for a retirement business either as a part-time or full-time operation. With good breeding stock started, experts in the business say, you should be able in about three hours' work a day to pack and ship about $14 worth of worms.

There are many species of worms to choose from. You will find many breeders of worms listed in gardening and hobby magazines and in the *Earthworm Buyers Guide*. Write to several asking for literature on the species they raise. The state agricultural college can help you in selecting the best type in which to specialize. One of the best booklets on the subject is *Raising Earthworms for Profit,* by Earl B. Shields, Shields Publications, P.O. Box 472, Elgin, Illinois, postpaid $2.00. Also by the same publisher, *Earthworm Buyers Guide,* $2.00.

Animal Sitter

There's a woman in a suburb of Los Angeles who is building up a thriving business as an animal sitter. Traveling about in a light truck, she visits about six "clients" a day. These vary from goats to goldfish. Her specialty is feeding and taking care of animals and pets in their own homes, while owners are away on vacation, in the hospital and so on. Her prices vary according to the animal or pet.

"Hotel" for Pets

Many dog owners would welcome a place to board their pets while they are away from home. They hesitate to leave their pets caged up in the small areas provided by veterinarians. One woman solved this problem by building a series of pens ten feet square in a barn with a cement floor. Long runs were built outside under trees so that the dogs could get exercise. During the vacation season there is a waiting list for available pens. The charge is $2.00 and up a day for room and board. A bath costs $1.00. Veterinarians and pet shops refer dog owners to her. She also runs small advertisements in the classified section of the local newspaper. This activity could be expanded to include obedience lessons and the selling of pet-shop accessories, such as dog baskets, blankets and harnesses. Good opportunities exist for this type of service in locations adjacent to city areas.

Small Animal Breeding for Pleasure and Profit

Many retired men and women make a comfortable living raising and selling small animals and birds. The secret of success is to specialize in something for which there is a demand and not too much competition. If raising dogs, pheasants, goats, rabbits, singing canaries or rare birds appeals to you, look into the market possibilities for selling your stock. Research organizations and hospitals buy mice, guinea pigs, rabbits and other animals for medical research projects. Hotels, clubs, restaurants, shooting clubs, private game preserves and other sporting organizations buy many thousands of pheasants each year. Rabbit meat is popular in some areas as a food item. Goat milk finds a good market in some localities. There is always a good market for select breeding stock of small animals and pets of all kinds.

Some states require licenses for raising fur animals in captivity. Information on this matter can be obtained from your state game commission. Some towns also have restrictive ordinances.

Parcel Delivery Service

One retired man I know bought a light secondhand delivery truck and had an attractive paint job done on it. He has a contract service with several retail stores to make parcel deliveries. He charges from 25 cents to 50 cents per parcel, depending upon the size of the parcel and the delivery distance. He makes store pick-ups once in the morning and once during the afternoon.

Investing in an Established Business

You may be offered the opportunity to buy an established business. Perhaps you can buy it at a good price if the owner is anxious to sell. Don't, however, concentrate upon buying a business at a bargain. Under normal conditions there are no bargains or "steals." Take plenty of time to make a careful analysis and appraisal of the business.

Try to find out the owner's reason for selling. It may be entirely different from what he tells you. He may be trying to unload a sick or dying business, a "white elephant," on an unsuspecting prospect. Here are some legitimate reasons why owners sell established businesses: desire to retire from active participation in the business, bad health, plans for moving to another region, need to settle an estate, disagreement among partners, marital differences, business not suited to their temperament. But watch out for these factors: location of business on the downgrade, main highway being relocated, new zoning laws which threaten future of the business, no demand for products or services in the area, the franchise to sell principal line is being lost, too much competition, lease expiring and landlord refusing to renew it.

Wisdom demands that you investigate the business proposition as thoroughly as possible before you get too deeply involved. Don't let the owner or his agent push you into buying a business before you complete your investigation. Ask the owner for copies of his business records, and also his income tax returns since he has operated the business he wants to sell. Find out when the business was originally established, how many times it has changed hands and if it has been consistently profitable. If you decide to buy, appraise each of the assets separately to determine what price you should pay. What is the value of the equipment and the stock on hand? Check every item. Unless you do so, you may find it necessary to discard a lot of material that you took for granted was in good condition. It might be a good idea to have an accountant check the financial records and make an evaluation of the business. Compare the business in its present state and the price asked for it with one you could start and develop yourself. Sometimes when a business is sold, the former owner wants to sell his receivables. These are accounts of customers who owe him money. If you take over these accounts, be sure that you are actually buying customers and not bad debts. Check the list of customer accounts receivable with the local retail credit association or banker. Engage a competent lawyer to draw up the purchase agreement.

The Small Business Administration May Help You

If you are truly serious in wanting to start a new business either before usual retirement date or at R-Day, the Small Business Administration of the Federal Government might well be of assistance to you. The SBA is a permanent, independent government agency created by Congress to help small business.

Congress has directed SBA to insure free competition as the essence of the American economic system of private enterprise and to strengthen the over-all economy of the nation.

Through its network of 73 field offices in the principal cities of every state, SBA offers to small business financial assistance including lease guarantees, management assistance, aid in obtaining government contracts, counseling services, and more than 300 publications covering practices in every small business field.

Any small businessman with a financial problem may come to SBA for advice and assistance. Agency specialists will review his problem and suggest possible courses of action.

If a businessman needs money and cannot borrow it on reasonable terms, SBA often can help. The Agency will consider either participating in, or guaranteeing up to 90 percent of a bank loan. If the bank cannot provide any funds, SBA will consider lending the entire amount as a direct government loan. Ninety percent of SBA's loans are now made in participation with banks.

How to Decide Whether a Small Business Is for You

People sometimes go into business for themselves without being fully aware of what is involved. Sometimes they're lucky and succeed. More often, they fail because they do not consider one or more of the ingredients needed for business success.

The Small Business Administration of the Federal Government offers a list of questions you should ask yourself.

This checklist is designed to help you decide whether you are qualified or have considered the various phases of going into business for yourself. Careful thought now may help you to prevent mistakes and to avoid losing your savings and time later. Use this list as a starter. Consider each question as it applies to your situation. Check off each question only after you've made an effort to answer it honestly. Before you omit a question, satisfy yourself that it does not apply to your particular situation.

Questions to Consider

Are You the Type?

1. Have you rated your personal traits such as leadership, organizing ability, perseverance and physical energy?
2. Have you had some friends rate you on them?
3. Have you considered getting an associate whose strong points will compensate for your weak traits?

What Are Your Chances for Success?

4. Have you had any actual business experience?
5. Do you have special technical skills, such as those needed

by a plumber, electrician, mechanic or radio repairman?

6. Have you obtained some basic management experience working for someone else?

7. Have you analyzed the recent trend of business conditions (good or bad)?

8. Have you analyzed business conditions in the city and neighborhood where you want to locate?

9. Have you analyzed conditions in the line of business you are planning?

10. Have you determined what size business you plan to establish (dollar sales per year)?

11. Have you built up a detailed set of figures on how much capital you will need to launch the business?

12. Have you figured how much time you will need until the business income equals the expenses?

13. Have you planned what net profit you believe you should make?

14. Will the net profit divided by the investment result in a rate of return which compares favorably with the rate you can obtain from other investment opportunities?

How Much Capital Will You Need?

15. Have you worked out what income from sales or services you can reasonably expect in the first 6 months? The first year? The second year?

16. Do you know what net profit you can expect on these volumes?

17. Have you made a conservative forecast of expenses including a regular salary for yourself?

18. Have you compared this income with what you could make working for someone else?

19. Are you willing to risk uncertain or irregular income for the next year? Two years?

20. Have you counted up how much actual money you have to invest in your business?

21. Do you have other assets which you could sell or on which you could borrow?
22. Have you some other source from which you could borrow money?
23. Have you talked to a banker?
24. Is he favorably impressed with your plan?
25. Do you have a financial reserve for unexpected needs?
26. Does your total capital, from all sources, cover your best estimates of the capital you will need?

Should You Share Ownership with Others?

27. Do you lack needed technical or management skills which can be most satisfactorily supplied by one or more partners?
28. Do you need the financial assistance of one or more partners?
29. Have you checked the features of each form or organization (individual proprietorship, partnership, corporation) to see which will best fit your situation?

Other sets of questions are listed under the following headings in a bulletin entitled "Checklist for Going Into Business," No. 71 in the Small Marketers Aids series of the Small Business Administration. (Washington, D.C. or your regional office.)

Where Should You Locate?
Should You Buy a Going Business?
Are You Qualified to Supervise Buying and Selling?
What Selling Methods Will You Use?
How Will You Price Your Products and Services?
What Records Will You Keep?
What Laws Will Affect You?
What Other Problems Will You Face?
Will You Keep Up to Date?

Five Steps in Establishing a Retirement Business

1. *Early Start in Preparation.* Find out as early as possible the type of business you would like to establish and operate in your retirement years. Your aptitude, interest and health are vital factors in determining whether or not you should engage in a particular business. Your knowledge of the business, practical experience in it and financial status are essential factors in determining the type of business you are likely to make a success of.

Most businesses fail because of the owner's lack of business capacity and lack of capital. An early start in planning will enable you to acquire by reading and studying, by part-time practical experience, the necessary business capacity to establish and operate the business of your choice. A carefully planned savings, investment and income-producing program, started early, will provide you with the capital needed to open or buy your business. By planning and organizing your spare time, you can make an interesting hobby out of preparing to establish a profitable business of your own when you retire. In doing this you will be storing up understanding and knowledge that you will need when you make the big plunge on your own.

2. *Studying for Business Operation.* You cannot have too much knowledge about the business you propose to engage in. Gaining more knowledge is a continuous process.

Government Helps. The publications of the United States Government are prepared in the form of leaflets, pamphlets, bulletins and books by the various agencies. The Department of Commerce publications include *Small Business Aids*—over five hundred titles covering such subjects as financing, selling, advertising, insurance and record-keeping; *Establishing and Operating Series*—mostly on retail and service trades. This series includes over forty books that thoroughly discuss the major problems of a particular type of business. Types of businesses covered range from small woodworking shop to service station, from restaurant to jewelry store; *Basic Information Series*—bulletins which are listings of governmental and nongovernmental publications, directories, trade papers and trade associations for various fields of business. Questions or problems which arise on which no publication has been prepared will be answered by specialists in the Department of Commerce. Address your letter to Bureau of Information, Department of Commerce, Washington 25, D.C. Published information is for sale by Superintendent of Documents, United States Government Printing Office, Washington, D.C. 20402.

Books on Your Specialty. Visit your public library every so often and take out how-to-do-it books on the subject of your business interests.

Trade Papers. Numerous general business magazines are published by each type of trade and business. Subscribe to the leading trade magazine of the business field you plan to enter. Reading these magazines will keep you in touch with what is happening in the business and keep you up-to-date on new products and new applications. Keep a clipping file of articles that are of particular interest to you.

Trade Associations. Many businesses and industries have active trade associations of their own. You can pick up a great deal of helpful information attending national and state conventions and trade shows. Watch local newspapers and trade journals for notices of conventions in your locality.

Manufacturers' Catalogs and Booklets often are textbooks on their lines of products. A study of their sales and instruction literature is well worthwhile. Manufacturers also prepare sales manuals on store layouts and sales techniques covering their products.

Schools and Correspondence Courses. Check with local public and private school and college administrators regarding classes available. Many courses, conducted at night, cover a wide range of vocational subjects and occupations. Enrollment in one or more of these courses may develop your skill, talents and technical training for a retirement occupation or business. Many a person has developed a successful new career by studying selected occupations by the correspondence method. Accredited correspondence schools train you, in your spare time, by regular lessons which are informative and practical.

3. *Getting Practical Training.* The records of those who have succeeded and those who have failed in business prove beyond a doubt that practical experience is one of the most important assets you can possess. Therefore, if you have never worked in the type of business you plan to establish when you retire, you will be wise to take a part-time job on weekends or during some of your vacations in such a business. You could, of course, wait until you retire and then work for six months or a year getting on-the-job practical training and experience in a well-established and successful business.

4. *Getting Occupational Tools and Equipment.* In some types of businesses, a woodworking shop, for example, you can begin to collect much of the necessary tools and equipment while you are still working on your regular job. You may be able to pick up bargains as they become available or buy new tools and equipment out of savings from your regular salary or wages. It is important to have good judgment in buying these things in advance, so that you don't load yourself with a lot of obsolete equipment.

5. *Selecting a Location.* Decide in which region of the country you wish to establish your business. Begin a study of the various towns and communities in the region. Find out which offer the best opportunities. Visit the area selected during your vacations for a personal checkup of general

business conditions. Study it carefully. Is the city or town lively, progressive, growing? How about competition? Is there any? What is the rent situation? What about sources for obtaining merchandise? Is there really a potential market for your proposed products or services? Study both sides of the picture—the disadvantages as well as the advantages.

Bibliography

BOOKS

How to Start Your Own Business ed. by William D. Putt (M.I.T. Press, Cambridge, Mass.)

Can a Smaller Store Succeed? by Jane Cahill (Fairchild, N.Y.)

Small Business Bibliography (The Useful Reference Series of Library Books) by Jessie C. Ellis (Faxon, Westwood, Mass.)

How to Buy a Franchise or Small Business by Robert Franks (WWWWWW Information Service, Rochester, N.Y.)

Your Own Craft Business by Herbert Genfon (Watson-Guptill, Cincinnati, Ohio)

One Hundred and One Businesses You Can Start and Run with Less than $1,000 by H. S. Kahm (Doubleday, N.Y.)

Help Yourself to a Job: A Guide for Retirees by Dorothy Winter (Beacon Press, Boston, Mass.)

Choosing Your Retirement Hobby by Norah Smaridge (Dodd, Mead, N.Y.)

Retirement Dollars for the Self-Employed by Steven S. Anreder (Crowell, N.Y.)

TRADE PAPERS DEVOTED TO SELECTED BUSINESSES

Antique Trader, Box 1050, Dubuque, Iowa 52001

Antiques Dealer, 1115 Clifton Ave., Clifton, N.J. 08109

American Paint and Wallcovering Dealer, 2911 Washington Ave., St. Louis, Mo. 63103

Leisure Industries Review, Beekman Pub., Inc., 53 Park Place, New York, N.Y. 10007

Ski Business, 380 Madison Ave., New York, N.Y. 10017

Journal of Accountancy, 1211 Ave. of Americas, New York, N.Y. 10036

Travel Trade, 605 Fifth Ave., New York, N.Y. 10017

National Real Estate Investor, 461 8th Ave., New York, N.Y. 10001
Real Estate Bulletin, 99 Church St., New York, N.Y. 10001
Greenhouse Newsletter: Cooperative Extension Service, Box U 67, Storrs, Conn.
  06268
Gift and Tableware Reporter, 1 Astor Plaza, New York, N.Y. 10036
Gifts and Decorative Accessories, 51 Madison Ave., New York, N.Y. 10010
For a complete list of trade papers in all classifications, see *Ulrich's
International Periodical Directory.* Your public library probably has a
copy.

FREE—SMALL BUSINESS ADMINISTRATION PUBLICATIONS

Available at your nearest SBA office or SBA, Washington, D.C. 20416
  Handicrafts
  Selling by Mail Order
  Marketing Research Procedures
  Retailing
  The Nursery Business
  Mobile Homes and Parks
  Bookstores
  Restaurants and Catering
  Basic Library Reference Sources
  National Mailing-List Houses
  Are You Kidding Yourself about Your Profits?
  Checklist for Going into Business
  A Pricing Checklist for Managers

HOME BUSINESSES

Are You Ready for Franchising?
Accounting Services for Small Service Firms
Retirement Plans for Self-Employed Owner-Managers

SMALL BUSINESS ADMINISTRATION PUBLICATIONS For Sale

Starting and Managing Series	Catalog No.	Price
Starting and Managing a		
Small Business of Your Own	SBA 1.15:1	1.35
Starting and Managing a Service Station	SBA 1.15:3	1.05
Starting and Managing a Carwash	SBA 1.15:14	1.10
Buying and Selling a Small Business	SBA 1.19:B99	1.60

HOW TO ORDER: Send check, money order, or Documents coupons to the Superintendent of Documents, Government Printing Office, Washington, D.C., 20402. Make check or money order payable to the Superintendent of Documents. Do not send postage or cash. These booklets are *not sold* by the Small Business Administration.

U.S. GOVERNMENT PUBLICATIONS

Occupations—Professions and job descriptions. Send for free bibliography and price list of books and pamphlets on these subjects to Superintendent of Documents, Government Printing Office, Washington, D.C. 20402.

9

If You Would Like to Retire to a Farm

Farming for those of retirement age should be undertaken only by people of two types. One is the couple who like country living and would be content with a small farm for fruit, vegetables, poultry and livestock, primarily for personal consumption, for the pleasure of producing for their own sustenance and for reducing the cost of living. The monetary income for them should be on a catch-as-catch-can basis, to produce extra dollars over budgetary needs.

Another type of farming would be for a vigorous person taking early retirement, a person of some means and a great yen for farm life. This person would have independent income in addition to some risk capital to try the new venture. He would have started ahead to gather the knowledge necessary for the type of farming he plans to enter—by attending classes, seriously studying, and probably by working awhile with some experienced farm operator. With his acquired specialized knowledge and a prior background in some other form of business management, this person could find a new career in the "farm business."

These types could find opportunity. On the other hand, many others might find that retirement farming may well open up years of strenuous activity, high risk, and a rigid binding to the occupation at the very time when most individuals want less work, less risk, and freedom of action to vacation and to enjoy life.

Acquiring a Farm before Retirement

If you decide to go ahead with farming you don't necessarily have to wait until you retire before acquiring farm property. It is a good idea to be on the lookout for a suitable farm or ranch some years prior to your tentative retirement date. If you come across property that meets your requirements, buy it—if the location, the time and the price are right, and if you have the money. Older people should not use their savings and mortgage their future, however. By the time your retirement date rolls around, you should own the property without substantial encumbrances against it.

If you acquire farm property at a location that is too far away from your present employment, you may be able to lease the property to a reliable tenant and use the rent income to help pay the taxes. Or you can make an arrangement with a farmer tenant to operate and maintain the farm or ranch on a share-the-income basis, during the years of your absentee ownership.

Be sure to select a farmer tenant who is experienced, industrious and conscientious. The owner, in addition to furnishing the land and buildings, pays the taxes, insurance and repairs on buildings. A farmer tenant usually owns his own machinery and sometimes half the livestock. Each stands half the cost of seed, fertilizer and hired operating services. Both owner and renter divide cash sales of farm production and normal increases in livestock on a monthly or yearly basis.

Have a contract in writing, setting forth the duties of each party and the division of the income. If you expect a good tenant to stay and work on your farm, he must receive a fair return for his time and labor. Working together you can make your farm more livable, more productive and profitable—hopefully.

Don't Try to Be a Pioneer

In any community, your success depends upon your choice of a farm. Other important factors are your knowledge of soils, crops, livestock and the use of farm machinery. Don't try to be a pioneer at retirement age. The hardships that are part of the settling of new lands should be left to the younger generation. Your best chance for success and happiness is in an established agricultural community. There you will find those facilities that make a desirable place to live and neighboring farm families to aid you in making adjustments to life on a farm.

Remember a farm home is a way of life. Be sure you want it before you start. Location with respect to good roads is important. So are churches, schools, hospitals and other services. The availability of electricity, telephone service, RFD, water supply, radio and television service, all should be looked into.

If you are not familiar with farm values in the community, see the county agricultural agent, then have an appraisal of the property made by a qualified appraiser before you buy. The county agricultural agent can tell you the factors influencing the productivity of the farm and whether the price is right.

If You Merely Seek a Farm Home

A small farm home could provide a satisfying way of life and reduce the cost of the family food budget, if carefully planned and properly managed.

In most localities, an acre or two has been found to be adequate for a small farm home. That is about all the land that can usually be cared for by elderly persons, or by one person in his spare time. The California Agricultural Extension Service even says: "A half acre will provide space for a house, an outdoor living or recreational area, garage and tool shed, vegetable garden, berry patch, ten to twenty fruit trees, and an area for a few chickens and rabbits."

The average rural resident on a small farm home of this size will have difficulty marketing his surplus products, if he has any. Surplus may be sold to or traded with neighbors, sold to roadside-stand operators or retail market stores or stored in a frozen food locker. An acre is not enough to provide much cash income, except as it reduces one's cost of living.

Larger Farm Needed to Produce Income

For those seeking a farm to produce the income they need for family living, the actual acreage needed will depend upon the type of farming undertaken, the productivity of the soil and the region in which the farm is located. Medium-size farms are usually the most economically operated and, in the long run, the safest, particularly for those lacking experience in the operation of a large-farm business.

There are a sufficient number of successful cases among people of retirement age to lure others to the soil. There are also many instances of failure among people of this age group. For them the farm business was a drain on their nonfarm income.

With this thought in mind, we will review some of the types of farm occupations and opportunities that can be considered by the prudent person who dreams of life on the farm and who can step cautiously and wisely—looking well before he leaps.

What to Grow

In general, crops that cost more to produce bring in a greater return per acre, although they are more hazardous. Intensive crops, such as vegetables and fruit, require added labor, and higher expenses for seed and fertilizer.

Cotton, corn, soybeans and peanuts require smaller expenditures for labor and supplies, but larger acreage. Cattle or sheep ranching requires the most extensive acreage.

Dairying calls for more constant attention than any other type of farming. Cows need to be milked morning and afternoon seven days a week. Dairy cows require 140 hours per cow per year of labor as compared to 40 hours for beef cattle. The continuous heavy work and sanitary housekeeping around the barns are too strenuous for most retired persons.

Some crops can be sold on the vines or on the trees to canneries or to packers. Of course you will not make as much money from your crops selling in this way. On the other hand, you will not have the bother of a harvesting problem.

Truck Crops

Early market and high quality bring in highest returns. Melons, sweet corn, tomatoes, radishes, carrots, celery and asparagus are a few of the cash crops that lend themselves to specialization. Truck farms from twenty to fifty acres provide opportunities for a good income. But—truck farming on this scale becomes a business, requiring considerable energy, farming acumen, capital and employees.

Berries bring in high returns from relatively small acreage devoted to their cultivation. Strawberries, raspberries, blackberries, blueberries and cranberries provide a good living on five to ten acres. Knowledge of timing, fertilizing, irrigating, spraying and harvesting operations is essential for success. Marketing is usually done through an association of growers.

Orchards

The quickest and easiest way to become an orchardist is to purchase an established orchard. The other way is to start with small trees called whips. It takes five to ten years, depending upon the kind of fruit, to bring whips into commercial production. If you buy a mature orchard, check on the age and condition of the trees as well as the market potential for the fruit. Orchards require several sprays a year, as well as pruning and harvesting. About ten pickers are needed at harvest time to pick the fruit that one man can care for during the rest of the year. Pickers are very scarce and high-priced labor.

Mild climate, soil fertility and irrigation or rainfall are important factors for orchardists. Bees are necessary for pollenization. Most commercial orchards run from ten acres upward. You can specialize in citrus fruits, papayas, avocados, guavas, figs, pears, peaches, apples, almonds, walnuts, and so forth, depending upon the climate, soil and frost conditions. Write to the college of agriculture in the state you plan to settle in for detailed information on full-scale fruit farming.

Nursery Stock

With specialized nursery stock, planted twenty-four inches apart on forty-two-inch rows, you can grow over six thousand plants to the acre. In central and southern Florida, from seven thousand to ten thousand rose plants are planted to the acre. Fifty to seventy-five saleable cut roses per plant can be grown each year, depending on the variety of rose and general conditions. Ferns provide a good source of revenue in Florida. Ferns and other foliage plants are potted and sent to department and five-and-ten-cent stores in all parts of the country, where they are sold.

A few acres of flowering shrubs, though they take four or five years to reach market size, will bring you high return per acre. A rotation system of harvesting and planting new seedlings can produce a perpetual source of income.

Christmas Trees

Since good returns can normally be expected from the sale of Christmas trees in eight to ten years after planting, a number of persons in their fifties are planting them on their farms now so that the trees will be ready to harvest when they retire. However, they do require some yearly care.

If the tree seedlings are spaced four feet apart with four feet between rows, you can plant 2,720 Christmas trees to the acre. The tree sizes most in demand by the Christmas trade are those between five and eight feet high. Planting stock is usually obtained from public or private nurseries. Names and addresses can be obtained from the Forest Service, United States Department of Agriculture, Washington, D.C. 20250.

Mushroom Sales on the Increase

Cultivated mushroom growing is not a seasonal activity; they can be grown the year round. By rotating the plantings in mushroom beds, you can have three plantings a year in the same beds. The normal crop from each planting is about two pounds from each square foot planted. Beds come to bearing in four to eight weeks after the spawn is planted, and bear mushrooms over two months from each planting. For optimum growth, a fifty-eight- to sixty-two-degree temperature is essential. In some parts of the country this means summer cooling and winter heating. Mushrooms grow best in poorly lighted or dark places. That is why mushrooms are often grown in caves and abandoned mines. You can build mushroom houses of cinder blocks, with solid walls and no windows. Mushrooms can be shipped fresh or dried. However, fresh mushrooms are the better profit-makers. As a rule, the larger the mushroom, the more it brings. Because they weigh so little, there are several dozen mushrooms in the ventilated pound and half-pound boxes in which they are shipped to hotels, groceries and restaurants. Wholesale prices are usually fairly stable through any single marketing season; Pennsylvania price averaged 59 cents lb., in 1976. They can also be sold to roadside stands, produce wholesalers and canneries. Mushroom growing, however, is a highly competitive business on a commercial basis. Be sure to inquire of the agricultural college in your state before investing in it.

You Can Make Money Selling Honey

Beekeeping is a practical and money-making specialized activity. Few occupations require so little capital. Many hobbyists and back-lot beekeepers get considerable pleasure and relaxation from a few hives of bees. In addition to direct returns from the sale of honey, the beekeeper has some monetary return from the sale of beeswax. There are some fifty-four crops that are dependent upon the honeybee for pollination. Many beekeepers truck colonies of bees to orchards where substantial fees are collected for their pollenization work. About fifty million pounds of honey are used each year by the baking industry. Other large-quantity users are manufacturers of confectionery, ice cream, beverages and similar products.

In San Diego County, California, there are hundreds of registered apiaries with many hundreds of colonies of bees. At Rutherfordton, North Carolina, there is an apiarist who has thirty-four colonies of bees. From these colonies he harvests five hundred pounds of deluxe sourwood honey and three thousand additional pounds of tulip poplar and clover honey.

Orchardists pay $15 to $20 each to rent hives for a week in the blossom season. One hive is required for about every fifty fruit trees. During the blossom season which may last from a few days to a month, depending upon the locality, hives may be rented to five or six fruit growers at group rates.

The initial cost in beekeeping is about $40. This includes the cost of one hive, the bees, a queen, mask, bee smoker and a hive tool for withdrawing the honey combs. Beginners seeking information should write to Bureau of Entomology, United States Department of Agriculture, Washington, D.C., and ask for all available free publications on beekeeping, as well as a list of those which may be purchased. Several of the state agricultural colleges have specific bulletins applying to beekeeping in their particular areas. A recognized "bible" in the field is *The A,B,C, and X,Y,Z of Bee Culture* published by A. I. Root, Medina, Ohio. Price, $3.95 a copy.

Poultry: Highly Competitive—Big Business

The poultry industry is being integrated by feed companies, so that today there is little money to be made by a private poultryman unless he has volume.

Poultry raising is less seasonal than other types of farm production. However, eggs and broilers run in fairly well-defined cycles of high and low prices. Intelligent management calls for planning production so as not to overproduce in periods of low prices. Eggs bring highest prices during the fall and winter. Broilers usually bring good prices in winter and holiday months because most poultry raisers unload their flocks in late spring or early summer.

In some localities turkey raising and turkey egg production are important farm activities. Young turkeys require particularly close attention. Most states do not produce enough turkeys for local consumption.

Where can you sell quality poultry products at good prices? Neighbors are good prospects for limited quantities. They are easy to serve and are dependable customers. At home or at the roadside you can attract customers by using an attractive roadside sign. Also, stores and roadside-stand operators want a good source of quality eggs. A good egg business can be built up this way. The same goes for hotels and restaurants which make a specialty of serving eggs with uniform yolks. You can also run an egg route. Housewives like to buy eggs at the kitchen door.

Homemakers will pay more per dozen than the wholesale price for eggs, if they are top quality and attractively presented. Quality and freshness are the most important factors in marketing eggs, followed by price and size.

Consult with a feed company service man, the county Agricultural Extension Agent (County Agent) or the State

Agricultural Experiment Station for assistance in getting started in poultry.

A Private Fish Pond

Hundreds of farm families in the South have fish ponds where they can catch fish almost any day of the year. These fish ponds provide outdoor recreation for all members of the family and their friends.

In most states soil conservation technicians will aid in planning and locating a good fish pond site. The United States Fish and Wildlife Service, as well as state fish and game departments, will furnish fish to stock the pond *free* for the asking. Some states charge a small fee for delivering the fish.

The pond must be fertilized at about four-week intervals, after it is stocked with hatchery fish. The fertilizer is not for the fish but to aid the growth of green microscopic plants in the pond water. Thousands of small insects feed on the green plants. Bluegills feed on these small insects, while bass in turn feed on the small bluegills. From an acre of fish pond you should catch from one hundred to two hundred pounds of fish each year. Also, a well-landscaped fish pond can be a source of great enjoyment and an asset in increasing property values.

Soilless Gardening

If you want to get into a new and fascinating branch of gardening, try hydroponics—the culture of plants without soil.

Hydroponics outyields traditional soil farming in a number of crops. It can produce crops where soil fertility is lacking or water is scarce, as in some regions of Florida, Arizona and New Mexico. The basic equipment for soilless gardening is a basin to hold the nutrient solution. This can be a small tank made of sheet metal, concrete or wood. Regular basins or tanks, for amateurs, are five to seven inches deep, two to four feet wide and six to twelve feet long. Commercial operators use basins that run the entire length of their greenhouses.

The seedbed for plants, which rests on top of the basin, is made of a simple, open, six-inch-wide wood frame with a fine mesh chicken wire fastened over the bottom side. Coarse materials, such as straw or excelsior, are mixed with fine materials such as wood sawdust, sphagnum moss or glass wool, and placed within the frame.

The nutrient solution can be purchased at seed stores or you can prepare your own from standard formulas. The basin or tank is filled with the nutrient solution to within one and a half inches from the bottom of the seedbed. Some of the popular plants adaptable to hydroponics are vine crops, such as tomatoes, cantaloupes, cucumbers, watermelons and squashes; potatoes; root vegetables, such as carrots, radishes, beets and parsnips; leafy vegetables, such as lettuce, cabbage and celery; field crops, such as tobacco, barley, rye, oats, rice, etc.; herbaceous annual flowers; flowers from bulbs, corms, tubers and rhizomes; roses, gardenias and fuchsias. Yields claimed for hydroponics are from four to ten times the average yield from soil. The production of crops by hydroponics, however, is costly and noncompetitive in price with those produced in the soil.

Grassland Farming for Cattle

Grassland farming, especially for the production of beef cattle, is becoming a popular and prosperous agricultural enterprise for those who have the capital to invest. It involves fertilizing the soil, sowing grasses and legumes for pasture grazing, for hay and for silage, and the conversion of this feed into livestock products. When properly limed, fertilized, seeded and managed, an acre of grassland pasture will produce three times as many feeding units as an average acre of corn.

Beef cattle, dairy cows, sheep, horses, swine, poultry and goats depend for food upon grasses and legumes. They can feed on the grasses right off the ground and return much of the fertility to the soil. Grasses furnish almost the entire feed supply of beef cattle for at least half the area of the United States. Grasses furnish grazing pastures for the entire year in many areas of the southern states, and along the coastal area and Central Valley of California.

The opportunities in grassland farming for beef-cattle production are: (1) As a breeder, you sell purebred cattle to farmers who want to improve their herds, or young range stock to feeders. (2) As a feeder, you buy calves and yearlings to fatten and finish out to a weight of one thousand to twelve hundred pounds and sell them to a packing house or to a livestock-marketing organization.

The cattle business, like other agricultural enterprises, has its ups and downs. But cattlemen who keep their herds young, have plenty of feed (especially grassland pastures) and avoid overborrowing make excellent returns on their investments over the years.

Hickory-Smoked Meats Sold by Mail Order

Some country residents who have developed specialized skills have turned them into profits. One example is selling hickory-smoked meats by mail order. High-quality hogs are butchered and cured country style in a preparation that includes special seasonings. The meat then goes into an old-fashioned smokehouse where it is kept until proper tenderness is achieved in an atmosphere of hickory smoke.

Specialized products like these are advertised in small space in magazines, reaching homemakers with high incomes who do considerable entertaining, as well as those who like to serve unusual dishes. If you *can* produce a specialized farm product that is *better* than the average on the market, *package it attractively,* tell people about it and offer it for sale *at a reasonable price* that assures you a profit, it is possible to make a good living from your efforts.

Farm Home-Restaurant Business

City residents and travelers appreciate the pleasures of a home-cooked meal in farm surroundings, prepared with freshly killed poultry and farm-grown vegetables. Old-fashioned home cooking is so scarce in restaurants today that people will drive miles out of their way to patronize places offering real on-the-farm meals. Meals should be cooked with skill and served the way "mother used to do it." A farm operator strategically located on a much-traveled highway, with an attractive roadside sign out front, can make a good supplementary income serving meals from products of the farm. A small farm home-restaurant can serve meals in one or two front rooms as a start and expand as the business grows.

Farm or Ranch Vacation Resort Home

Many city folk, as well as artists and writers, enjoy spending a few weeks resting quietly "back on the farm." If you have a few spare bedrooms, you can probably build up a clientele of paying guests during the vacation season. You can offer horseback riding, fishing, swimming and hay rides. A farm or ranch located on a lake or brook, near a national or state park, near the seashore, mountains or summer theater colony, provides additional recreational facilities. You can, if you prefer, build small sleeping cabins on the property and have your guests come up to the main house for meals. Small advertisements in city newspapers would help to keep your rooms or cabins rented for the season. A reputation for providing good accommodations, as well as good farm meals from home-grown food, are essential for success. You can also arrange with nearby motels and tourist courts to take overflow guests. Many country homes with spare rooms offer board and lodging to persons without established homes, such as school teachers, nurses and others residing temporarily in the area.

Sell Farm Products at Retail

Many farmers sell a good percentage of their farm products at retail. If you are on a road with a good volume of automobile traffic, you might want to set up your own roadside stand close to your home. To be successful, a roadside stand must be visible some distance ahead and must provide adequate parking space for customers.

An attractive businesslike sign in front of your home is an asset. It can help you sell breeding stock, honey, eggs, poultry, vegetables, fruit, special services and sidelines. A distinctive name for your farm or roadside stand is a great help in advertising your enterprise.

Fruits and berries can be sold as fresh products or marketed as jams, jellies or preserves. Direct-to-the-home selling is often profitable if you don't have to travel too far. You can do a weekend business selling farm products by advertising in nearby town newspapers or mailing postcards to a list of selected people. It is also possible to build up a steady business selling farm products to city people, shipping by parcel post. Smoked hams and turkeys, fruit gift baskets, honey and similar products are ideal for mail-order selling. Be sure to grade and ship only high-quality products so that your customers will reorder.

Farm Caretaker

A retired man and wife, who once operated their own farm, act as caretakers while the farm owners take a vacation. They move out to a farm and run it for the owner while he and his wife are away. This retired couple even take care of the owner's children. Because they are trustworthy and dependable, they are paid well for their services.

Personal-Service Job Opportunities in Farm Communities

"In almost every farming community there are various jobs and services which farmers want done and are willing to pay for. Such jobs can sometimes be combined well with a small, part-time farm, or can be done to piece out the income of a man living in a village."

This quotation, and the suggested farm service jobs that follow, from the United States Department of Labor in *Occupational Outlook Handbook,* point up the opportunities open for enterprising persons to earn supplementary income from personal services associated with farming.

Custom Farm Mechanization Work. Threshing, combining, tractor plowing, potato digging, hay and straw baling, and so forth, provide part-time work for a man who owns (sometimes rents) specialized farm implements. Ordinarily, the owner of the equipment will go from farm to farm doing the job on a custom-work contract, usually having a list of jobs scheduled ahead.

Livestock Trucking. A specialized job that requires a truck with a body especially fitted to handle animals, it provides virtually a year-round job in certain regions.

Whitewashing Service. In the dairy and poultry regions, a

man with a whitewashing outfit can keep busy the year round. This necessitates a light truck with spray rig large enough to do this kind of work. A man offering such a service usually has a regular route which covers a large number of farms. He goes back over the same route perhaps once every three months. Ordinarily the farmer pays a flat fee for the job, depending upon the size of the buildings. A whitewashing outfit can usually do several jobs a day.

Fruit-Spraying Service. In the orchard sections, tree spraying will usually occupy a man with a mobile spraying outfit several months of the year. The equipment is usually a light truck with a good spray rig which will reach to the height of fruit trees. Charges are either by the job, by the tree or, in some cases, a flat rate by the season to keep the orchard properly sprayed.

Mobile Repair Shop. The outfit usually consists of a covered truck, its interior equipped with tools for both metalwork and woodwork. It must have a forge as well as ordinary bench equipment and supplies. The mobile repair truck stops at farms or comes on call to fix anything from a broken plow handle to a heavy tractor. Some outfits furnish a good income to the owner, but an investment of $1,000 to $3,000 is necessary for the essential equipment.

Variations are the mobile welding outfit and the mobile blacksmith shop, operated as separate businesses or connected with shops in town.

Electrical and Carpenter Services. Electricians and carpenters are in great demand in rural areas. Such services require a car or a light truck and usually a small workshop at home. Carpenters in slack seasons usually turn out such products as ladders, potato crates and fruit baskets.

Mobile Grocery Store. Another established institution in many farm sections, providing a good year-round income for the merchant. This enterprise requires a covered truck, often containing a refrigerator, and equipped for carrying all kinds of groceries. Some kind of store or warehouse building in town is necessary to serve as a base of operations. The traveling store covers a fixed route each day, sometimes covering the same route twice a week.

Recreation Jobs. In areas offering recreation facilities, there are seasonal jobs as guides, camping experts and recreation leaders. Many men are so employed from the beginning of the spring fishing season to the close of fall hunting. Some of these are part-time farmers or ranchers. For these jobs a man often needs nothing more than an expert knowledge of the region and skill in outdoor matters; in some cases, he may own or lease considerable equipment, including boats, horses, guns, fishing tackle.

Get to Know the County Agent

The county agent is a public employee selected and paid jointly by the United States Department of Agriculture and the state agricultural college and county board of control. He is the local fountainhead of agricultural information, the farmer's counselor and troubleshooter. The county agent's headquarters is usually at the county courthouse or county U.S.D.A. centers. The county agent can help you a great deal in getting established in farming in his county.

The agricultural extension services of the state agricultural colleges, as well as experimental farms, also provide valuable practical information on the types of agricultural products best suited to local areas. Many state school systems offer vocational agricultural classes. The United States Department of Agriculture, Washington, D.C., publishes hundreds of pamphlets on all phases of agricultural living.

Seeking the Farm You Want

Build up a mental image of the farm you'd like to own, and then look for one that meets your specifications. Study the offerings of farms for sale with an open mind. You may have to examine many farms of the desired type, size and locality before you find one that approaches the specifications you have in mind. Seeking a farm calls for much inquiry, traveling and patience. It is rarely possible to find on any particular farm all the desirable features you are looking for.

Correspond with, or interview, those familiar with farm real estate in the locality to which you plan to move. Friends living there, bank officials having foreclosed properties, real estate agents, secretaries of farm loan associations, staffs of agricultural colleges, county agents—all are good sources of information. Subscribe to the leading local newspaper and study real estate listings. If you do not know the name of a reliable real estate agent, ask the chamber of commerce or a local bank to recommend one.

Before making a definite decision as to the type of farming you should undertake, visit the region of the country which you prefer for retirement living. See for yourself what each area of the region has to offer. Consult the county agents. Talk to farmers who have already settled there. Visit the nearest agricultural experimental stations in the regions under investigation. Check the chamber of commerce or realty boards for land prices, information about living conditions, taxes, climate and other general information.

After the decision has been made to purchase a particular farm, it is important to know the legal status of the property and to make sure the title is clear. Have a lawyer check on these points for you.

Best Areas for Retired Persons to Operate a Farm

The 1970 census reveals that the fastest-growing regions of the United States are the Pacific Coast, Mountain, and Southern states. The indications are that these sections of the country will continue to grow in population faster than the rest of the country. From the standpoint of climate, length of growing season, outdoor living conditions and opportunities in agricultural production, the Southern states and California offer the best advantage for persons who wish to retire to a farm.

Opportunities in California

One-Family Commercial Farms. Since the plane of living in California is rather high, an average net income from $7,000 to $10,000 is desirable for successful farm living. This sum varies according to the needs of the farm family. Those who consider small commercial farming must study well the market for their products. Usually it must be an outlet they establish themselves, like a hotel, a restaurant or a roadside stand. It would be most difficult to compete with the regular commercial producers and distributors who have invested six figures in their operation and operate like big business.

The Southern California Area. This region occupies the southern quarter of the state. The coastal zone extends inland a few miles at Santa Barbara to about seventy miles east of Los Angeles and south to the Mexican border. The chief crops of the area are oranges, lemons, walnuts, avocados, berries, a variety of vegetables and a few field crops. This is the major citrus area of the state. There is also an intense local poultry industry. Land values are among the highest in the United States, bare land costing $2,000 to

$4,000 an acre and good citrus orchards costing as high as $8,000 to $10,000 an acre.

The mountain and desert regions of Southern California are not important from an agricultural standpoint. Farming is possible only in irrigated valleys. Imperial Valley is a large and important agricultural area. Irrigated field and truck crops cover most of the acreage. The citrus fruits, grapes and dates are of minor importance. Coachella Valley, irrigated by deep wells, produces dates, grapefruit, cotton, alfalfa and out-of-season vegetables. The length of the growing season in Southern California is 365 days on the coast to 270 days in the interior.

The Central Coast Area. This region extends from about 80 miles north of San Francisco to about 260 miles to the south. The region is largely one of large commercial farms. Only near the cities are there many small and part-time farms. Considerable livestock is produced on the grassland and range pastures. In the valleys and on some hill slopes, production is in grain, dairying, poultry, berries, fruits and vegetables. Good opportunities are open in Salinas Valley, where large acreage is under irrigation. The length of the growing season is 204 to 310 days.

The San Joaquin Valley Area. This area is bounded on the east by the Sierra Nevada Mountains and on the west by the Coast Range, joins the Sacramento Valley on the north and borders Southern California on the south. This is the largest agricultural region in California. Here are grown grapes, deciduous fruits, citrus fruits, figs and olives. Field crops, however, occupy most of the land. The region is the most important dairy district of the state. Poultry raising is scattered throughout the area. Livestock is produced in the Valley, some being pastured on the ranges and national forests.

The Sacramento Valley. This is the northern half of the Great Valley of California. Being north of the San Joaquin

Valley, it is colder and has more rainfall. The region is largely devoted to field crops and general farming with some dairying. It also contains several important fruit districts producing peaches, prunes, almonds, pears, walnuts, olives and some citrus fruit. Commercial poultry farms are found in several localities. Livestock, both cattle and sheep, are wintered in the Sacramento Valley to be pastured in private range lands and national forests in the mountains during the summer.

The North Coast Area. This region runs up to the Oregon line and is largely occupied by the Coast Range. The mountainous area is covered with forest or brush. Farming is limited to the valleys and a narrow shelf along portions of the coast. Beef-cattle and sheep ranches occupy most of the country. This is popular wine and grape growing area. Most of the good farmland is fully utilized. Growing season is 210 to 277 days.

Opportunities in Florida

Florida's agriculture has been characterized by its diversity and continuous growth. The state has a relatively abundant supply of land and water. While much of its land is not naturally very fertile, it responds well to proper management and fertilization. Availability of water causes some concern, but water is abundant and high quality, compared to most farming areas of the world. Florida's warm winters and long growing season permit intensive production of citrus and winter vegetables. They encourage intensive forestry and they favor the beef business with a long grazing period.

A rapidly growing population has resulted in a greatly enlarged local market for farm products. Beyond its borders, Florida is a key supplier of fresh vegetables for the nation from October to June.

One-Family Commercial Farms. No state-wide standards can be set down for the most desirable size of farms on which to make a good living. Reports from the College of Agriculture, University of Florida, indicate that one needs at least fifteen hundred to two thousand good hens to make a fair living from poultry. At least one hundred good beef cattle are needed to make a fair living from raising livestock, fifteen to twenty cows from dairying, thirty acres from citrus fruits, fifty to one hundred cultivated acres of general farming depending on the nature of the crops. Ten good acres of truck land may be enough for some vegetable production, while other vegetables may require twenty or more acres. However, a man and wife alone can't produce ten acres of vegetables, and hired help is necessary to make a good living at truck farming.

It costs less to buy farmland capable of producing a specified net income in Florida than it does in California. Most farm dwellings are inadequate, according to the standards and needs of northern people. Many truck and citrus farms have no dwelling at all—the owners living either in nearby cities or towns or in the North.

Some of the improved Florida pasture will support a head per acre for cattle raising. The average on improved pasture is one head to three acres. A new grass coming into use promises to support as high as four head to the acre. Cattle raising in Florida does not require the heavy investment in buildings necessary in other areas.

Small Farm Homes for Greater Security. An important and growing group of residents of Florida live on small farms that contribute some subsistence but little or no cash income. If these farms are carefully selected, retired persons can supplement retirement benefits by raising home-grown food for the family. The optimum size of such an undertaking for elderly persons appears to be about one acre. In most cases, they should limit their efforts to producing vegetables and poultry. In selecting a farm, investment should be kept low in order to maintain as much of the accumulated savings of the family as possible.

A well-managed small commercial farm offers a means of supplementing the incomes of retired persons, and of those who live on a farm but whose major employment is off the farm. They should have no physical handicaps or medical ailments, and not be too elderly for the strenuous work needed to make the farm productive. To be successful, adequate family labor or hired labor must be available when the farm needs attention. The type of farming followed should be that of the area where the farm is located. In a study of thirty-one broiler farms in the Palatka area, conducted by the Florida Department of Agriculture, it was found that one-fourth of the producers had retired from other occupations. It is easy to overinvest in a part-time farm. Care should be exercised lest the extra investment be too great for the returns.

The Northern Florida Zone. The chief farm produce here is tobacco, cabbage, potatoes, beans, peanuts, oats, watermelons, berries, tung nuts, pecans, livestock and poultry. There is also some production of various legumes and feed crops. Turpentine and resin are obtained from the pine forests. Some citrus groves are found in the southern districts of the zone. Nursery stock for transplanting is produced in the section. The growing season is 300 to 320 days.

The Central Florida Zone. A good portion of the land is planted in citrus groves. This is the orange, grapefruit and tangerine belt of Florida—the location of the largest packing houses, juice canneries and frozen concentrate plants. Many farms specialize in truck crops. Celery, cabbage, field peas, tomatoes, sweet corn, strawberries and watermelons are the favorites. Nurseries of flowers, plants and ornamental shrubs are numerous throughout the area. Beef cattle, dairy cattle and poultry are raised extensively. The growing season averages 320 days.

The Southern Florida Zone. The climate is much warmer in this zone during the winter months. Occasionally frost occurs in the northern part of the zone. For the most part, this is the subtropical part of Florida. Winter vegetables are the big crops. They include cabbage, beans, celery, sweet corn, potatoes, peppers and tomatoes. Palm Beach County ranks first of all counties in the nation in acreage of vegetables harvested for sale. Some citrus fruits and tropical fruits, such as the avocado, mango, papaya and guava, are grown commercially. Ferns and orchids are grown commercially. Sugar cane has become a major crop, with over 225,000 acres harvested. The grasslands provide grazing for livestock. The eight-foot-deep muck of the Everglades has been compared with that of the Nile Valley. Three plantings a year are harvested. Growing season is 320 to 365 days.

Opportunities in North Carolina, South Carolina and Georgia

These are states of comparatively small farms, the average being 168 acres. Average size in Georgia is 233 acres, South Carolina 166, and North Carolina only 106. The variations in types of soil, topography and climate conditions give rise to considerable variation in the types of farming in different parts of the region.

The agricultural pattern in the past has been centered mainly around cash crops, especially cotton, tobacco and soybeans. But the agricultural picture of this section of the South is undergoing considerable readjustment. The trend is toward greater mechanization and the use of labor-saving farm equipment. Additional sources of income from a diversity of crops and livestock is being added to the traditional "one cash crop" system of the old South.

The Coastal Plains of the Carolinas and Georgia offer some of the best cropland in the United States. But demand of land for highways, dwellings, shopping centers and other urban development has helped to move prices of land up sharply. Today farmland in the entire State of North Carolina has increased to an average of $686 an acre, a 232 percent increase since 1967. Comparable increases can be expected throughout the area. Even steep mountain soil, unproductive for crops, demands high prices for recreation and retirement homes. People are coming into South Carolina and Georgia by the hundreds from many other states.

Authorities say that beef production can be multiplied four times without encroaching on other kinds of agriculture. It takes two acres of southern range to support one animal against as much as fifty acres in the West. Beef production is strong in this area.

One of the promising crops is soybeans, which can be handled almost entirely by mechanization with a good return for the investment.

Egg production, once up sharply, has fluctuated up and down in recent years while remaining a major farm product. South Carolina counties eggs ranked as the number one cash farm commodity.

There are many farm communities throughout the entire region, where persons with modest retirement incomes can establish a semi-rural home on a small farm and achieve the independent security of producing part of the family's food requirements. Subsistence and part-time farming is increasing and is centered mainly around cities and towns where part-time employment can be found in local industries.

The topography exerts a very important influence on farming. There are four distinct regions from the mountains to the seashore. The mountain region covers the western portion of the area. Many mountain valleys are at elevations up to two thousand feet, and peaks rise to as high as six thousand feet. The Piedmont Plateau forms the central region and is characterized by rolling hills with a general elevation of five hundred to nine hundred feet. The Sandhills region has elevations from four hundred to six hundred and fifty feet. And the coastal plains run from sea level to elevations of three hundred feet. The growing season is shortest in the mountains, where it is about 190 days. The growing season becomes longer as one goes eastward and southward toward the coast, where it is from 240 to 300 days.

The Mountain Region. Agricultural production is devoted to general farming, beef cattle, apples, poultry and dairying. The farms are small, with many classified as subsistence farms.

The Piedmont Region. The main agricultural products are cotton, peaches, apples, poultry, dairying, beef cattle, hay, seed production, soybeans with some truck farming in local areas. There are good opportunities for beef-cattle raising on pastures.

The Sandhills Region. The major crops are cotton, tobacco, soybeans, peanuts, hay, peaches, poultry, turkeys and some truck crops in local areas.

The Coastal Plains Region. The most extensively grown products are cotton, tobacco, corn, sweet potatoes, beef cattle, dairying, poultry and turkeys, hogs and truck crops. Good opportunities for greenhouse and nursery crops.

Opportunities in the Gulf States

Alabama's chief cash crop for many years was cotton. The state is now the center of one of the greatest land opportunities in the United States for grassland farming and the production of livestock. The Black Belt section offers one of the best land investment opportunities in the nation today, according to a survey made by one of the country's leading land appraisal organizations.

The state produces annually over four million pounds of honey. In 1965 there were 176,000 colonies of bees in Alabama. Alabama leads the nation in number of tree farmers and its timber resources are abundant. In broiler production the state ranks third and this industry continues to expand at a rapid rate.

Baldwin County is the largest county in Alabama. It is considerably larger than the state of Rhode Island. Baldwin County has a mild climate, a growing season of three hundred or more days and sixty-two inches of rainfall annually. Farmers in the area raise two crops a year. Modern farming methods have brought great yields in the many agricultural products raised in the county. For example, yields of 100 bushels of corn per acre are not uncommon on farms using recommended practices. Among the twenty-five agricultural crops are Irish potatoes, soybeans, sweet potatoes, pecan and tung nuts, corn and numerous truck crops. Year-round grazing makes beef cattle and dairying popular. Hogs and poultry are profitable operations. Almost any kind of flower is grown by the acre.

Mississippi. This region offers similar opportunities to those of its neighbor states of Alabama and Louisiana. It is an important area for early and late fresh vegetable production. Pecans are widely grown.

Louisiana is one of the nation's leading producers of sugar and rice and the leading cultivator of yams. The state produces large crops of timber, forestry and nursery products, cotton, soybeans, corn, lilies and other flowers. Opportunities exist in this area for growing early and late market vegetables. As in the rest of the South, cattle raising and grassland farming is rapidly expanding. The rich soils, temperate climate, abundant rainfall and long growing season combine to make the area ideal for agricultural production on a year-round basis.

Texas. The state of Texas is broken down into eighteen major farming areas and many sub-areas. The coastal prairie area is mainly devoted to cattle ranching, cotton and rice production, with dairying and vegetables in limited production around the larger cities. The Lower Rio Grande Valley area, with its long growing season and irrigation, has a wide range of crops including cotton, corn, grain, onions, sugar cane, watermelons and winter vegetables. Citrus fruits are grown primarily in the Rio Grande Valley and some sub-areas. The Panhandle area is in cotton, corn, sorghum and wheat production.

Cotton ranks first in value of Texas crops in most years with grain sorghum the leading grain crop. Grazing land comprises about 73 percent of the area of the state with beef cattle the leading livestock industry. Some of the best grazing lands are in the Trans-Pecos and the Edwards Plateau. Sheep and Angora goat-raising are important enterprises on many farms. Poultry and eggs are produced in every county, but the greatest egg production is in Fayette, Gonzales, and Shelby counties.

Opportunities in Arizona and New Mexico

Arizona and New Mexico are arid states, and cultivation of crops requires irrigation. Because most of the water rights are claimed, new farmland is not being developed in significant amounts. Therefore, the purchase of existing farms is recommended.

The northern part of Arizona and New Mexico is primarily devoted to livestock production. Farms generally produce forage or hay crops for this purpose. Ranches throughout these two states generally contain private, state and federal lands. The public lands are grazed under permit.

Some goats in North Eastern Arizona and in Southern New Mexico are raised for their mohair. Opportunities for part-time farming are rather limited. Poultry does offer an opportunity for those who would like to supplement their income. Poultry meat is below the consumption demands in both Arizona and New Mexico.

Intensive farming of more diverse crops is limited to the valleys in the southern half of these states. Important crops grown include citrus, some cotton, vegetables, small grains, pecans and alfalfa. The water quantity and quality in these areas is highly variable.

The population growth of Arizona has been dramatic in the last few years. This has resulted in many thousands of acres of farmland being converted to urban development. The development of tracts with lot sizes from one to ten acres has also become popular. These lots offer a rural setting where supplemental production of agriculture products may be undertaken. However, the initial investment for these lots is usually high.

Greenhouses, when used to produce out-of-season vegetables as well as flowers, hanging baskets, and other ornamentals, are a growing opportunity to make money on minimum acreage. Greenhouse production and use is on a steady increase. Look into opportunities for hydroponics (soilless gardening).

A Few Case Histories of Farming in Retirement

Nine years prior to retiring, at the age of fifty-seven, a former executive of one of America's leading corporations purchased ten acres of land near Lakeland, Florida. He had nine acres cleared and planted in grapefruit trees. One acre was set aside for his home, lawn and flower and vegetable gardens. Upon his retirement from business, he moved to his Florida home. Once there, he set himself up in a mail-order fruit business and developed it into a profitable enterprise that he operated until four years ago. The job of managing the grapefruit grove and selling the fruit he turned over to a cooperative association. This man, now eighty-eight years old, has lived a happy and profitable retirement life. During many of these years, he grossed over $11,000 a year from his Florida activities. His advice to those contemplating retirement is: "Have a plan, a goal, a vision to live by."

Here is the experience of a West Virginian who was formerly in the grocery business. At the age of sixty, he decided to retire. He bought an abandoned farm of 186 acres and started to farm it as a hobby. Without any previous experience as a farmer, he learned to farm by observation, by reading good farm papers, by asking advice of other farmers. His friends laughed when he bought the farm and said they were afraid he was too old. Because he lacked experience they thought he would fail as a farmer. By his personal determination and love of the land, he has made more progress than many farmers in the county within the last four years. His fields were originally overgrown with briars and weeds and sage grass. He cut and burned the briars, grubbed the thickets with a bulldozer, plowed under the weeds. Next he applied lime and commercial fertilizer, and sowed mixed grass seeds. His progress in four years is almost beyond belief. The fields are now beautiful pastures that carry fifty-five head of fine beef cattle, along with horses, goats and other livestock. He practices strip farming and grows alfalfa, Ladino clover and other kinds of grass mixtures. A new barn has been erected to store fifty tons of hay. He has a purebred Hereford sire to head his fine herd of cattle. This man, who began farming at the age of sixty, without any previous experience, is an inspiration to anyone about to retire or already retired. The secret of happy retirement is to transfer your main interests to a new field, to change your occupation and do some of the things you have dreamed of when alone with your thoughts.

Check This List Before You Decide

The College of Agriculture, University of California, advises prospective purchasers of a farm to answer the following questions frankly to evaluate their preferences and desires.

1. Why do I wish to engage in farming? Is my object primarily investment, a home or a home and business? Do I assume none, some or all the manual tasks and management responsibilities?

2. Do I really want to live in the country? What proof have I?

3. Where do I hope to locate? What are my preferences regarding climate? Regarding distance from stores, doctors, schools, places of entertainment?

4. What sort of dwelling am I seeking? Must I have certain conveniences and luxuries?

5. What sort of neighbors do I like?

6. What do I want to produce?

7. How big a farm should I buy?

8. What annual income do I require to take care of personal needs?

9. How much money can I command to make initial payments, to buy equipment and to provide necessary seeds, fertilizer, water, taxes and other operating expenditures?

10. Am I willing to invest my savings, and possibly pledge my future earnings, for the maintenance of a farm?

11. What knowledge of farming do I possess that I can utilize to good advantage? Have I an inquisitive mind that will cause me to delve further into agricultural lore?

12. Have I the required experience and training?

13. Have I the ability to select, direct and supervise hired help?

14. Have I the physical strength for farming?

15. Have I the courage?

16. What are my chances to resell or lease in case of future dissatisfaction? In other words, is this property really marketable?

What to Do to Prepare for Farming in Retirement

Once you have definitely decided that you would like to engage in farming when you retire, here's what you should do next.

Your First Step. Begin to acquaint yourself with some of the down-to-earth problems of work and living associated with your choice of farm activity. Begin a long-range self-education program. The earlier you begin to shape your program along specific lines, the easier it will be to progress rapidly when you actually take up farming.

You should, of course, continue about the everyday business of earning a living as you have been doing. This program of acquiring information on your retirement farm specialty is your after-work hobby activity. You are merely laying the foundation of a program that will save you time and money later on.

If you have had no previous farm experience, begin by systematically reading some of the good farm papers. There are a number of monthly and weekly publications that cover farming in general from a nationwide viewpoint. Other farm magazines confine themselves to the agricultural activities of a particular state. Still others are devoted to a specialized branch of farming.

Perhaps the easiest way to acquaint yourself with the various publications on the market is to ask your local librarian to let you look at the bound volumes of back issues of the various farm publications on file at your local library.

Pick out one or more publications that appeal to you and subscribe to them. The features, news stories and advertisements will give you a good background on the latest developments as they occur, experiences of successful farmers, how-to-do-it counsel, market prices, new farm equipment—and much information on various aspects of farm living.

Your Second Step. Begin to study and to accumulate a library and reference file of clippings of pertinent information on your farming specialty.

The United States Department of Agriculture spends millions of dollars each year in research and development on a great many phases of agriculture. Briefly, these activities cover studies on the growing, harvesting and marketing of better farm products, advice and guidance on improved methods and how to use them, the successful solution of farm management problems, farm home and living.

Publications are prepared in the form of leaflets, pamphlets, bulletins and books by various bureaus of the Department of Agriculture. Many present information in a detailed, step-by-step manner. They are extremely helpful to farmers and prospective farmers. A number of these publications are distributed free. For a complete listing of publications both free and for sale write to Division of Publications, United States Department of Agriculture, Washington, D.C. 20250. Ask for a copy of *List of Available Publications,* Miscellaneous Publication No. 60. Publications that are for sale should be ordered from the Superintendent of Documents, United States Government Printing Office, Washington D.C. 20402.

Personal counseling by specialists in the various bureaus is available on many problems which confront farmers. Direct your correspondence to Office of Information, United States Department of Agriculture, Washington, D.C.

20250. You can even borrow 16 mm. sound motion picture films. For listing and where to borrow films write to Motion Picture Service, Office of Information, United States Department of Agriculture, Fourteenth St. and Independence Ave., S.W., Washington, D.C. 20250.

Many of the state agricultural departments and agricultural colleges also publish bulletins on various farming activities more specifically related to areas of their states. When you decide on the state where you want to retire, write to these departments and colleges for information pertaining to problems that confront you. Some agricultural colleges offer correspondence courses on various phases of farming.

Your Third Step. Perhaps you are thinking by now that you will get a lot of book learning but no practical experience from this self-education program. The more information you have, the easier it will be to acquire the necessary practical knowledge. But how about some practical experience?

At this stage of your program, it would be a good idea to get to know a farmer who is specializing in the type of farming you have chosen. You will see how some of the knowledge you have gathered is actually used in practical farming. Perhaps you can arrange to work part-time for him, say on weekends or during your vacations. In this way you can get some practical experience along with your book learning. If you can't find such a farmer in your locality, get in touch with the county agent. He will be glad to arrange for you to meet a progressive farmer whom you can call on.

Attend state and county fairs and talk with attendants at the various exhibits. You will pick up a lot of practical information.

Your Fourth Step. Plan your home and living arrangements for your new way of life on the farm. Include in your planning a program of recreation and participation in the community life. Your financial program should be arranged so that you can take over your new farm free or nearly free of mortgage debt. You should have money to buy the equipment, fertilizer, seeds and livestock, and to cover the other operating expenses required to run the farm. In addition, you should have some surplus cash to provide for emergencies.

Bibliography

MAGAZINES DEVOTED TO FARMING

Covering Farming in General

Progressive Farmer, Box 2581, Birmingham, Ala. 35202
Farm Journal, 230 W. Washington Sq., Philadelphia, Pa. 19106
Farm Digest, 1999 Shepard Rd., St. Paul, Minn. 55116
Successful Farming, 1716 Locust St., Des Moines, Iowa 50336

Covering Farming in Various States

Arizona Farmer-Ranchman, 434 W. Washington St., Phoenix, Ariz. 85003
California Farmer, 83 Stevenson St., San Francisco, Calif. 94105
Florida Agriculture, 4350 S.W. 13th Street, Gainesville, Fla. 32601
Mississippi Farm Bureau News, 429 Mississippi St., Jackson, Miss. 39205
Carolina Cooperator, 125 E. Davie St., Raleigh, N.C. 27605
South Carolina Farmer, P.O. Box 754, Columbia, S.C. 29203

Covering Various Farm Products

American Bee Journal, Hamilton, Ill. 62341
Sheep Breeder & Sheepman, P.O. Box 796, Columbia, Mo. 65202
The Cattleman, 410 E. Weatherford St., Fort Worth, Tex. 76102
National Livestock Producer, 733 N. Van Buren, Milwaukee, Wis. 53202
American Fruit Grower, 37841 Euclid Ave., Willoughby, Ohio 44094
Citrus & Vegetables, Box 2349, Tampa, Fla. 33601
American Poultry & Hatchery News, 521 E. 63rd St., Kansas City, Mo. 64110
Poultry Digest, Garden St. Bldg., Sea Isle City, N.J. 08243
Flower and Garden, 4251 Pennsylvania Av., Kansas City, Mo. 64111
For additional farm magazines see *Ulrich's International Periodical Directory.*

Farm Management—Including agricultural marketing. Send for free bibliography and price list of books and pamphlets on this subject to Superintendent of Documents, Government Printing Office, Washington D.C. 20402

Also bibliographies on
Forestry
Fish and Wildlife
Animal Industry—Farm animals, poultry and dairying
Plants—Culture, gardening, marketing, storage of fruits, vegetables, grass, grain

10

Good Climate Is Part of Good Living

Location Is Important

Climatologists and physicians are in general agreement that, for persons past sixty years of age, a mild, warm year-round climate is best. The southern states, as well as Southern California, with their distinctly mild winters, plentiful supply of sunshine, absence of snowfall, warm, moist summers, and generally settled weather, afford good climate for retirement living.

In the cold and stormy regions of the United States, people live on a high plane of both physical and mental energy. As we get past 65 years of age, the body does not respond as easily to weather changes. In the warm sunny climates, the need of the body to make adjustments is considerably less. Existence is at a more relaxed pace and consequently persons are less susceptible to diseases of fatigue.

Dr. Clarence A. Mills, M.D., Ph.D., Professor of Experimental Medicine, University of Cincinnati, in *Climate Makes*

CLIMATIC DATA FOR SELECTED U. S. CITIES

City	Ft. Elevation	Temperature °F				Precipitation		%
		Winter	Summer	Highest	Lowest	(in.) Rain	(in.) Snow	Relative Humidity
Albuquerque, N. Mex.	5,130	36.4	74.4	104	–16	8.06	7.0	50
Amarillo, Tex.	3,590	34.9	74.0	107	–16	20.99	20.1	–
Atlanta, Ga.	1,054	44.0	77.9	103	–8	49.75	2.3	72
Asheville, N.C.	2,192	39.2	71.6	99	–6	38.02	10.5	75
Bismarck, N. Dak.	1,670	12.0	67.3	114	–45	16.39	34.3	70
Boise, Idaho	2,842	32.5	69.8	109	–13	12.66	15.0	61
Boston, Mass.	15	29.7	69.4	104	–18	40.14	43.1	72
Brownsville, Tex.	16	61.2	83.3	104	12	31.05	–	81
Buffalo, N. Y.	693	25.5	67.8	97	–20	36.00	74.9	77
Burlington, Vt.	331	20.2	67.4	101	–29	32.30	65.6	72
Charleston, S. C.	9	51.3	80.4	104	7	45.22	.3	79
Cheyenne, Wyo.	6,144	27.1	64.2	100	–38	14.99	56.7	58
Chicago, Ill.	594	27.0	70.9	105	–23	32.81	33.4	73
Cincinnati, Ohio	761	33.6	75.1	108	–17	38.40	18.2	76
Cleveland, Ohio	787	26.7	69.9	103	–17	33.82	41.4	72
Denver, Colo.	5,221	32.1	70.2	105	–29	13.98	55.1	52
Des Moines, Iowa	800	24.0	73.6	110	–30	31.74	32.3	72
Detroit, Mich.	619	26.4	70.4	105	–24	31.47	39.7	74
El Paso, Tex.	3,920	46.6	80.9	106	–5	8.86	2.3	41
Fort Worth, Tex.	688	47.5	83.0	112	–8	32.16	0.2	67
Galveston, Tex.	6	55.6	82.6	101	8	46.55	0.2	80
Helena, Mont.	3,893	23.1	64.6	103	–42	12.69	54.4	60
Huron, S. Dak.	1,282	16.0	70.3	111	–43	19.51	28.2	–
Jackson, Miss.	316	49.5	80.8	107	–5	51.46	1.3	–
Jacksonville, Fla.	18	56.6	81.2	104	10	49.74	–	81
Kansas City, Mo.	741	31.9	77.1	113	–22	36.32	21.4	68
Knoxville, Tenn.	974	40.5	76.1	104	–16	48.10	9.4	73
Little Rock, Ark.	265	43.6	79.8	110	–12	47.61	4.8	71
Los Angeles, Calif.	312	56.4	69.5	109	28	15.40	T	68
Memphis, Tenn.	271	43.0	79.6	106	–9	47.66	5.2	71
Miami, Fla.	11	68.2	81.4	96	27	58.83	0.0	76
Minneapolis, Minn.	830	16.7	70.4	108	–34	27.19	41.1	72
Montgomery, Ala.	201	50.0	80.8	107	–5	51.50	0.7	72
New Orleans, La.	8	56.0	82.1	102	7	60.27	0.2	78
New York, N. Y.	10	32.4	71.9	102	–14	42.99	30.9	70
Norfolk, Va.	11	42.5	76.9	105	2	42.25	9.1	76
Oklahoma City, Okla.	1,254	39.2	79.8	113	–17	31.65	7.6	68
Omaha, Nebr.	978	25.3	74.9	114	–32	27.83	27.7	–
Pensacola, Fla.	11	54.2	80.4	103	7	58.60	0.1	78
Philadelphia, Pa.	26	34.3	74.1	106	–11	40.41	22.4	70
Phoenix, Ariz.	1,107	53.4	88.1	118	16	7.81	–	42
Pittsburgh, Pa.	1,248	32.0	72.4	103	–20	35.95	34.2	71
Portland, Maine	61	24.7	65.7	103	–21	42.16	70.6	72
Portland, Oreg.	30	40.9	65.3	107	–2	41.62	12.9	73
Raleigh, N. C.	400	42.9	77.3	104	–2	46.56	7.6	75
Reno, Nev.	4,397	34.1	67.5	106	–19	7.16	28.6	53
Roseburg, Oreg.	508	42.6	65.6	109	–6	32.28	5.9	74
St. Louis, Mo.	465	34.1	77.5	110	–22	39.23	17.5	68
Salt Lake City, Utah	4,260	29.8	72.7	106	–30	13.72	46.2	58
San Antonio, Tex.	782	54.1	82.9	107	4	27.09	0.5	68
San Diego, Calif.	19	55.7	67.0	110	25	10.03	0.0	71
San Francisco, Calif.	52	51.4	59.0	101	27	22.08	0.2	78
Sault Ste. Marie, Mich.	724	14.1	60.3	98	–37	29.94	79.3	80
Seattle, Wash.	14	41.8	62.9	100	3	33.93	11.2	75
Spokane, Wash.	1,954	30.0	67.3	108	–30	15.78	35.8	64
Tampa, Fla.	6	61.9	81.4	98	19	48.91	T	79
Washington, D. C.	72	35.6	75.0	106	–15	41.85	20.5	70
Wichita, Kans.	1,372	34.2	78.1	114	–22	30.13	13.7	67

Sunshine Hours	Days with					90° or Fog	32° or Higher	0° or Lower	0° or Lower
	Clear	Pt. Cloudy	Cloudy	Rain	Snow				
3,408	197	114	54	50	5	4	49	126	1
3,495	198	109	58	75	14	6	52	102	2
2,776	129	108	128	122	2	20	57	43	0
2,519	122	131	112	134	25	31	4	82	-
2,658	146	114	105	94	70	5	18	183	48
2,768	124	95	146	93	14	17	40	120	1
2,561	118	118	129	125	42	14	9	106	3
2,723	112	146	107	75	-	14	104	3	0
2,346	74	130	161	165	98	12	1	128	3
2,144	73	111	181	148	48	9	4	148	19
2,945	130	134	101	111	*	14	27	9	0
2,926	124	152	89	96	69	14	7	175	12
2,645	117	120	128	124	59	10	11	109	8
2,670	112	118	135	131	19	10	26	89	1
2,344	90	121	154	154	45	5	4	114	3
2,966	146	152	67	84	49	2	22	136	8
2,766	124	118	123	104	50	6	24	128	16
2,367	97	124	144	134	38	11	9	124	4
3,546	216	112	37	50	2	1	88	44	*
3,610	158	115	92	76	4	6	90	29	6
2,850	148	123	94	99	*	18	13	4	0
2,666	101	125	139	98	42	2	9	153	22
2,856	136	132	97	94	-	8	24	169	35
-	-	-	-	100	-	-	-	-	-
2,802	125	142	98	121	0	11	59	6	0
2,880	148	112	105	106	34	9	39	96	4
2,603	124	122	119	134	17	18	30	63	*
2,831	141	107	117	107	7	9	51	40	*
3,217	179	128	58	39	*	24	14	*	0
2,808	142	107	116	111	3	5	45	40	*
2,931	101	151	113	134	0	2	6	*	0
2,614	104	114	147	107	71	8	14	147	30
2,866	133	119	113	113	2	5	67	19	0
2,642	119	139	107	119	-	15	53	4	0
2,685	106	133	126	125	35	21	7	92	*
2,735	133	115	117	125	6	15	25	41	0
2,999	163	109	93	83	6	8	64	70	*
2,817	132	120	113	97	22	8	30	120	14
2,914	135	125	105	112	*	14	16	7	0
2,627	114	121	130	124	29	10	13	79	*
3,752	228	90	47	39	-	-	152	10	0
2,303	85	129	151	149	64	24	16	102	2
2,586	130	109	126	237	37	28	3	135	6
2,155	93	100	172	153	14	9	6	27	0
2,724	133	114	118	120	4	12	37	50	*
3,370	195	100	70	49	39	3	32	154	2
2,293	110	121	134	134	5	47	15	33	*
2,693	138	118	109	111	31	10	36	79	2
3,064	136	113	116	85	59	9	49	132	5
2,721	133	132	100	83	-	16	104	12	0
3,015	180	109	76	46	0	21	1	0	0
2,935	157	115	93	67	*	15	1	*	0
2,125	85	101	179	155	73	18	1	158	29
2,049	77	107	181	150	14	27	1	21	0
2,583	97	107	161	111	54	17	19	112	4
3,019	122	159	84	114	*	16	62	1	0
2,583	126	120	119	124	12	11	26	83	*
2,827	161	113	91	86	12	10	52	95	3

Source: United States Department of Commerce, Weather Bureau, Washington, D.C.

the Man, gives this advice:

> There are several large classes of northerners who would benefit from seasonal or permanent southward migration. The largest of these includes the millions of elderly people whose tissue fires have pretty well burned out or become choked with clinkers of degenerative disease. With their arteriosclerosis, diabetes, chronic nephritis, heart troubles, and a host of other chronic ailments, they are no longer fit for the physical struggle it takes to survive the stormy cold of northern winters.

This is good advice for folks living in the North, past middle age, who find the weather increasingly burdensome. It is especially true for any person who suffers from the illnesses mentioned. He may add years to his life by getting away from the too-invigorating cold climate. The farther people of retirement age move into the southern warmth, the better it will be for many of them.

CLIMACTIC DATA TABLE NOTES

* Less than one

T Trace

Elevation. The ground elevation at the Weather Bureau Office.

Temperature:
> *Winter.* The average of the daily maximum and minimum temperatures for December, January, and February.
> *Summer.* The average of the daily maximum and minimum temperatures for June, July, and August.
> *Highest.* The hottest temperature on record.
> *Lowest.* The coldest temperature on record.

Precipitation. Average annual.
> *Rain.* Includes actual rain plus the water equivalent of solid forms (hail, sleet, and snow).
> *Snow.* Average depth of unmelted snowfall.

Relative Humidity. An average based on the 7:30 A.M. and P.M. records for all months.

Sunshine. Average annual hours.

Days with: Annual averages.
> *Clear.* Number of days that the average cloudiness does not exceed 3/10 of the sky.
> *Partly Cloudy.* Number of days that the average cloudiness is 4/10 to 7/10.
> *Cloudy.* Number of days that the average cloudiness is 8/10 or more.
> *Rain.* Number of days with 0.01 inch or more of rain.
> *Snow.* Number of days with 0.1 inch or more of snow.
> *Fog.* Number of days with fog.
> *90° or higher.* Number of days with maximum temperature 90° or higher.
> *32° or lower.* Number of days with minimum temperature 32° or lower.
> *0° or lower.* Number of days with minimum temperature 0° or lower.

It is a common experience to have more colds, more nose and throat irritations and other respiratory diseases as soon as the cold weather sets in and we must rely on artificial heat. The dry, parched air of northern homes, offices and factories, and the atmospheric pollution of industrial areas, are largely responsible for the high rate of respiratory diseases.

It is in the winter months that the greatest differences in temperatures occur between different regions of the United States. Midwinter mean temperatures as low as ten degrees occur over the northern interior as compared with fifty-five-degree mean temperatures in Florida, the Gulf Coast and Southern California. In midsummer the distribution of average temperatures is more nearly uniform between the Northern and Southern states. A migration in summer from the South to the North in search of cooler weather does not offer nearly the advantages of a trip to the South in winter in search of warmer weather.

The mean annual range of temperatures between the heat of midsummer and the cold of midwinter in the North is as much as sixty degrees. In the South and in Southern California, the range between the hottest and coldest parts of the year is only twenty-five to thirty degrees. Some localities, like San Francisco, have a difference of only ten degrees between mean summer and mean winter temperatures.

Below the Snowfall Line

Generally speaking little or no snow falls and lies on the ground in winter south of an irregular line stretching from Cape Hatteras in North Carolina on the Atlantic Coast, through the southeastern section of South Carolina, Georgia and the Gulf States, across southern Texas, across southern New Mexico and southern Arizona (except at mountain altitudes) and over the lowlands of central California to the coast of California (except in the mountains). During exceptional cold spells, an occasional light snow may fall in parts of these regions. But when it does fall it is such a rarity that it causes considerable excitement and little discomfort. The continent's stormiest region is around the Great Lakes and southern Canada. As we go south from this region, storminess diminishes. Florida has a moderate degree of stormy weather. Southern California, southern Arizona and southern New Mexico are the least stormy parts of the United States.

What Makes a Good Climate?

You often hear people say that a certain place has a "perfect" climate. But climatologists tell us that a perfect climate as such does not exist. Every climate has its own advantages and some disagreeable features at certain seasons. A southern climate, with its mild winters, abundant sunshine and opportunities for outdoor living the year round, may be hot and moist in summer. The invigorating climate of the North may be too cold and stormy for elderly people in winter. Coastal climates may be too damp and foggy for many persons afflicted with respiratory diseases. The high altitudes and chilly climates of mountain regions are too rugged.

The best climate for the majority of older men and women is one that encourages them to spend a great deal of their time outdoors, with frequent but moderate weather changes, temperatures rarely above eighty degrees during the daytime and fifty-five degrees at night, relative humidity around 55 percent and variety in the amount of cloudiness. Such a climate is neither too hot nor too cold. Some change in weather is desirable to avoid monotony.

Don't undertake the impossible task of trying to find the one perfect climate spot in the United States. Select one out of four or five possible locations, any one of which is suited to your physical and mental condition of health and your personal preference. Live in the selected location for a year on a temporary basis before making it your permanent retirement residence.

From a retirement point of view, the ideal way to live is to reside in the South or in Southern California from November through May. Then migrate to New England, the Great Lakes peninsula or to the mountains of North or South Carolina from June through September or October. Migrants should leave the North or mountain altitudes before the winter storms set in. Because this way of living would require the support of two household units, it is beyond the financial reach of the average retired person.

The next best thing for retired people to do is to take up permanent residence in one of the better all-year-round climate regions that provide an easy, more relaxed existence. This calls for getting away from the rigorous climatic conditions of cold, snow, ice and blizzards of winter.

Control Hot Summer Weather by Air Conditioning

Probably the greatest disadvantage of the climate of the Southern regions is the heat and humidity of the summer months. Yet the trade winds and on-shore sea breezes, especially in the coastal regions, make the Southern seaboard more desirable in the summer months than many regions in the north.

Even though a man may work or spend considerable time outdoors during the hot summer months, he can be refreshed by a good night's sleep in a cool house. The heat of the day is not nearly so depressing when a comfortable night's sleep is possible.

If the climate is too humid, air conditioning removes the surplus moisture from the air but leaves enough moisture to insure a healthful humidity. Through air conditioning, people living in the South can control the temperature and humidity in homes, offices, stores and other private or public buildings.

Air conditioning is no longer a luxury item only for the wealthy. Room air-conditioning units, placed in a window, can be purchased for about $230. Console or floor units are more expensive, costing $500 and more, depending upon the horsepower rating of the unit. Air-conditioning manufacturers are developing complete weather-controlled home units. The latest units, run on gas or oil, provide solid comfort the year round by keeping the inside of the house at an even and comfortable temperature no matter what the weather is outside.

Additional Ways to Keep Cool

Here are a few things you can do in order to keep cool during the summer's heat: A light-colored roof will deflect the rays of the sun . . . insulation under the roof and in the side walls keep out heat . . . an attic fan will remove heat . . . attic vents let in fresh air . . . light-colored outside walls reflect heat, dark colors absorb heat . . . cool colors on inside walls and in decoration materials make you feel cool . . . wide overhanging roof and awnings provide shade and keep direct rays of sun from reaching the side walls . . . cross- or through-ventilation carries away the heat . . . vent fan over the stove removes heat . . . fluorescent lighting is cooler . . . portable fans circulate the air . . . trees and a vine-covered trellis on the west side of the house lessen the severity of the heat.

Another way to beat the heat is to wear white or light-colored and loose-fitting clothing. Dark clothes in summer absorb heat and act like a blanket-warmer around the body. Don't stay too long in the direct sun in the middle of the day. Eat light but balanced meals.

Climate and Health

While there are certain areas of the United States where average persons suffering or convalescing from certain illnesses feel better and more comfortable, there are no peculiar properties in natural climates which act specifically to prevent disease. Some local areas, however, do have dusts, pollens, smoke and acids that pollute the atmosphere and cause discomfort to persons susceptible to them.

Temperature, winds, variability in weather changes, humidity and barometric pressure are the factors that make a climate good or bad. Every time there is a sudden or severe change in weather, the body has to make adjustments to meet these changes. Normally healthy younger folks make the adjustments easily. For people in ill health, weather changes make demands on the body. They also have a depressive or a stimulating effect on the mental state of the ill person.

People who diagnose their own illnesses and treat themselves run great risks of unnecessary suffering and possible permanent harm. The same is true with reference to choosing a climate for health purposes. *Don't make a drastic change of climate, because of illness, without the guidance of your doctor.*

Beneficial Regions for Sufferers of Ailments

Doctors and climatologists recognize, under certain conditions, that some regions are preferable for persons suffering from specific ailments. Your doctor should be consulted regarding your particular problem.

For alleviating asthma, sinus, bronchitis, arthritis, rheumatic infections and hay fever, southern Arizona has been found to be helpful.

The dry and cool mountain area of the Southwest, at altitudes high enough to escape summer heat, has long been a popular area for persons afflicted with tuberculosis. Today, however, good sanatorium care near the patient's home usually gives him the best chance of recovery. If you move to another state, you may not be able to get state tuberculosis hospital care unless you are a legal resident of the state. In some states a person becomes a legal resident only after three years of residence.

For hay fever, have your doctor diagnose the pollens and dusts to which you are allergic. Check with the United States Department of Agriculture, Washington, D.C., to learn in which regions of the country the plants with pollens that affect you have their natural growth and which regions are generally free of such plants. Generally speaking, the Southwest desert regions are beneficial to sufferers of hay fever, because pollen-bearing plants do not grow in these regions.

A change of climate often has helped people who suffer from certain ailments, but it has also failed. For this reason those who seek relief by change of residence should try the new location for several months before making a permanent decision to relocate.

Bibliography

Climate in Everyday Life by Charles E. Brooks (Greenwood Press, Westport, Conn.)
Climate and Weather by Herman Flohn (McGraw-Hill, N.Y.)
Man and His Environment by David N. Gator (Harper & Row, New York)
Climate and Man's Environment, by John Oliver (Wiley, New York)

For climate information on specific areas, write to the National Climatic Center, Asheville, North Carolina 28801 (Attention Publications Div.)

U.S. GOVERNMENT PUBLICATIONS

Weather, Astronomy, Meterorology. Send for free bibliography and price list of books and pamphlets on these subjects to Superintendent of Documents, Government Printing Office, Washington, D.C. 20402

11

Selecting a Location for Retirement Living

Since personal preferences vary so widely, it is impossible to list every location that offers good prospects for retirement living. However, the localities described in the pages that follow are those most frequently recommended in my research of important retirement areas. The omission of any specific location does not necessarily mean that the particular city or village has little to offer for enjoyable retirement.

The localities included in this survey are significant because they are all below the regular snowfall line. We recognize that many people will surely find their choice retirement locales in other parts of the nation. Others may prefer migratory retirement living as a means of escaping the ruggedness of the winter season in the North, and find the Southern locations of value in the selection of a *winter* retirement site.

The principal points to consider in selecting a place for retirement are: *Climate,* which has much to do with physical comfort and good, healthful living. *Avocation, hobby and work opportunities*, as they fit into your retirement plans and desires for keeping busy. *Facilities for intellectual and cultural outlets*, covering libraries, museums, lectures, concerts, art, adult education classes, and so on. *Recreation facilities*, such as golf, fishing, yachting and shuffleboard, depending upon whether you want an active or quiet community life. *Social and religious groups*, providing opportunities to meet congenial people and to make new friendships according to backgrounds and interests. *Scenery, altitude and topography*, with reference to the charm of the place and facilities. *Financial requirements*, because in many desirable locations the cost of a home, taxes and other living expenses may be too great a strain on your retirement income. The problem is to find the best locations within your means. In some instances, the answer will be to settle in a new suburban development or in a neighborhood village which is part of a larger community offering the advantages you are looking for. *Personal preferences*, which may be influenced by any number of considerations, such as nearness to relatives or friends, availability of medical care, the tempo of living, preference for urban or rural living, opportunities to engage in a small business enterprise and other special and personal reasons.

Each of these considerations carries a different degree of importance for each individual. Decide for yourself which are most important for you, which will assure the rich life you are looking forward to in retirement.

Keep in mind, however, that there are many things about a place that cannot be measured statistically. These have to be discovered by pesonal experience while actually living in the community. If you plan to move to a new locality, it is wise to live there on a temporary basis for a while. Try it out through all seasons of the year before taking up permanent residence.

An early start in planning where to live in retirement will

avert errors in judgment, save a good deal of money and make adjustments to retirement easier. Somewhere in the United States, there are retirement localities seemingly made to order for your needs and desires. The earlier you start searching for them, the better your chances of finding them.

12

California

Southern California, Coastal Areas

Climatologists classify the climate of Southern California as Mediterranean in type—one of the best four-season climates in the world. The summers are tempered by sea breezes with almost no rain for two to six months; winters are mild with light to moderate rain coming in periods of a few days' duration separated by many days of brilliant sunshine.

Because of the proximity of the Pacific Ocean, freezing temperatures are extremely rare. Average temperatures along the coastal plain range from forty-eight degrees to sixty degrees during the winter months, with a daily range of about twenty degrees. In the summer months the temperatures vary from seventy-two to seventy-eight degrees during the daytime to around sixty degrees at night, with a daily range of about fifteen degrees.

Southern California has about forty-five days of rain, amounting to ten to twenty inches, as an annual average.

There are normally twelve rainy days in spring and nineteen in winter. Relative humidity at noon in winter averages 45 to 56 percent and during the summer months 52 to 60 percent. This region has 179 clear days and 77 cloudy days annually. During daylight hours in winter, the sun shines 68 to 71 percent of the time, and in summer 70 to 80 percent.

In the interior valleys, winter temperatures are sometimes below freezing at night and summer temperatures rise to ninety-five degrees. Low humidity, however, moderates the effect of high temperatures. The nights are usually cool and comfortable. The desert areas of the southern part of the state, near Nevada and Arizona, are hot and dry —among the most arid places on the North American continent.

The coastal areas and nearby foothill districts are subject to night and early morning fogs which are more frequent in summer than in winter. The fog increases as latitude and altitude increase.

San Diego. Pop. 770,344. Alt. Sea level to 1,586 ft. County seat of San Diego County. The oldest Spanish settlement in California is 125 miles south of Los Angeles and about 15 miles from the Mexican border. The large city (305 square miles) offers diversified terrain. One may dwell by the shore or the scenic bay, in agricultural valleys or in the cosmopolitan city. The city and county enjoy a dry subtropical climate, considered by many experts as one of the world's finest climates. High temperatures are almost unknown. Nights are cool and light blankets are needed year-round.

The city is built around beautiful, fourteen-hundred-acre Balboa Park, which contains a large zoo, museum, art galleries and many diversified recreational facilities, exposition buildings and outdoor organ recitals. Back of the city is the Coastal Range, affording snow sports in season, as well as camping and hunting. San Diego is well equipped to satisfy every cultural desire. Art galleries, floral gardens, symphonies-under-the-stars, theaters, starlight operas, social clubs, churches, missions—all are here in numbers and quality. Every form of diversion from deep-sea fishing and boating to golf, surfing and shuffleboard is available in the area. San Diego Public Library has thirty-two branch libraries.

Condominiums start at about $40,000. Apartment rentals for two-bedroom units are from $185. Average mobile home space rental is $55 to $200.

La Jolla. Pop. 30,000. A suburb of San Diego, is one of the most delightful retirement communities in the United States. It is located on a picturesque rocky headland, fronted by many pleasant sandy coves, with beautiful and comfortable homes around the beaches and on the hill slopes.

The shopping center has charming shops with unique names, such as The Green Dragon. At the Scripps Institution of Oceanography there is an aquarium and marine museum for the study of ocean life. For golf there is the La Jolla Country Club, and championship tennis is played at the Tennis Club.

Many retired business executives live in this distinctive and cultural community, which is blessed with some of the best climate in the United States. Ranch-type homes with three bedrooms are listed from $70,000 to $250,000 up. You will need about $1,000 a month to participate in, and enjoy, the community standard of living.

Coronado. Pop. 18,000. Alt. 25 ft. San Diego County. A fashionable community of beautiful homes, resort hotels, modern apartments, fine restaurants, shady avenues, parks, beaches and a famous yacht harbor, located across the bay from San Diego. Recreation facilities include yachting, deep-sea fishing, golf, tennis, lawn bowling, swimming in ocean or bay, in a climate where every month is an out-of-doors month. Rather on the expensive side for retirement living.

Escondido. Pop. 51,500. Alt. 660 ft. San Diego County. A number of retired and semi-retired families have chosen Escondido because of its excellent year-round climate and happy, healthful, informal way of living. Many families live on a small acreage and grow avocados, citrus fruits, vegetables and poultry. Escondido (meaning valley) has beautiful rolling hills, canyons, highlands and lowlands, and affords ideal locations for diversified types of farming and retirement homes. It possesses practically everything for healthful and comfortable living.

You will find the usual number of clubs, social and service groups here; fifty-four churches, representing every important denomination; an excellent school system; opportunities for many forms of outdoor recreation; twenty-five golf courses within forty-five minutes' drive; a philharmonic society; painting and art groups and devotees of the drama; a well-stocked library and a well-equipped hospital. Five shopping centers provide excellent stores and, combined with the downtown area, are the reason Escondido leads all cities in per capita buying, according to tax figures provided by the State Board of Equalization. Escondido is the southern gateway to the famous Palomar Mountain Observatory and its two-hundred-inch telescope. Very close to the area are the Warner Hot Springs and Rincon Springs. The town is situated beyond and above the coastal fogs, lying fifteen miles inland from the Pacific Ocean. The Chamber of Commerce reports that opportunities for establishing small businesses exist in the community. Real estate offerings: rentals for one and two bedroom apartments and duplexes range between $150 and $300 per month; many suburban residential areas within ten miles of Escondido offer homes from $25,000 to $75,000; there are thirty-three mobile parks, most of which have swimming pools and recreational facilities.

Oceanside. Pop. 60,000. Alt. 50 ft. San Diego County. Located on the coast, thirty-eight miles north of San Diego, this community at the mouth of the San Luis Rey Valley offers good prospects for retirement. The four-mile beach is considered one of the cleanest and safest in California. A huge municipal pier, picnic facilities, open-air theater, fishing, swimming and playground equipment add to the attractiveness of this fine resort town. The Mission San Luis Rey and the estate of the Rosicrucian Fellowship are located here. One of the largest United States Marine Corps bases adjoins Oceanside. A multi-million dollar pleasure marina with 600 berths and alongside docks for transient craft and large yachts is operated by the Ocean-side Small Craft Harbor District. The year-round harbor is a home port for an enormous inland area as well as a haven for distressed craft and headquarters for avid sportfishing fans.

Laguna Beach. Pop. 16,400. Alt. 0–1,000 ft. Orange County. This attractive village is the home of a number of distinguished playwrights, musicians, actors, ceramists, photographers and artists and craftsmen of every imaginable media. At the L. B. Museum of Art you will find painters and sculptors mingling with guests at monthly teas. Here, too, you will find schools of painting, photography, ballet, sculpture and ceramics. Some artists' studios have uniquely shaped roofs and bright-colored shutters. If you like to live in an atmosphere of art, lectures and concerts, where living is easy and informal, you'll enjoy Laguna Beach. The Festival of Arts and Pageant of the Masters, presented each summer, is a famous and popular attraction, as are three additional large arts and crafts shows. Galleries, shops and artisans wares abound. As recreation, you can enjoy surf fishing and bathing, motorboating, and nearby, sailing, golf, tennis, lawn bowling, beautiful trails for riding or hiking. Laguna's churches represent almost every denomination. All the principal service clubs and fraternal organizations are represented. The Orange Coast Junior College, Santa Ana College and University of California at Irvine provide academic and college sports atmosphere.

Here you will explore pleasure islands, palm-fringed coves, green valleys, orange groves, old Spanish missions and snow-capped mountains that rise right up from the ocean surf. Beyond the mountains are the vast deserts with palm jungles, oasis resorts, dude ranches and ghost towns.

It is strategically located fifty miles south of Los Angeles and eighty miles from the Mexican border, in the center of Southern California's famous climate belt. Laguna is a town of artistic homes and gardens noted for individuality and hospitality. It is very popular as a retirement community. Attractive homes start at $80,000; condominiums, at $40,000.

Santa Ana. Pop. 155,762. Alt. 133 ft. Seat of Orange County. Over four hundred clubs and service organizations. More than eighty churches. Community players, Municipal Stadium, Bowers Memorial Museum and Prentice Park Zoo.

Santa Ana is the professional, financial and retail center of Orange County. The city reflects the gracious, easy, California way of life, and the varied life styles available here have one thing in common: an emphasis on alfresco pleasures centered around the patio, the outdoor grill, and swimming pool. Buying a home here makes good financial sense, too, since Santa Ana homeowners enjoy one of the lowest property tax rates in Orange County.

Rentals for one- and two-bedroom apartments and duplexes range from $140 to $400 per month. Rentals for two- and three-bedroom houses range from $250 to $750 per month. Sales prices of existing homes were from

$30,000 to $100,000 during 1974–75. There are numerous suburban residential areas within five miles of Santa Ana offering homes priced from $30,000 to $250,000.

Pasadena. Pop. 125,000. Alt. 700 to 1,200 ft. Metropolitan Los Angeles Area. Located ten miles northeast of the city of Los Angeles, at the foothills of the Sierra Madre Mountains in the San Gabriel Valley, it is a city of above-average homes, gardens and estates. It is best known as the site of the annual Tournament of Roses and Rose Bowl football games. The California Institute of Technology, Huntington Library and Art Gallery, the Norton Simon Museum, Pasadena Civic Auditorium, Beckman and Ambassador Auditoriums and Pasadena City College provide plenty of opportunities for lectures, plays, concerts and other cultural activities. Brookside Park's five-hundred acre recreational preserve and fifteen other parks afford a variety of outdoor recreational activities.

Most houses for sale in this location are advertised at from $35,000 to $65,000 and more. This includes homes in San Marino, which is a rapidly growing suburb of Pasadena. Many millionaires have large estates here, and thousands of moderately wealthy families also live in retirement throughout the Pasadena area. You'll need a monthly income of $600 or more for reasonable retirement living. People with more moderate financial incomes will find good living in nearby in Sierra Madre and Altadena.

Long Beach. Pop. 350,000. Alt. 35 ft. A celebrated seaside resort and year-round playground, about twenty miles southwest of Los Angeles. For many years this has been a haven for retired folks. It was here that Dr. Francis Townsend organized his famous old-age pension movement. There are many organizations and clubs catering to retired people. Many people now consider Long Beach too commercialized with too much tourist activity for peaceful retirement living. However, thousands of retired families have settled here.

A thirty-year average shows only fifteen degrees variation between the mean average temperature; fifty-five degrees in the winter and seventy degrees in the summer. Average annual rainfall is 12.6 inches (City of Long Beach). Average number of sunny days per year is 305.

An eight-mile smooth and wide ocean beach plus stillwater beaches provide for swimming, aquatic sports and fishing. In its one thousand acres of parks and playgrounds are numerous recreation facilities for retired folks—everything from shuffleboard and horseshoe pitching to flycasting and picnics. Lectures, plays, concerts and community programs are held throughout the year at the Municipal Auditorium. Homes in the residential areas range from modest bungalows to pretentious estates.

City-owned oil wells have brought in huge revenues for the city government which has resulted in lower tax rates for residents. A municipal golf course is located at Recreation Park, and in addition there are six other public courses. There are more than two hundred churches representing forty-six denominations. The library system includes the main library, ten branch libraries and one bookmobile. Bixby Park is a picnic park noted as the site of state society picnics. More than six hundred industries are located in Long Beach, and it is the home port of the United States Navy Battle Fleet. Ten equipped hospitals provide modern facilities.

Santa Monica. Pop. 88,848. Alt. Sea level to 400 ft. Located sixteen miles from Los Angeles in an area of scenic beauty "where the mountains meet the sea," Santa Monica is in the ideal year-round climate zone where frosts, thunderstorms and strong winds are virtually unknown. A great many of the Hollywood movie stars have their residences here. This is a city of attractive homes and estates with beautiful gardens. Residential districts extend from the ocean front up into the foothills of the Santa Monica Mountains. Santa Monica with its palm-lined streets is the kind of city Eastern people dream about.

The nearby University of California (UCLA) and Loyola University provide college-town atmosphere, as well as excellent facilities for social and cultural life. The Community College offers classes for adults. Things to do in Santa Monica include visits to Municipal Pier, fishing, swimming, paddleboard, yachting, bathing along three miles of beaches; tennis in city parks, bowling on the green, shuffleboard; golfing and riding nearby and attending the open-air theater. The city has fifty churches, the usual social and service clubs, and an excellent public library and art gallery. It is an easy place in which to make friends and is a popular retirement location for people from the Midwest.

The average ocean-water temperature in summer months is sixty degrees and in winter months, fifty-five degrees. The average air temperature in July is seventy-nine degrees and in January, sixty-one degrees. Rainfall averages only about twelve inches a year.

Oxnard. Pop. 89,000. Alt. 45 ft. Ventura County. The climate is about ten degrees cooler than that of Los Angeles in summer and winter. Maximum average temperature for January is sixty-seven degrees; for July, seventy-four degrees. Minimum average for January is forty-one degrees and for July, fifty-five degrees. There are fogs in the spring and fall seasons. Thunderstorms are a rarity. The area is practically frostless and relatively smog-free. Oxnard is located sixty-two miles northwest from Los Angeles and thirty-eight miles from Santa Barbara, on the Pacific Ocean. It is in the center of a rich agricultural empire of lemons and truck crops.

Everything in recreation and relaxation is within minutes of the community—deep-sea and surf fishing; sun bathing and swimming; hunting and fishing in mountain and stream country. Riding, hiking, golf and other outdoor recreation are easily accessible. Adult evening classes furnish added diversion, as do the many musical, dramatic, art and cultural groups which are active throughout the county. Practically every denomination is represented in Oxnard's sixty area churches, as well as most of the nationally recognized fraternal and civic organizations.

Mindful of the importance of water supply, Oxnard has taken a lead in the development and preservation of adequate future water supplies by planning river-source dams, open and underground reservoirs. Average annual rainfall has been 14.72 inches for the past five years.

Ojai. Pop. 5,700. Alt. 700 ft. Ventura County. Here is an unusual, cheerful and active community, whose cultural and recreational facilities, blended with leisurely living, have attracted many people looking for a place to settle in retirement. Lying in a sunny and fertile valley in the mountains of the Los Padres National Forest, Ojai Valley is called the "Valley of Enchantment." The Ojai community enjoys smog-free air, warm summer days and cool summer nights. July temperatures reach a maximum of ninety-two degrees, with night temperatures around fifty-three degrees. The dry climate has helped many who suffer from asthma and hay fever. Arts and crafts flourish in the community aided by classes and exhibitions of the many outstanding artists and craftsmen who reside in Ojai Valley. Late in May, a week-long festival presents outstanding artists of the music and concert world. Many attractive resorts and hot springs are located in the valley. Fishing may be enjoyed in the mountain streams and hunting in the hills. Golf, tennis, riding, picnics, and shuffleboard are a few of the outdoor activities to be enjoyed the year round. Other retired persons raise flowers, ornamental shrubs or citrus fruits.

Three-bedroom homes sell for $40,000 on up in the

village. Better homes on hillside locations start at $75,000. Because it has no industrial area and is off the beaten path, Ojai has been able to retain its spirit of peace and tranquality.

Santa Barbara. Pop. 70,000. Alt. Sea level to 850 ft. County seat of Santa Barbara County. For gracious living and an atmosphere of natural beauty in oak-covered hills, mountain background and expanse of seashore, Santa Barbara is a favorite retirement location for businessmen, professional people and ex-military personnel. A bright, clean city of flowers, red tile roofs, white stucco walls, it has a reputation for ease and leisure. Many internationally famous writers, painters, sculptors and musicians reside in this community. Flowers and shrubs grow the year round in home gardens and on the landscaped estates and ranches of the retired wealthy.

Average temperatures during summer are in the high seventies, and night temperatures average forty-nine degrees. Winter temperatures average sixty-five degrees maximum to forty degrees minimum. Annual rainfall is eighteen inches. Relative humidity averages 78 percent.

Santa Barbara stands out for its high level of cultural activities. The Civic Recreation Center is the headquarters for dance groups, plays, orchestra and singing groups, as well as card and chess games. Instruction in arts, crafts and trades is provided by the adult education classes. The University of California, Santa Barbara, has spent $50 million on a 600-acre campus, Goleta, ten miles from Santa Barbara. Santa Barbara has an outstanding museum of art, a museum of natural history, an historical museum, and a botanical garden.

From a social and recreational viewpoint, Santa Barbara has much to offer retired people with its social and service clubs and groups covering all manner of special interests. The Retired Business and Professional Men's Club (similar to the Old Guard) has over 150 members. Archery, base-ball, tennis, golf, lawn bowling, swimming, yachting, hiking, picnics, riding, rifle and skeet shooting and fishing are a few of the recreational facilities available. Outstanding concerts, plays, recitals and road shows are presented at the Lobero Theatre and the Arlington Center for the Performing Arts. The Santa Barbara Mission is said to be the most photographed of all the old missions.

Farming activities in the county include citrus, walnut and avocado groves, vegetable growing, cattle and horse raising, dairying and flower growing. Typical real estate values recently advertised include three-bedroom cottages with garden for $60,000 to $80,000; homes with "view" locations from $70,000 to $125,000. Apartment rentals range from $175 up per month.

Santa Barbara is so well thought of as a retirement location that you will find families from all sections of the country living in retirement there.

Southern California, Interior Areas

The climate of Southern California varies with the distance from the coast and the topography of the locality. In general, the climate is warmer and drier in Riverside County than in the coastal counties. Low average relative humidity, infrequent fog, predominantly clear skies and warm temperatures, are considered beneficial to persons afflicted with asthma, bronchial diseases, neuritis and sinus. During the summer months the maximum daytime temperatures are usually below ninety-five degrees and the relative humidity averages 45 percent. The effect of the low humidity is that, though the thermometer is high, people feel comfortable. Summer nights are cool, with temperatures in the fifties. In the winter months temperatures range between thirty-six degrees minimum to sixty degrees maximum, with relative humidity around 50 percent. There are about 233 clear days and wind averages seven miles per hour. This is a land of contrasts—rich valleys filled with orange, lemon, cherry, walnut and date palm trees, lakes cupped in wooded hills, famous desert resorts and hot springs. Those seeking a dry climate for health reasons, within accessible distances from a great metropolitan center like Los Angeles, will do well to consider retirement locations in Riverside County.

Riverside. Pop. 163,000. Alt. 854 ft. County seat for Riverside County, just 50 miles inland from Los Angeles. One of the outstanding inland cities on the Santa Ana River. The birthplace of the navel-orange industry in the United States. Riverside is famous for its Mission Inn Garden Hotel, unique for its collection of art objects and pioneer relics. The city has 106 churches.

Banning. Pop. 12,300. Located on the slopes of Mt. San Gorgonio, this town is in the midst of citrus fruit and almond groves.

Corona. Pop. 31,250. Alt. 678 ft. is a charming modern city, the second fastest growing community in Riverside County, having more than doubled its population in the past years. A diversified yet well balanced community industrially, commercially and residentially, it is situated in the Santa Ana Mountain Plains Region, nestled in a valley of orange and citrus groves with an atmosphere of rural as well as urban living. Cost of living is reasonable and there are many attractions in the area to interest retired families.

Corona is located approximately 45 miles east-southeast of Los Angeles in the northwest corner of Riverside County near its convergence with Orange and San Bernardino counties. Corona is situated at the base of a gently sloping alluvial plain extending northward to the Santa Ana River from the surrounding Santa Ana mountains on the west and south. Corona's southwestern boundary is contiguous with the Cleveland National Forest, whose nearby mountain peaks range from 3,000 to 5,700 feet, compared with a city elevation of 678 feet.

Beaumont. Pop. 6,075. Located in the San Gorgonio Pass, which is the principal pass connecting the coastal plain and Imperial Valley, it is the center of cherry, and apple orchards and the home of the Annual Cherry Festival.

Palm Springs. Pop. 28,700. Alt. 425 ft. A fashionable and fun desert and social resort nestled at the base of 10,831-foot Mt. San Jacinto, it is located 105 miles east of Los Angeles and is famous as both the Winter Golf Capital of the World and the site of healthful natural hot mineral waters. The golden desert is fertile; flowers and palm trees bloom profusely. This oasis in the desert, once the exclusive playground of Hollywood movie stars, artists and rich Americans, is now growing in popularity among tourists.

Many who come as tourists discover the benefits of the clean, dry desert climate and remain to join the ranks of the "villagers." The atmosphere is that of a friendly village. Some of the finest shops in California are located on the tree- and flower-lined streets of this fascinating desert city. With more than 5,600 swimming pools, and the Palm Springs Aerial Tramway, which climbs 8,300 feet to Mt. San Jacinto State Park, the golden sandpile offers beauty, variety and surprises in the desert.

The Palm Springs new 6 million dollar Desert Art Museum features some of the most famous artists in the world, showing their works on a rotating basis and is the site of the million dollar Annenberg Theatre donated by former Ambassador to the Court of St. James the Honorable Walter and Mrs. Annenberg.

Palm Springs is also the location of the world famous Bob Hope Golf Classic held in February of each year, as well as the Colgate-Dinah Shore Ladies Professional Golf Association tournament each year.

Central California, Coastal Region

This region comprises the counties of San Luis Obispo, Monterey, Santa Cruz, San Mateo, Marin, Contra Costa, Alameda and Santa Clara. These counties have a marine type of climate. Mild temperatures prevail the year round and result in the absence of clearly defined seasons although periods of gradual transition are apparent. The region is characterized by low temperatures near the coast and high pressures during the summer, while the interior is characterized by higher temperatures and low pressure. Saturated air passing over the colder water surfaces is cooled until the moisture condenses into fog. Strong westerly winds carry the fog inland. The entire coastal area is subject to fogs which occur most frequently during the evening and early morning in the summer months. The fog is usually "burnt off" by midmorning. These fogs cause a large number of partly clouded days and reduce sunshine to 60 percent of daylight hours. Average annual temperatures are seventy degrees maximum and forty-seven degrees minimum along the coast. Inland they reach into the eighty-degree range. Average rainfall varies from fourteen inches in the valleys to twenty-five inches in the foothills, with most of the rainfall occurring from November to March. During most days clear, sunshiny afternoons prevail. There is no snowfall.

San Luis Obispo. Pop. 33,800. Alt. 300 ft. County seat of San Luis Obispo County. This is an old mission community, located halfway between Los Angeles and San Francisco, in an area where everything is raised, from wheat and cattle to citrus fruits. Average January temperature is forty-seven degrees and average July temperature is sixty-eight degrees, which allows the community 320 growing days per year. This accounts for its marvelous vegetable crops and flower-seed industries. The California Polytechnic State University provides an academic and sports background.

One good testimonial for the city and its surrounding community is that a great many ex-servicemen have made this their home, as have quite a large number of retired persons. Deep-sea fishing, clamming and small-game hunting are all close at hand. The county is attracting many people who want to escape the congestion and smog of the urban areas to the north and south. Rentals for one- and two-bedroom apartments, and duplexes range from $175 to $350 per month. Sales prices of existing homes range from $35,000 to $150,000. Within one mile of San Luis Obispo, there are two suburban residential areas offering homes from $40,000 to $90,000. In spite of its rapid growth, San Luis Obispo manages to maintain a semi-rural atmosphere.

The Monterey Peninsula Area

Called the world's most spectacular meeting place of land and sea, the Monterey Peninsula has long been famous for its natural beauties, renowned pines and invigorating climate. It is popular as a retirement location. More than seventy-five years before the Pilgrims set forth to establish a colony in New England, Rodriguez Cabrillo sailed up the West Coast and sighted this great wooded promontory. Since then, many of those who have come to the Peninsula as visitors have fallen in love with it and settled there in retirement. Artists, writers, musicians, intellectuals, business and professional men and ex-military officers from all parts of the United States have chosen this part of California for their retirement. Robert Louis Stevenson made his home there. A seventeen-mile drive, one of the most beautiful scenic roadways in the country, follows the rugged coast. Sixteen golf courses, several of championship caliber, make the Monterey Peninsula the golf capital of the world. The Peninsula has come to mean a way of life and to be a haven for those more interested in living than in merely making a living. They live in Monterey, Carmel, Pacific Grove, Seaside, Del Rey Oaks and in several unincorporated areas. The location of these communities, only a few miles apart, affords easy participation in the assets of each community.

Carmel. Pop. 4,580. Alt. 20 ft. An informal, individualistic community, situated on Carmel Bay on the southwest side of the Peninsula. No concessions, hotels or other commercial activities are permitted to operate at the beach or its immediate area. It has grown from a village of artists and writers to a famous art and literary center of California, while still maintaining the flavor of a village. There are no sidewalks or street lights in the residential area and no house numbers. Villagers go to the post office to get their mail. The Carmel Bach Festival is ranked as one of the major music festivals in the country. Fine arts are fostered by the Art Association, whose members work in ceramics, metal, leather, plastics, wood and other materials. Carmel is said to have one of the loveliest beaches in California. It also has good schools, a library and an art gallery.

Monterey. Pop. 30,000. Alt. 20 ft. This community is rich in tradition and history. It was old California's first capital. Monterey Bay is popular for its deep-sea fishing, shore fishing, fishing from rocks, wharf or boat. The First Theatre in California, established over one hundred years ago, still holds to a regular schedule of productions each weekend the year round. Small two-bedroom ranch-type homes are selling at prices ranging from $40,000 and up.

Pacific Grove. Pop. 18,000. Alt. 20 ft. This is a quiet community on the spectacular shoreline of the Monterey Peninsula. The town maintains as a park its own rugged waterfront coastline, municipal swimming pool, sheltered cove beach with marine gardens, boating, picnic and barbecue facilities. It operates a municipal golf links, playground, tennis and roque courts, in addition to its museum and exceptional library. Scientists and students from all over the world come to the Hopkins Marine Station at Pacific Grove.

Los Gatos. Pop. 25,000. Alt. 428 ft. Santa Clara County. If you would like to retire to a delightful small community at the foothills of the mountains, yet not too far away from the ocean, and within easy distance of a large shopping center, take a look at Los Gatos. It is called the "Gem City of the Foothills." The community is located in sheltered hills at the mouth of a forest canyon, with lovely views and picturesque trails. According to one great English medical authority, Los Gatos has one of the world's most equable climates, like that of Assouan, Egypt. Average summer temperatures are eighty-four degrees maximum to fifty-two degrees minimum, and in the winter months the thermometer stays fairly steady at from fifty-six degrees maximum to forty degrees minimum. This community is recommended often to sufferers of asthma and bronchial troubles as a place where they may find relief. The cost of living is high. New two-bedroom and three-bedroom homes, on 75 × 125-foot lots, are available from $45,000 with an average price much higher.

There is an organized dramatic club, as well as several social clubs, a public library and active adult education groups. For recreation there is hiking, riding, fishing, hunting and golf. Santa Cruz on the Pacific Ocean is about twenty miles away. Many residents commute daily to San Jose. Four miles northwest is the community of Saratoga, which looks down on orchards as far as the eye can see. In this home and resort center is located Congress Springs, also Villa Montalvo, a haven for artists and writers.

Los Altos. Pop. 23,300. Alt. 200 ft. Santa Clara County. A retirement garden spot within an hour's rail commuting of San Francisco. Los Altos is ten minutes' ride to Palo Alto, twenty minutes from San Jose, an hour from the beaches of Santa Cruz. The town is proud of its Foothill College. With its auditorium, little theater and fine arts center, it has become the cultural hub of the community. Other nearby colleges and universities are the world-famous Stanford University, Santa Clara University and the University of California. This charming community is one of the choice retirement locations of the entire country. Every home has its garden, its trees; many have orchards and shady groves. Among its oak-studded hills, in cozy cottages and on estates, retired families enjoy gracious living in the California tradition.

Socially, Los Altos is democratic and modern. Much of the community life centers around the Country Club with its attractive clubhouse, golf course, tennis courts and swimming pool. College atmosphere and adult educational programs are within half-an-hour's drive, at Stanford University, the University of Santa Clara, San Jose State College and San Jose Bible College. Recreation facilities, libraries, museums, social clubs and organizations in nearby communities cover almost everything you can think of.

The climate is ideal, with summer temperatures averaging seventy-eight degrees maximum and minimum fifty-one degrees, while the average winter maximum is sixty-two degrees and the minimum forty degrees. Rainfall from September to March averages twelve inches, and for the rest of the year about two inches.

Palo Alto. Pop. 58,000. Alt. Sea level to 2,810 ft. Santa Clara County. A community where retired men and women of the arts, sciences, professions, business, including the late President Herbert Hoover, have chosen to live to enjoy the advantages of a university community and a mild, sunny and dry climate. A distinguished Palo Alto citizen, Kathleen Norris, described the community as an exquisite, tree-shaded city of beautiful, spacious homes, of gardens and tennis courts, of matchless climate, good neighbors and honest standards.

Stanford University, adjoining Palo Alto, is one of the world's great centers of higher education and cultural and college athletic activities. The Community Center has diversified indoor and outdoor recreational activities for everyone. Adults and children have their own theaters, libraries and swimming pools. The public school system offers adult evening classes in practical and cultural subjects. Adults enjoy civic theater programs, folk dancing, song fests, lectures and concerts. Museums include the Hoover Tower and Library, Stanford Museum, Stanford Art Gallery and the Children's Junior Museum. There are twenty-four parks, five libraries and forty-nine churches.

Average summer maximum temperature is seventy-seven degrees, average minimum fifty-four degrees, and for the winter months the average maximum is fifty-eight degrees, with thirty-nine degrees the average minimum. The relative humidity daytime average is 59 to 76 percent. Average rainfall for the year is fifteen inches. In 1977, homes are selling in the range of $45,000 to $275,000, depending on age and location; $75,000 to $95,000 is average for an attractive, modern home with 2 or 3 bedrooms. Home rentals range from $300 to $750 monthly.

Palo Alto Yacht Harbor is located three miles from the center of the city on the shore of San Francisco Bay. Many residents commute daily to San Francisco, which is only thirty-one miles away. Other residential communities within a six-mile radius are San Carlos, Redwood City, Woodside, Atherton, Menlo Park, Los Altos, Los Altos Hills and Mountain View.

Berkeley. Pop. 108,000. Alt. Sea level to 1,300 ft. Alameda County. On the eastern shore of San Francisco Bay, facing the Golden Gate, is the charming and cultural city of Berkeley. It is situated on a gently-sloping wide plain that stretches upward to a range of tree-clad hills and wooded canyons. While Berkeley is the home of the world-famous University of California, it is more than a college town. It is a suburban city of comfortable homes from which thousands of people commute daily to work in San Francisco. Berkeley is also a thriving business and industrial center. The topography of the land affords a wide choice of residential sites with picturesque views, suiting the means and tastes of various groups. A tunnel through the Berkeley Hills provides quick and easy access to a fertile valley where many retired families have settled.

The beautifully landscaped University of California is the center of numerous musical, dramatic, educational and sports activities. Open-air musical and dramatic performances are given in the Greek Theatre, which seats over seven thousand persons. The California Memorial Stadium, seating capacity seventy-eight thousand, is the center of college sports activities. The University offers various correspondence courses and class instruction covering a wide range of subjects of interest to adults.

Other interesting sidelights for Berkeley residents are the Pacific School of Religion, the 14,900-acre East Bay Regional Park, the Berkeley Aquatic Park, the Berkeley Yacht Harbor, the Tennis Club, the University Art Museum and Gallery and the Botanical Gardens. Golf is played at Tilden Park the year round. Berkeley residents can also enjoy the advantages of its neighboring city, Oakland, or drive across the bridge to San Francisco.

Marin County Area

Across the Golden Gate Bridge from San Francisco is the broad triangular peninsula of Marin County. This is a region of garden communities, forests of redwoods and eucalyptus trees, rolling hill ranges, beaches, bays and lagoons, dominated by Mt. Tamalpais. The seacoast and bayshore provide swimming, yachting and motor boating. In the waters of San Francisco Bay bass fishing is famous, and salmon and steelheads are caught. The lakes and streams afford trout fishing. Hunters bring down deer in the fall months; in winter months they shoot ducks. Golf and tennis are played at all seasons of the year. Hiking and horseback riding are popular.

Marin County services include 5 modern hospitals with bed capacity of 500. Twenty-eight convalescent hospitals, nursing and rest homes. Many health and social services. Medical laboratories and ambulance service.

Residents of Marin County enjoy a rich community life amid delightful surroundings. The typical residence stands within a large lot or estate. It would be hard to find a home without a garden. Roses bloom from June to June. Service clubs, women's organizations and other civic groups contribute to the fullness of community life. Fifty churches are established here. A wide variety of events, from fiestas to rodeos, mark the year-round activities. New residential districts are being developed in many localities. Dairy farms and poultry ranches, stock ranges, truck farming and orchards are inviting many rural residents. It is only about half-an-hour's drive to downtown San Francisco. The leading residential areas are:

Sausalito. Pop. 5,331. This area has many delightful homes on wooded hills overlooking the bay.

Mill Valley. Pop. 10,411. This charming community at the

base of Mt. Tamalpais, with a good climate for retirement living, is surrounded on three sides by wooded hills. Attractive homes are advertised from $50,000.

San Rafael. Pop. 47,000. Seventeen miles north of San Francisco. Average temperature forty-seven degrees minimum seventy degrees maximum. Marin County has been rated as one of the world's six best climate areas. Fog infrequent. Average rainfall—38.63 inches. Average humidity—67.5 percent. This popular retirement area is largely populated by commuters to San Francisco. Average homes are priced from $65,000. It is the pleasure-boating center for the Bay Area. Docking and launching facilities are available. Seven thousand boats are registered.

Santa Rosa. Pop. 66,400. Alt. 167 ft. County seat of Sonoma County. Situated fifty-two miles north of San Francisco, twenty-five miles from the Pacific Ocean, its climate is moderate, winter and summer, with an average temperature of fifty-seven degrees and average rainfall of thirty inches. Trade breezes from the Pacific Ocean prevent hot spells and insure cool summer evenings. Pride of ownership is exemplified in well-kept lawns and flower gardens that bloom the year round. The rich soil and gentle climate so delighted Luther Burbank that he chose this place for his experiments in plant breeding. There are eight parks, a city symphony orchestra, churches of all denominations. The famous recreational area of the Russian River and the Redwood Empire is fifteen miles away. Petaluma, one of the foremost poultry districts of the world, is sixteen miles south of Santa Rosa. The slogan of Santa Rosa is: "The city designed for living." If you would like to retire to gardening and relaxation, as so many have already done, take a look at Santa Rosa.

Paradise. Pop. 19,500. Altitude ranges from 1300 to 2400 ft. An unincorporated community in Butte County, on the western slope of the Sierra Nevada mountains above the floor of the northern Sacramento Valley, located 100 miles north of Sacramento.

Paradise retains much of the charm of a mountain village. While not a farming community, the Paradise apple, which is grown here, is famous. Industry is active in the valley communities, and Paradise has become "the residential" community. It is a beautiful rural community, offering its residents the advantages of many fine stores, shopping centers and medical and dental facilities. Many clubs and organizations offer active cultural and educational programs. Twenty-six churches of various faiths are located here.

Mountain streams can be found within the community, and within a few minutes' driving distance is excellent trout fishing in rivers or lakes. Steelhead and salmon are also accessible to the fisherman willing to drive a few more miles. Deer often graze on the lawns, and upland game birds are taken nearby, while a few miles west the Pacific Flyway numbers ducks and geese in the thousands.

With the completion of the great Oroville Dam, Paradise has become a recreation area as it has the added advantage of lying within six miles of one of California's finest and largest water-sports complexes. Homesites are scattered spaciously throughout the abundantly forested pines creating a parklike separation among the homes. Life in Paradise can be exciting or leisurely—just as one chooses.

13

Florida

In survey after survey among people contemplating retirement and in polls taken throughout the nation as to where Americans would most like to live, Florida rates at or near the top in popularity.

If you take a look at a map of the United States, you will see that Florida lies farther south than any state of the Union. The northern boundary of Florida is one hundred miles south of San Diego, California. The sweeping curve of the Atlantic Coast pushes Florida directly south of eastern Ohio, while Florida's northwestern boundary lies directly south of Chicago. Within a few hours, by air, Miami can be reached from the entire East and Midwest, eastern Canada, Central America, the Caribbean, Colombia and Venezuela.

Climate is one of Florida's great assets. While the greater part of the nation is freezing and the North and East are blanketed in snow, the January average temperature in southern Florida is sixty-eight degrees and for north Florida, fifty-four degrees. Winters in Florida are nearly fifty degrees warmer than in the northern states.

In the summer months the highest temperatures are no higher than those of New York or Chicago. July average temperature for the whole state of Florida is eighty-one and eight-tenths degrees. Florida's hot days are relieved by afternoon semitropical rains of short duration that cool the atmosphere so that evenings are almost always cool. In addition, prevailing breezes from the ocean speed evaporation of perspiration and keep the body cool.

Florida offers other advantages for the retired person. A modern two-bedroom house costs about 30 to 40 percent less to build than the same type of house would cost in the Northern states. Comfortable, simple, small homes can be bought on the outskirts of cities and towns or in rural sections from $18,000 on up.

There is no Florida state income tax. Personal and property taxes are low. Because of Florida's Homestead Exemption Law, the first $5,000 of assessed valuation is free of property tax. For residents who have lived in the area for five years or more and are 65 years of age or older, another $5,000 of assessed value is not taxed.

It is not fair to judge Florida from the publicity of showgirls and the "sports" who crowd Miami, the horse-race followers who flock to Hialeah, the millionaires hibernating in Palm Beach. These people congregate along the Gold Coast, a narrow coastal strip stretching 75 miles from Palm Beach to Miami. Florida is more than 400 miles wide at its northern boundary, 150 miles wide across the middle of the peninsula. From north to south it extends more than 500 miles. In this vast territory there are many excellent communities for retirement.

What about hurricanes? The chances of hurricane-force winds reaching the Florida coast in any given year are, for Miami, about one in seven; for Daytona Beach, one in thirty; for St. Petersburg, one in twenty; for Jacksonville, one in fifty. The United States Weather Bureau at Miami says: "Damage totals have been declining over the past twenty-five years, due to 'Hurricane Building Codes' and other concerted efforts to protect property. Protective measures consist primarily in building 'hurricane-proof' homes according to the codes, and staying in them during the storm." If a building is properly constructed, with proper type of roof, and is securely anchored to the proper kind of foundation, it will probably not sustain serious damage in a hurricane of major intensity. It is apparent that Florida residents have no fear of hurricanes. If one does come along, the Weather Bureau gives from three to four days' warning, people stay away from the waterfront and settle down in their homes until the storm passes by. The months of greatest hurricane frequency are September and October.

The rapid growth of Florida's tourist business, now a year-round activity, increase in agricultural activities, industrial development and business expansion, comfortable climate the year round, wide choice of inexpensive recreational opportunities, low cost of living, friendliness of residents to retired persons—all add up to new and expanding opportunities for retired people.

East Coast Section

Coral Gables. Pop. 44,000. Alt. 10 ft. Dade County. The city of Coral Gables is not a tourist resort. It is a refined and preplanned community of comfortable homes set in parklike surroundings. People make Coral Gables their permanent home and live in houses mostly of Mediterranean-type design, though zoning permits French and Dutch Colonial architectural designs in certain sections, and in other subdivisions, adaptations of West Indian, African and Chinese add a foreign note. The name Coral Gables is well known as a "hundred million dollar" real estate development of George E. Merrick at the end of World War I. Through the years, the high standards of building and landscaping conceived by Merrick and his original city planners have been adhered to. Though Coral Gables is at the back door of Miami, it is not "tourist" as are Miami and Miami Beach.

Coral Gables is a university city, the home of the University of Miami, the cultural center of south Florida. The campus contains the Ring Theatre production center of the Drama Department, Lowe Art Gallery, Playing Field for college sports events. Coral Gables has many cultural facilities and an active little theater group, music and garden clubs, concerts, and over fifty social and service organizations. The Coral Gables Library and Community House, Art Center and Country Club all contribute to good living. You can fish in Coral Gables' canals or move over to Biscayne Bay, Miami Beach, where some of the world's finest fishing is available. Salvadore Park maintains tennis courts, shuffleboard, horseshoe, croquet and other adult recreation facilities. Golf can be played at Coral Gables Country Club, Riviera Golf Course and Biltmore Country Club. Since Coral Gables is adjacent to Miami, local residents have the opportunity to participate in the cultural and social life of Miami and Coconut Grove, and to take advantage of the entertainment, recreational, shopping, beach, parks and sports facilities of Miami and Miami Beach. One great advantage is that one can always withdraw from the tourist stream to the relaxing tranquility of life at Coral Gables.

Fort Lauderdale. Pop. 156,000. Alt. 10 ft. County seat of Broward County. This is a city of waterways, rivers, bays, canals and inlets, with the Atlantic Ocean at its front door. There are about two hundred miles of ocean, river and canal waterfronts within the city limits, bordered by tropical gardens, palms, lawns and lovely homes. Many wealthy residents with homes on the waterfront keep their yachts and pleasure craft tied up to private docks in their front yards. Other yachtsmen tie up their craft at Bahia-Mar Yacht Basin where they find every provision for pleasant living. Fort Lauderdale has long been famous as a yachtsman's and fisherman's paradise. Both inshore and deep-sea fishing rank with the best in Florida. The city is in the heart of the Gold Coast, twenty-five miles north of Miami. The Gulf Stream is only two miles offshore. New River, which flows through the center of the city, is connected by a canal with Lake Okeechobee. Hugh Taylor Birch State Park is in the city.

There are fifty-three golf courses in the area, many shuffleboard clubs, community centers with day and evening adult programs for canasta, bridge, dancing, arts and crafts. Surf bathing and sunbathing can be enjoyed the year round on a six-mile ocean beach. Fort Lauderdale's library has 200,000 volumes. There are forty-nine churches representing sixteen religious denominations. For those who desire excitement and activities, there is always something going on—regattas, concerts, festivals, fishing tournaments, forums. And Miami is only a half-hour drive from the city.

Fort Lauderdale is popular as a retirement location with New Englanders, New Yorkers and Middle Westerners. The standard of living is rather high, and an income of at least $150 a week is required to enjoy living in this community.

As to climate, January temperatures average seventy-six degrees maximum to sixty degrees minimum, and for July, ninety degrees maximum to seventy-three degrees minimum, with the usual onshore sea breezes to temper the hot weather.

Hollywood. Pop. 124,000. Broward County. This is a resort city located seven miles south of Fort Lauderdale. It is an attractive resort community with a six-mile ocean beach, wide palm-bordered streets and many attractive homes. Twelve parks provide facilities for shuffleboard, tennis and other recreation. There are fourteen golf courses in the area. Hollywood has an annual fishing tournament and the kennel club holds dog races. There is also horse racing at Gulfstream Park, Jai Alai and harness racing at nearby Pompano Park. Evening bandshell concerts are scheduled nightly during the winter season, free to the public. In Hollywood you can enjoy quiet living in the shadow of Greater Miami, which is only fifteen miles to the south.

Daytona Beach Resort Area. Altitude 7 ft. Volusia County. A high percentage of this resort area's permanent residents settled here because they fell in love with the surroundings while vacationing at the beach. They found that the 23-mile long, 500-foot wide (at low tide) beach was only one of many assets to recommend the place as a year-round home.

Eight communities make up the Daytona Beach Resort Area, with a combined population of more than 155,000. They are Daytona Beach, Ormond Beach, Holly Hill, South Daytona, Port Orange, Daytona Beach Shores, Ponce Inlet and Ormond-by-the-Sea. The population also includes surrounding unincorporated areas. The area's principal industry is tourism, which brings four million visitors yearly.

Climate and physical beauty are the drawing cards for visitors and permanent residents. The average year-round temperature is 70.5 degrees; January average maximum temperature is 70 degrees, with a minimum of 50; in July, the average maximum is 89, with 71 the minimum. Afternoon showers and pronounced sea breezes during the summer months keep temperatures from soaring to uncomfortable levels. Average rainfall is 48 inches. The average ocean temperature in January is 60.3 degrees and in July 78.9 degrees.

In addition to the beach, which is most popular for picnics, fishing, walking and feeding the birds, the area has lovely parks graced with tall palms and bright flowers. Its residential sections also abound in palms, mossy oaks and flowering shrubs of all subtropical varieties.

You may live as luxuriously or as economically as you like in the Daytona Beach Resort Area. The oceanfront estates of the wealthy sell for $100,000 and more. But a few minutes walk from the beach will find neat two-bedroom homes priced from $18,000 to $25,000. There also are hundreds of three- and four-bedroom homes, many with pools, in the $35,000 to $45,000 range.

Summertime events include beauty contests, open-air band concerts at the beach bandshell, races at the Speedway and a full schedule of Florida State League baseball games featuring the Daytona Beach Islanders. The Montreal Expos play Spring Training games here in March and April.

Ormond Beach, eight miles north of Daytona, is a popular cottage and resort colony. Wide beaches are ideal for surf casting; pier fishing is also popular.

Beauty pageants, theater festivals, band concerts under the stars, music festivals, greyhound racing, Jai Alai—all of these and more for those who choose to recreate by watching and relaxing. There's a great variety of attractions and activities nearby.

Central Section

Lakeland. Pop. 52,000. Alt. 227 ft. Polk County. A city of well-kept homes amid rolling hills in almost the exact center of Florida, Lakeland is located on one of the highest elevations in the state and is built around thirteen lakes within its corporate limits. Temperature in January is seventy-two degrees maximum to fifty-one degrees minimum, and for July, ninety-one degrees maximum to seventy-two degrees minimum. Sunshine during daylight hours is 72 percent. Annual average rainfall is 51.37 inches.

Numerous retirement housing facilities are available. Lakeland's Lake Mirror Center is the focal point for recreational activities. Lakeland's new $13 million Civic Center provides year-round entertainment such as circuses, ice shows, musical reviews, rodeos and many other events with international stars.

Florida Southern College, the only college with an orange grove for a campus, has exceptionally fine schools of music, art and dramatics. It is architecturally famous for its college buildings designed by Frank Lloyd Wright.

Lakeland has a Little Theater group, Civic Music Concert Association and four eighteen-hole golf courses. Munn Park has facilities for horseshoe pitching, card and checker playing, while Municipal Park has barbecue pits, picnic tables and a swimming pool.

The Detroit Tigers have had spring training quarters here for 35 years. The Orange Cup World Championship Motorboat Regatta on Lake Hollingsworth is held in February.

Comparing living costs with other areas of the nation, central Florida has one of the most reasonable living costs today. Retirees are finding that they can live comfortably on a modest income. Homes range from retirement communities to luxury houses depending on personal desires. In Florida the accent is on outdoor living in a comfortable and informal atmosphere. Retirement homes range from ranch-style homes to high-rise apartments, especially designed for retirees.

Winter Park. Pop. 30,000. Alt. 100 ft. Orange County. This charming community, nestled in the heart of Central Florida's picturesque lake region, has earned the name "City of Homes." The city's fourteen springfed lakes provide background for its showplace residences. Built around a chain of lakes and their network of canals, the city can boast of unexcelled cultural centers and an appetite for gracious living.

Rollins College, Florida's oldest co-educational college, is located in the heart of the city. The campus is an integral part of the community, offering theatre at its finest, and continuing education programs for students of all ages. The campus houses the Beal Maltbie Museum, reputed to contain the finest collection of shells in the world. The Walk of Fame, with over 700 stones gathered from the homes of the great the world over, is located at Rollins.

Boating and fresh water fishing are daily recreations, not seasonal ones. Golf courses abound in the area and several major stock brokerage houses are represented here.

The City of Winter Park covers eight square miles, with sixty-eight acres devoted to city parks. From November to May the days are usually dry and sunny with an average temperature of sixty-five degrees. The nights are cool with the winter climate similar to the sunny fall weather of the north. The temperatures from May to October average seventy-five degrees, with cooling evening breezes and showers to moderate the summer heat.

The Shuffleboard Club, with over 400 members, holds weekly social meetings, tournaments, and occasional picnics. Winter Park Women's Club has a membership of over 500. The public library, Genius Drive with its free roaming peacocks, Kraft Azalea Gardens, Mead Botanical Gardens, the annual art festival, the Bach Festival at Rollins College, and the John Young Museum are all features of interest. Shuffleboard, croquet, and regularly scheduled card games offer additional recreation and entertainment for its residents and visitors.

Close by, without altering the conservative year-round living atmosphere, are such world-renowned attractions as

Walt Disney World, Cypress Gardens, Cape Kennedy and the exquisite beaches of Florida.

Orlando. Pop. 135,000. It is the largest inland city in Florida. Orlando is a popular residential and resort center that has attracted an enthusiastic retired colony. There are fifty-four lakes within the city limits and over 2,000 in the area. As home of the nationally acclaimed Florida Symphony Orchestra, Orlando boasts the only all-professional symphony group in the state. Orlando also offers plenty of drama at three theaters—the Studio Theater, Central Florida Civic Theater and Rollins College's Annie Russell Theatre.

Shuffleboard is one of the several sports enjoyed in Sunshine Park, one of the country's most modern recreational centers. The park has lawn-bowling greens, roque courts, horsehoe pits and three air-conditioned clubhouses for cards and chess. Other recreational facilities include seventeen tennis courts, a trapshooting range, ten bowling centers and twelve scenic golf courses.

The Minnesota Twins' spring training camp is here. Another top Orlando sports attraction is the city-owned Ben White Raceway, the world's largest training center for trotters and pacers. Other sports activities here include greyhound racing, sailing regattas, Jai Alai, golf courses, and water ski shows. Disney-World, with its myriad attractions, is only a short distance away.

Gainesville. Pop. 75,000. Alt. 185 ft. County seat of Alachua County. You may retire from your business, work or profession, but you need not retire from life, from cultural, recreational and sports activities if you locate in this college town in central Florida. You will find a bonus in the University of Florida located at Gainesville. The University offers courses in many fields for people of retirement age. Your experience in life meets all the admission requirements to enroll for a course in two hundred fields of knowledge through seventeen colleges and four schools of the University. Retired persons who plan on settling down on a small or large farm can benefit from courses offered by the College of Agriculture. Noted lecturers, authors and musicians regularly make appearances at activities sponsored by the various University groups. Other active cultural groups are the Civic Music Association, Fine Arts Association, Little Theatre, Philharmonic Society and Twentieth Century Club, as well as the Florida State Museum and numerous civic and social organizations and clubs.

Gainesville has a full-time recreational program. There are three eighteen-hole golf courses at the country club, skeet shooting at the gun club. Close by Gainesville are many fine fishing lakes famous for their bass. An abundance of quail, turkey, duck, rabbit, deer and bear await sportsmen.

The hill country of this area enjoys low humidity, a factor appreciated by sufferers of bronchial ailments. Maximum average temperature in January is 69.4 degrees, the minimum, 47.3 degrees—somewhat cooler in winter than points further south. In July maximum temperatures reach 90.8 degrees and drop to 71 degrees in the evenings. Average annual rainfall is 52.45 inches. The United States Veterans Administration selected Gainesville as the site for one of its regional hospitals. Agricultural products of the area include cattle raising, poultry, truck farming, citrus orchards and the commercial growing of flowers and bulbs. Several trailer parks are located in Gainesville; many occupants are year-round residents.

West Coast Section

Naples. Pop. 19,000. Alt. 5 to 16 ft. Collier County. The Tamiami Trail from Miami through the Everglades turns north at Naples, a pleasant resort community that is the most southerly city on Florida's west coast. Naples is renowned for its fishing and attracts many anglers. A free fishing pier extends 1,000 feet into the Gulf of Mexico. In addition to pier and surf fishing, there is excellent fishing in the Bay of Naples and in the various passes and canals. Many fishing boats are available for charter, manned by experienced guides. A few miles south of Naples are the ten thousand islands, an angler's paradise, which stretches for fifty miles along the coast of the Everglades National Park.

Naples is growing very rapidly. It is the fifth-fastest-growing city in Florida, and many retired folk have settled there. The city is known as the home of many wealthy retired industrialists and corporation executives, but is also making attempts to attract those in the medium-income group. There are new subdivisions for realistically priced homes and many new apartments, including cooperatives.

Naples has ten golf courses, six of which are open for public play. Besides fishing and golf, its other recreational activities include year-round swimming, boating, water skiing and shuffleboard. Naples is also culturally active. It supports five art galleries, various musical events including community concerts, and an excellent public library.

Naples is in subtropical Florida. Its average temperature for January is sixty-five degrees; for July, eighty degrees. In January the temperature frequently climbs into the seventies, but in July, because of cooling breezes from the Gulf, it seldom gets above ninety.

Naples Airlines runs three round-trip flights every day to Miami, and six round-trip flights daily to Tampa. There is also frequent bus service via Greyhound and Trailways.

Venice. Pop. 20,000. Alt. 10 ft. Sarasota County. True to its namesake, Venice is becoming a city of bridges, spanning the Inland Waterway. High-rise apartment and condominium buildings are going up on Gulf beach property, and mobile-home parks are being constructed to accommodate a growing demand for retirement housing.

In the early twenties, the Brotherhood of Railroad Engineers selected Venice as the site of an ideal retirement haven for its older members. The Brotherhood called in experts to help plan a city of the future. Wide streets, avenues divided by parkways and parks dotted with pines and palms attest to the fact that Venice is one of the nation's few planned cities.

Venice is located directedly on the Gulf between Sarasota and Fort Myers. A seven-mile beach is in the town's front yard. Swimming, sunbathing, shelling, searching for shark teeth and fossils, fishing and picnicking are the rule. There are many golf courses in the area, as well as theater groups, shuffleboard, and an excellent library.

Homes can be purchased from $25,000 up, depending upon location and type of construction. Many retired teachers, army officers and business people have settled here. Artists, writers and others interested in creative arts and crafts have also been attracted to Venice. Situated in the practically frost-free belt, the surrounding countryside is ideal for truck farming, cattle raising and subtropical fruit growing. There are good opportunities to establish small businesses and services catering to the needs of tourists.

Fort Myers. Pop. 35,000. Altitude from 3 to 15 ft. Seat of Lee County, Fort Myers is the city made famous by the late Thomas Alva Edison, inventor of the electric light. Edison perfected the first incandescent light in Fort Myers with the use of a fiber product of the tropical bamboo tree, which grows in abundance along the banks of the Caloosahatchee River. Edison's home, where he spent the winters for almost half a century, remains today as a public shrine to the city's first late citizen. Edison's good friend Henry Ford also built a winter home in Fort Myers, adjacent to his estate on the Caloosahatchee.

Fort Myers is located about seven miles from the Gulf of

Mexico and is within thirty minutes' driving time from the islands of Sanibel and Captiva, world famous for their shelling beaches; Pine Island, noted for its ample fishing grounds; and Fort Myers Beach, said to be the world's safest, with absolutely no undertow. Lee County is the gladioli-growing capital of the world. Flower crops bring in over $10 million from the northern markets. It is also the home port of some 250 shrimp boats.

Tourism is Lee County's greatest industry and increases the population during the winter months (November through April) by two-thirds. Spectator sports include the Kansas City Royals Baseball Club Spring Training, Feb.–Apr., Greyhound Racing, sailing races, water ski shows. The Edison Pageant of Light, the Shrimp Festival in February and the Shell Fair in March are highlights of the winter season. The Tourist Center, a municipal facility maintained for senior citizens and winter visitors by the Metropolitan Fort Myers Chamber of Commerce is devoted entirely to entertaining the city's visitors with daily programs and recreational quarters. The City Yacht Basin is equipped with 200 boat slips.

Fort Myers is the western terminus of the 120-mile cross-state Okeechobee Waterway, connecting the Atlantic Ocean and the Gulf. There are twelve golf courses in the area and five municipal bowling lanes. Tennis courts are provided by the City and the Tourist Center provides shuffleboard courts and card rooms. The Fort Myers Symphony Orchestra, Edison Junior College Fine Arts Programs, community concerts, little theater and five art leagues make up the cultural activities. Dozens of senior citizen organizations and hobby clubs are also popular. The city has churches of every denomination, good schools and a junior college. The average annual temperature is 73.7 degrees and prevailing winds from the Gulf cool off the summer evenings.

Sarasota. Pop. 47,134. Alt. 5 to 17 ft. Seat of Sarasota County. Sportsmen, artists, writers and professional people, as well as seekers after health and good business locations, all find what they are looking for in this friendly community.

Sarasota has miles of sandy beaches along Sarasota Bay and outlying keys or islands that extend twenty miles north and south, fronting the Bay. On these keys are beautifully planned residential subdivisions. Siesta Key, Longboat Key and St. Armands Key are as good retirement spots as you will find anywhere in the United States of America.

Sarasota also claims the honor of being the cultural center of Florida. The Ringling Museum Complex now includes the Museum, the Residence and the Circus Museum. The Art Association, Asolo Summer Festival, several art schools, and galleries—all provide stimulus for those who follow some form of art as a hobby. The Players (an accomplished little theater group), the West Coast Symphony, Community Concerts Association, choral society and music club all present full programs. Near the Museum, the Jungle Gardens feature exotic plants and bird life. Mayakka River State Park, one of the most tropical woodlands in the state, is sixteen miles east of the city. There are year-round fishing tournaments. Sarasota has excellent facilities for yachts, sailing craft and motor boats. The recreation center has facilities for bowling on the green, shuffleboard, card parties, tennis and indoor games. There are nine eighteen-hole golf courses in the city. The Chicago White Sox hold spring training here and play exhibition games. Ringling Circus makes its winter home in Sarasota County in Venice, Florida.

As to climate, the winter is mild with daily temperatures around seventy-two degrees maximum and fifty-three degrees minimum. Daily average summer temperatures are ninety degrees maximum to seventy-two degrees minimum with cool breezes at night. Homes on the keys and around the waterfront run from $65,000 upward, depending upon type of construction and location. Sarasota is a quality place for retirement, with luxurious apartments and condominiums, delightful golf courses, marinas and cultural activities to enjoy. It has been called an ideal place for tourism, business, and clean light industry.

St. Petersburg. Pop. 260,000. Pinellas County. Many thousands of retired men and women have taken up residence in St. Petersburg to regain their health, to lengthen their lives, to enjoy the companionship of people of their own age and yet to be near people of all ages. A recent Census Bureau study of St. Petersburg population indicated 27 percent of the residents to be 65 and over, 18 percent to be age 50 to 64 years, and 55 percent under age 50. The vast majority of residents in the County were born elsewhere. The largest group of transplants, in order of numbers, came from New York, then Ohio, then other cities in Florida, Illinois, Pennsylvania, Michigan, New Jersey, Massachusetts and Georgia—in that order.

They keep busy at the many senior centers in the area with an infinite variety of hobbies and sports. A recent survey quoted some of the most popular as being cards, gardening, fishing, chess, dancing and shuffleboard.

Asked why they had decided to spend their later years in St. Petersburg, most people mentioned the climate, its healthfulness and the recommendation of relatives and friends. In answer to another question. "What do you think is best about St. Petersburg?" the climate and the friendliness of its people were mentioned most often. Most retired people were enthusiastic about the community and found little to criticize. More than any other city, St. Petersburg has gone out of its way to attract and entertain elderly people. St. Petersburg's Shuffleboard Club (world's largest) with over seven thousand members is another famous institution. For comfortable living, a retirement income of at least $350 a month is recommended.

Climate is a *great* asset. The average mean temperature for the year is 71.6 degrees. For the winter months it is seventy degrees maximum and fifty-six degrees minimum, and for the summer months between eighty-eight degrees maximum and seventy-five degrees minimum. The sun shines, on an average, 360 days a year, with six and one-half hours of sunshine per day during winter months. Relative humidity averages 80 percent at night, drops to about 54 percent in midafternoon.

A number of senior citizens centers in St. Petersburg offer all manner of outdoor activities from shuffleboard (over two hundred courts) to card playing, checkers, chess, horseshoe pitching, lawn bowling and similar forms of recreation. The municipal pier extending a half-mile into Old Tampa Bay is a popular spot for fishermen and a favorite social center. Treasure Island and St. Pete Beach have their own residential beach communities. St. Petersburg has over four hundred social, cultural and hobby clubs and organizations where one may meet others with similar interests. The New York Mets and the St. Louis Cardinals maintain spring training camps in St. Petersburg. There are seven eighteen-hole golf courses within the city limits, excellent fishing facilities, fine boating, yachting, swimming and sunbathing.

Clearwater. Pop. 85,000. Alt. 30 to 75 ft. County seat of Pinellas County. Situated on the coast between the Gulf of Mexico and Old Tampa Bay with the highest coastal elevation of any city in the state, it is practically surrounded by salt water, which assures a temperate climate throughout the year. Average temperature for the winter is 64.40 degrees and for the summer 77.30, with temperate breezes drifting back and forth across the city. Pinellas County, in which Clearwater is located, enjoys more hours of sunshine than any other section in the eastern United States. Relative humidity averages 54 percent during the daytime. There are practically two springs, two distinct seasons of new vegetation growth—February to March and June to July. A committee of the American Medical Association is said to have selected this area as the healthiest spot in the entire United States.

Clearwater is a popular vacation resort both winter and summer. It has excellent facilities for year-round bathing, boating, fishing, tennis, golf, lawn bowling and shuffleboard. The tourist center provides opportunities for newcomers to meet and get acquainted. There are over 700 clubs and organizations offering participation in music, art, dramatics and social and recreational activities. The Gulf Coast Art Center at Belleair maintains programs of exhibitions, lectures and instruction in painting, silk screening, woodworking and ceramics. The Clearwater Art Group also sponsors exhibitions and lectures. A series of musical programs is presented by the Community Concert Association. Since Clearwater is surrounded by the residential communities of Belleair, Largo, Dunedin and Safety Harbor, the facilities of these communities are easily accessible. St. Petersburg and Tampa are each approximately 22 miles distant. There are over thirty-two golf courses in the area. Clearwater is the spring training camp for the Philadelphia Phillies. Safety Harbor has mineral springs offering therapeutic values. Clearwater Beach, one of the best bathing beaches on the West Coast, has a fishing pier and a yacht club.

Attractive homes in Clearwater range in price from $25,000 up to ultramodern three-bedroom homes in the $60,000 class—and up. Small two-bedroom homes outside the city are listed at $20,000 to $30,000. In the Belleair Estates, a community which is restricted, home sites range up to $50,000, and plans for construction of homes must be approved.

Clearwater Beach, a part of the city itself, is Clearwater's outstanding attraction. Lying along an island on the Gulf of Mexico, it is reached from downtown Clearwater by Garden Memorial Causeway, which winds two miles across scenic Clearwater Harbor and is landscaped as a tropical garden the entire distance.

The beach community has residential and business sections, and the wide, white sand playground offers fine swimming, boating, and other water sports. The Clearwater Marina docks one of Florida's largest sports-fishing fleets. Big Pier 60, along the Beach, provides the thrill of deep-sea fishing for those who prefer to stay ashore.

Retirement Housing Developments

Many retirement communities are being promoted in various sections of Florida, often in the outskirts of well-established and growing cities and towns. They provide for low-cost living for persons with modest incomes, pensions and annuities. They serve a mixture of age groups.

The sponsors of these properties assemble large-acre tracts which they subdivide usually into quarter-acre home site lots. The lots provide room for a small home, vegetable garden and a dozen or more fruit trees.

The developers usually have standardized plans for houses containing one-, two- or three-bedrooms, bath with shower, kitchen-living room combination, a breezeway and carport.

Recreational and social activities center around the community clubhouse and the facilities of the nearby town, beaches or lakes.

The postal clerks maintain a Postal Colony Company, at

Clermont, that operates a large acreage of citrus groves for retired members.

The Penney Retirement Community in Penney Farms is a model community for retired clergymen and their families. A couple buys a residential annuity costing $9,000 for their lifetime home. Single person annuities are $8,000. There is also a monthly maintenance fee. At death the apartment-home reverts to the Penney Retirement Community.

The Brotherhood of Railway Engineers sponsors a retirement colony for members in Venice.

The United Brotherhood of Carpenters and Joiners of America operates a national home for retired members at Lakeland.

At St. Cloud there is a retirement community of war veterans.

The Attraction of Lower Living Costs

For those living in northern big city suburbs, living budgets in many Florida communities sound like a dream. At the Beverly Hills Retirement Community, some 75 miles north of Tampa, a one bedroom home can be bought for $16,990 and a two bedroom unit goes for $22,990. Most of the residents had sold larger homes up north and with this money were able to pay cash for their Florida retirement homes, and have some capital left over. Yes, inflation provides the impetus for the steady migration of retirees to Florida. They seek lower living costs and the profit from the sale of their northern home at today's top prices.

In the Florida climate, your clothing bill is light, you're not inclined to chase around so much in your car. Florida offers a $10,000 homestead tax exemption for people over 65 years of age. At Beverly Hills, for instance, total maintenance costs for taxes, water, light, heat, and insurance would run about $150 per month.

Sociability runs high in communities like Beverly Hills. In this community there are already some *40* organizations and new ones keep popping up. Although everyone mixes with everyone, residents find special attachments to their past by forming little chapters of the type of ethnic club or fraternal lodge they formerly belonged to back home.

14

Georgia, South Carolina and North Carolina

Nature has favored this area with a moderate climate. It is not quite so warm as Florida, not so cold in winter as New England and does not have the wide range of annual climatic extremes of the Northern and Central states.

Along the coastal plain section, the mean temperature in January averages sixty degrees maximum to thirty-eight degrees minimum. Oranges and grapefruit grow in the sheltered seacoast regions as far north as Cape Hatteras. Cold waves are of short duration and practically no snow falls. There is no record of zero temperatures in any coastal county and hard freezes are rare.

In the interior sections, winters are cool enough to be invigorating. Snow almost never falls before Christmas, and many winters have none at all. When snow does fall, it disappears quickly. A series of frostless zones, called the "thermal belt," are found in the Carolinas where the winter climate is milder than that of the surrounding mountain areas, with the temperature on the slopes from one to fourteen degrees warmer than at the top of the mountains or the valleys at the bottom. These favored locations are popular as both summer and winter resort areas.

Summers in the coastal counties are tempered by ocean breezes. July mean temperatures average around eighty degrees. In the interior, summer temperatures generally are about ten degrees warmer than in the coastal plains, but at rises of altitude of one thousand feet the temperature usually is five degrees lower. That is why the nights are cool in the mountains during July and August.

Georgia, South Carolina and North Carolina offer an abundance of small, congenial communities where retired couples can find good friends and may live in pleasant surroundings without high costs. Those who wish to do a little farming, or to raise poultry or turkeys, can find many opportunities to do so. Average land prices are not high. In some localities there are opportunities for part-time or full-time work in the many new industries locating throughout this part of the South.

In selecting a site for retirement, you can choose between beautiful mountain areas and moss-draped, low country near and along the seacoast. Modest incomes are frequently sufficient for economical living, particularly in rural areas not fully developed and in areas that are past their population peaks. There are many places where life can be taken as quietly or as vigorously as anyone could wish—and in which retirement life can be budgeted to almost any income.

Georgia

Georgia's altitude ranges from sea level along the Atlantic coast to nearly 5,000 feet in the Georgia Appalachians. The State has three distinct topographic sections. Northern Georgia is mountainous. The central upland, known as the Piedmont Plateau, has broadly rolling terrain trenched by deep, narrow valleys and cut through by numerous streams and rivers. The Coastal Plain area, lying south of the "fall line" comprises approximately three-fifths of the state. Hilly in sections—particularly in the northern area—this Coastal Plain is generally an expanse of gently rolling level land.

Bordered by the Atlantic Gulf Stream on the east and to the north by the Appalachian Mountains, Georgia uniquely offers one of the world's best climate zones. Contrary to some opinions, Georgia summers are only slightly warmer than those of Chicago or New York areas. Humidity averages the same in mid-Georgia as Chicago, giving the State an advantage over many areas along the eastern seaboard. Rainfall is usually plentiful, with yearly averages ranging from more than 75 inches in the northeast corner to about 42 inches in the driest part of the east central section.

Few states can equal the variety of scenery and recreational facilities. Georgia has 40 developed State parks, 4 undeveloped parks, 27 wildlife refuges, and 6 national historical areas. Scattered throughout the State from the Blue Ridge Mountains to the Okefenokee Swamp and within 50 miles of any town, Georgia's State parks offer an amazing variety of altitudes, temperatures, scenery and recreational facilities.

Good hunting and fishing abound throughout the State. There are 700 miles of cold-water trout streams in North Georgia. Mountain trout, river perch, lake bass and deep-sea tarpon are all native to Georgia. Quail, wild turkey, deer, bear, fox and fowl provide great hunting sport.

Stretching across the State are 17 large rivers covering 2,818 miles. Georgia has more than 400,000 acres in large lakes for recreation.

Construction costs in Georgia have been consistently about 15 percent below the national average. Out of 145 areas Georgia ranks in the lower 10 percent in construction cost.

Albany. Pop. 90,000. Alt. 215 ft. County seat of Dougherty County. Albany is located on the banks of the Flint River, which is one of Georgia's largest streams in the southern coastal plain section of the state. The climate is characterized by short, mild winters and long warm summers. Only rarely does Albany have any measurable snowfall, and then only in small fractions of an inch. The normal temperature for the winter season is 60 degrees maximum, 42 degrees minimum. Some winters are so mild that very little heat is needed in the house. Mean summer temperatures reach 90 degrees during the day and drop to the low seventies at night. Heat is not oppressive, owing to the relatively low humidity, which averages 50 to 63 percent. Rainfall averages 49 inches for the year.

The Community Concert Association brings nationally known artists to Albany each season. The Albany Little Theater Group is very active in its restored pre-Civil War mansion. Several choruses for men and women and a symphony orchestra provide concerts throughout the year. Radium Springs, one of the South's finest resorts, is located four miles south of Albany. Chehaw Wild Animal Park, a natural animal habitat, providing all kinds of recreational opportunities, including swimming, boating and fishing.

The Metro Golf Course has nine holes and excellent golf courses are found at Radium Springs and the Doublegate Country Club. Albany is the site of the Marine Corps Logistics Support Base, Atlantic. The Albany Public Library, with its several branches, is easily accessible from any area of the city. One hundred and twenty churches represent the leading denominations.

Albany has recently been cited in several surveys as one of the most progressive cities in the nation, and is renowned as a medical, trade and educational center for the Southwest Georgia area.

Columbus. Pop. 172,000. Alt. 248 ft. Seat of Columbus County. This is one of the few cities whose site was deliberately selected and laid out in advance. It is located on the banks of the Chattahoochee River, on the fall line between the Piedmont Plateau and the coastal plain, in a region famed for its scenic beauty. Retired persons will like its tree-lined streets, green lawns and home gardens. Attractive well-planned residential neighborhoods and numerous home developments are in evidence throughout the metropolitan area.

During the winter months, temperatures range between sixty degrees maximum and thirty-nine degrees minimum. Snow rarely falls. Moderate winters reduce the cost of heating and winter clothing costs. Average summer temperatures reach ninety degrees and fall to sixty-eight degrees at night. Relative humidity at noon is around 59 percent, rising to 71 percent at night. Total annual rainfall is fifty-three inches.

Columbus College, operated by the University System Board of Regents, offers four years of advanced education, and the University of Georgia maintains an off-campus center in Columbus offering a variety of courses. Over four thousand persons are enrolled in adult education courses in the public school system. A full-time recreational department plans year-round recreational programs. A little theater group and numerous clubs and organizations foster special interests such as literature, drama, art and music. Columbus has an excellent library, nineteen parks and playgrounds, four golf courses, an auditorium and a stadium for college and high school football games. Golden Park is the home of the Columbus Astros. Pine Mountain State Park, one of Georgia's state parks, is twenty-five miles away. There is good fishing and hunting in the neighborhood area and in nearby forests and streams. Warm Springs, the famous health resort, and the famous Little White House are little more than thirty minutes' drive away. Fort Benning and Lawson Army Airfields are located three miles south of the city. Columbus offers good opportunities to retired United States military service personnel, who can take advantage of the facilities of the commissary, post exchange, Martin Army Hospital and Officers' clubs of Fort Benning. For nonmilitary people, too, who prefer retirement in an inland community, Columbus is well worth serious consideration.

Atlanta. Pop. 445,300. Alt. 1,050 ft. The county seat of Fulton County and capital of Georgia, Atlanta attracts people from every section of the country and every part of the world. Metropolitan Atlanta, with a population of 1,841,-200 embraces eighty-three towns and municipalities. Situated high on the Piedmont plateau, Atlanta's topography is responsible for a favorable climate of moderate summers and mild winters that permits year-round activities without interruption, makes living and working more comfortable, fuel and clothing less costly.

Atlanta averages less than three consecutive days of ninety-degree-and-above temperatures in the hottest periods of summer. The nights are uniformly cool. In the winter, there are no prolonged periods of extreme cold. The normal annual rainfall is 47 inches; the annual mean temperature is sixty-one degrees. With twenty-five degree-granting colleges and institutions of higher learning, residents enjoy a great many opportunities to participate in the colleges' educational, cultural and sports activities. Within easy driving distance are mountain and coastal recreational areas, public boating, hunting and fishing facilities, and three of the state's major lakes.

Cultural activities literally abound. The city has its own 89-piece symphony orchestra, a community orchestra and chorus, a concert band and pops orchestra. Seasons of light and grand opera, ballet festivals, popular concerts and art-ist-series are held throughout the year. Atlanta's enthusi-asm for sports and recreation can be traced to its four major league sports teams, International Raceway and five thousand acres of parks and playgrounds. Golf can be played at fifteen public and commercial courses, tennis at one hundred and fifty courts. Library facilities are excel-lent, with a large public library and seventeen branches, plus the state and college libraries. There are about two thousand churches and synagogues representing forty creeds and denominations. Every section of Atlanta has attractive tree-shaded residential areas. Homes are for sale or rent in all price ranges. There are many one-, two- and three-bedroom apartments in both high-rise buildings and garden apartments.

South Carolina

Beaufort. Pop. 12,500. Alt. 25 ft. Seat of Beaufort County. Located midway between Savannah and Charleston on the Atlantic seacoast. Beaufort is one of the historic spots on the American continent. It was these shores on which be-ginning 450 years ago the Spaniards, the French and the English first settled and over which they fought for two hundred years. The flags of six nations have floated over this section—a fact worth noting as indicative of the historic visual interests of the area.

Beaufort's rich historical background offers dozens of pre-revolutionary and ante-bellum homes and plantations beautifully preserved, as well as great resort areas; nearby Beaufort County is a county of islands, and among them are famed Hilton Head and Fripp Island resort communities.

Beaufort is a small community, pleasant in summer and winter. Average temperature in winter is around sixty degrees maximum to forty degrees minimum, while in summer temperatures are ninety degrees maximum to seventy degrees minimum. With a constant southwest breeze blowing, summer climatic conditions are enjoyable. Beaufort is wholly surrounded by salt water and the air has a sea tang. Here you will find magnolia trees, oleander, palmetto palms, camphor trees, as well as olives and oranges. Moss-draped live oaks, flowers and birds are everywhere, and the forests are green all winter. Practically every farmhouse has its own home orchard, and homes have beautiful lawns and flower gardens.

The area is a sports paradise, with unlimited amounts of shrimp, blue crab, oysters, and clams. Fish too, abound, with sea trout, channel bass, sailfish, blue marlin. It also has the longest deer season in America, with no limit on bucks. Turkeys, dove, quail and duck also abound.

Hunting Island across from Beaufort is a state park and wildlife sanctuary with long, wide beaches for picnics, swimming and surf fishing. Golf is played on sixteen major golf courses.

The County has several retirement communities, peopled by many former corporate executives, bankers, and military officers.

Charleston. Pop., 69,800. Alt. 25 ft. Seat of Charleston County. This is a fascinating, quaint Colonial city of narrow streets, homes and churches that date back to the seventeenth century. Widely known as a shrine of history and as a superb seaport, it is famed as an all-year resort. Six miles from the city limits is Sullivan's Island with a fine beach. Three miles further along the coast is a delightful beach community at the Isle of Palms, where a number of retired families live the year round. South of the city is Folly Beach. Resort and residential developments are located on nearby Kiawah and Seabrook Islands.

Located in Charleston are the College of Charleston, the

oldest municipal college in America; The Citadel Military College; The Baptist College at Charleston; and the Medical University of South Carolina. The city has an excellent school system. There are nearly two hundred churches of all leading denominations, and eight hospitals. Magnolia Gardens, Middleton Place Gardens and Cypress Gardens are outstanding showplaces. Bulls Island, near Charleston, is a semitropical island noted for its great number and species of birds, both migratory and native. The Footlight Players present original and Broadway successes at the Dock Street Theatre. Art classes are conducted by the Carolina Art Association. A series of concerts is given by the Charleston Symphony Orchestra. Residents enjoy excellent salt- and fresh-water fishing and swimming, sailing, good hunting in season, golf and home gardening.

Charleston enjoys sunshine during 65 percent of daylight hours. Winter temperatures average fifty-eight degrees maximum to forty-three degrees minimum. There is no snow. Summer temperatures average eighty-eight degrees maximum to seventy degrees minimum. The average year-round temperature is sixty-four degrees. Annual average rainfall is forty inches. Rentals for small unfurnished apartments range from $150 to $250 two- and three-bedroom unfurnished houses rent for $175 to $300 per month. Charleston has many lovely suburbs where real estate costs are from $25,000 to $45,000 for two- to four-bedroom houses.

Georgetown. Pop. 12,261. Alt. 9 ft. Seat of Georgetown County. There are many retired persons living in this area, some on small farms, some on large plantations and others in town. Georgetown is South Carolina's third oldest city. It is not a resort area but a substantial residential community with fine old streets lined with giant oaks and elms and many quaint historic buildings and famous plantations. Climatic conditions are similar to those of Charleston. The mean annual temperature is sixty-four degrees. Pawley's Island, twelve miles from the city, is noted for its quiet, uncommercialized residential area, surf fishing, shady beaches, surf bathing and plenty of golfing nearby. Brookgreen Gardens is an outdoor museum of American sculpture. The Musical Arts Club presents three or four concerts during the year. The Yacht Basin is a favorite stopping place of yachtsmen using the Intracoastal Waterways. This is a restful community for those who enjoy easy living.

Columbia. Pop. 113,000 (in city limits), 370,000 (in metro. area). Alt. 332 ft. Seat of Richland County. This is the capital of South Carolina and is located in the geographical center of the state in the Sandhills section. The mean annual temperature in January is forty-six degrees. There is an annual snowfall of about 3.8 inches. In July, the mean annual temperature is eighty-one degrees.

Columbia is the site of the University of South Carolina, Columbia College for Women, Lutheran Theological Seminary and the Columbia Bible College. The Midlands Technical Education School offers courses for adult education. There are nearly two hundred churches representing practically all denominations.

The city provides twenty-five parks. At Sesquicentennial Park, fifteen miles from the city, there are excellent picnic facilities and a lake for fishing. Within the Columbia area are four public golf courses and two country clubs, each with an eighteen-hole golf course. Excellent fishing is available in nearby lakes and streams. Hunting is primarily for deer, bobwhite quail and wild turkey. Collegiate sports are provided through the University. The Town Theatre, Music Festival Association and other literary and art groups provide cultural outlets.

Cost of living ranks in middle range. Property taxes have been among the lowest.

Spartanburg. Pop. 46,000. Alt. 875 ft. Seat of Spartanburg

County. This residential community has attractive assets for retirement living. Located in the rolling country of the Piedmont, in close proximity to the thermal belt. The climate is mild and bracing. During the winter months, the mean temperature is fifty-two degrees maximum with a mean low of thirty-five degrees. A chain of mountains to the northwest serves to block the movement of the cold waves from reaching the city. Year after year goes by without any snow observed or at most only a trace. In summer the average daily maximum is eighty-eight degrees, with night temperatures in the high sixties. Summer nights are usually cool and pleasant. Annual rainfall is about fifty-four inches. Relative humidity averages 55 percent around the middle of the day.

The cultural and intellectual atmosphere is heightened by Wofford College, Converse College, the University of South Carolina—Spartanburg and the Spartanburg Methodist College. Residents enjoy the faculty recitals, chorus, orchestra and glee club concerts, also the Lyceum, which presents outstanding lectures and speakers. A little theater group presents several plays each year. Summer stock presents a full program in the nearby mountain playhouse. Symphony orchestra and Civic Music Association presentations afford a balanced series of concerts. Croft State Park, five miles from town, has excellent picnic grounds and fishing lake. Spartanburg is located close to several resort areas. Other retirement advantages are good fishing in streams and lakes, four golf courses, three hospitals, more than 120 churches and three good libraries. Spartanburg County is the fresh-peach capital of the United States.

North Carolina

Wilmington. Pop. 55,600. Alt. 32 ft. Seat of New Hanover County. Hundreds of families from every state in the Union looking for cultural and intellectual activities, combined with an agreeable climate and economical cost of living, have selected Wilmington as their location for retirement. These include ex-military personnel, businessmen, educators and professional people. During the short winter season, the average daily maximum temperature is fifty-seven degrees with a minimum of thirty-nine degrees. Very rarely does any snow fall. Several varieties of palm trees grow in the city and many varieties of flowers bloom throughout the winter. For the summer months the average daily maximum temperature is eighty-seven degrees with average minimum of seventy-two degrees. The sun shines during 65 percent of daylight hours. Annual rainfall averages forty-nine inches. The cost of living in Wilmington is estimated to be from 5 to 10 percent lower than in Northern states.

Wilmington is famous for its formal flower gardens. Greenfield Lake and Park, Orton Plantation and Airlie Gardens are ablaze in the spring with blooms of azaleas, roses, camellias, dogwood, wisteria, magnolia trees and other flowers and shrubs. The Azalea Festival, in April, is attended by more than one hundred thousand people. The Community Concert Association brings in foremost concert artists during the fall and winter season. The Thalian Association, oldest little theater group in the country, produces several plays each year. Nationally known speakers are brought in by the Executives Club and other organizations. All the leading religious denominations are represented by over a hundred churches. Health welfare is provided for by five hospitals. All kinds of recreation are available from organized sports to golf, tennis, boating, fishing and hunting. In the immediate vicinity of Wilmington are five popular beach resorts.

The city has a well-defined historic section, with many

homes of architectural and historic distinction, and also pre-Civil War churches.

Additional coastal towns where life moves at a slow tempo and living is inexpensive are New Bern (pop. 15,812), Edenton (pop. 6,458), Elizabeth City (pop. 14,-062) and Southport (pop. 2,034).

The Outer Banks (estimated population 6,500). The country's first national seashore recreational area is on the famous Outer Banks. This area consists of a chain of islands along North Carolina's coast and is the most extensive tract of undeveloped seashore remaining on the Atlantic Coast. Here you can find year-round ocean and inland fishing that is without equal. Living can be as primitive and easy-going as you would like, and as inexpensive. A moderate income is sufficient for economical living, particularly if relative isolation is desired. For the retired, leisured person, the area is adapted for hunting, fishing, beachcombing, golfing, gardening and solitude.

January and February, the coldest months, boast an average maximum temperature of 50 and an average minimum of 34; and this leaves the other ten months for a most enjoyable climate. Nothing else is like the Outer Banks. More and more people are discovering them. Principal communities are Hatteras (pop. 500), Buxton (pop. 500), Manteo (pop. 571), Ocracoke (pop. 500), Nag's Head, Kill Devil Hills and Kitty Hawk.

Chapel Hill. Pop. 25,500. Alt. 501 ft. Orange County. You will find many well-to-do people, as well as those academically inclined, living happily in retirement in this college town, the site of the University of North Carolina. The cultural, social and sports life of Chapel Hill is dominated by "the University." There are no industries in the town. The atmosphere is informal and friendly, and the community is in no way stuffy or reserved. Annual events include statewide Dramatic Festival; Folk Festival; University Day and major college sports. Entertainment is provided by Playmakers Theatre, Forest Theatre, Grass Roots Opera Company, University Memorial Hall, Hill Music Hall, the Morehead Planetarium and the Ackland Art Gallery. The University library contains over one and one-half million volumes and is open to the public. In this community you can enjoy lectures and forums, concerts and plays, discussions and conferences with faculty members. Chapel Hill offers golf, swimming, fishing and hunting. Medical facilities are tops.

Climatically, the winters are temperate with average daily temperature of fifty-two degrees maximum and thirty degrees minimum; summers average maximum temperatures of ninety degrees and average minimum temperatures of sixty-seven degrees. Only a few days in winter are unpleasantly cold, and a few days in summer can be called hot. About nine inches of snow fall during the winter season, but snow does not stay on the ground long. Average rainfall is forty-seven inches.

Southern Pines. Pop. 8,000. Alt. 519 ft. A charming town of fine homes, tree-shaded streets and ideal year-round climate in the scenic Sandhills, home of a large colony of retired industrialists, military officers, writers, and others from all professions. Noted as the "Mid-South Resort," it has eleven fine golf courses, clubs, hotels, motels and outstanding stores and specialty shops. It is the home of the fifty-six-year-old Moore County Hounds and the site of many horse activities, which include hunts, horse shows and gymkhanas.

An adult education program is offered at Sandhills Community College. There are churches of all major denominations.

It is doubtful if there is another community of comparable size anywhere in the country that can boast of the health care Southern Pines offers. The doctor-patient ratio is 1 to

800, with specialists in all major fields. Moore Memorial Hospital has a surgical intensive care unit, a cardio-pulmonary unit and the most outstanding inhalation-therapy department on the Eastern Seaboard.

Friendly and congenial people, picturesque location and colorful but temperate change of seasons add to the gracious living in Southern Pines.

Tryon. Pop. 3,200. Alt. 1,200 ft. Polk County. Located on the southern foothills of the Blue Ridge Mountains in a thermal belt, Tryon affords a fairly even climate the year round. This is a well-established residential community and popular resort area, most attractive in the spring and fall, but maintaining an all-year season. The surrounding countryside is known for its vineyards and fruit orchards. Winter temperatures average maximums of fifty-three degrees with minimums of thirty degrees. About seven inches of snow fall during an average winter. In summer, temperatures average eighty-six degrees maximum to sixty-five degrees minimum. On the average, fifty-eight inches of rain fall during the year.

Many well-to-do retire here. There is swimming and tennis in addition to the golf courses at the Tryon Country Club and Red Fox Country Club. Several lakes and streams are near for fishing. The town has a fine library, also a Polk County library with a Bookmobile. There are active women's and men's garden clubs, a forward-thinking Chamber of Commerce, and churches of many denominations.

Artists, writers, handicrafters, musicians and actors have long found congenial surroundings in Tryon, many maintaining homes here. Sidney Lanier, F. Scott Fitzgerald, Margaret Culkin Banning, H. V. Kaltenborn, John Burroughs, William Gillette and Donald Peattie are but a few of the famous personalities who have discovered Tryon as a place for both work and relaxation.

They have a Fine Arts Center with a beautiful auditorium where they have access to such live music as the Tryon Concert Association brings, and the little theatre group. All kinds of crafts are offered; enameling on copper, weaving, knitting, crewel, needlepoint, rugmaking—hooked, braided and rya; ceramics, millinery, sculpting, painting, and many others.

Hendersonville. Pop. 7,000. Alt. 2,200 ft. Seat of Henderson County. A beautiful community located in a broad plateau region of the Blue Ridge Mountains. This attractive town affords all the modern conveniences of a larger city, only on a smaller scale. It is the center of prosperous agricultural and industrial activity, and is a vacation resort area. The chief sources of income of Henderson County are tourists, $11 million; industry, $43 million; agriculture, $30 million.

Hendersonville has been called the "dancingest town in America," because of its numerous community street dances. Recreational events include dramatic performances, Vagabond Players at the Flat Rock Playhouse, which is the N.C. State Theater, golfing, county fairs, fishing, hunting, swimming and shuffleboard tournaments, North Carolina Apple Festival and religious conferences and camps are outstanding summer events. This section is also the youth camp center of eastern America.

The mean maximum temperature during the winter months is forty-nine degrees and mean minimum is twenty-seven degrees. Snowfall averages about nine inches for the winter months. In summer the maximum daily temperature is eighty-three degrees at midday, dropping to sixty-one degrees at night. Retirement on small farms is quite in vogue in the Hendersonville territory. The area has a wide appeal to those retiring, and has already built considerable reputation among people of the Midwest, New York, Florida and the Panama Canal Zone. There are good buys in comfortable homes priced at $25,000 and up.

Asheville. Pop. 60,192. Alt. 2,203 ft. Seat of Buncombe County. Asheville, the "Land of the Sky," is situated on a plateau between the Blue Ridge and the Great Smoky Mountains. Here you can retire and take it easy, or engage in as active a life as you choose. Whatever your tastes, you'll find yourself in good company, for many retired military personnel, business executives, professional people, educators and many others live in retirement in the countryside of this happy inland community.

From the point of view of climate, the area is far enough south and sufficiently protected by mountain barriers to escape the extreme severity of winter storms and cold. Average daily temperature in the winter months is forty-eight degrees maximum to twenty-nine degrees minimum. Snowfall averages eleven inches for the winter season. In summer, daily maximum temperatures reach eighty-three degrees and drop to sixty-three degrees at night. Asheville is popular with northerners in January and February and with southerners in July and August. It has long been a favorite health area for those afflicted with pulmonary and similar ailments, as well as nervous disorders.

Asheville offers all kinds of recreational facilities associated with resort areas, plus social activities at numerous clubs and community organizations. The Annual Mountain Dance and Folk Festival is noted for its picturesque revelry. Many religious groups maintain summer assemblies and conferences throughout the area. There are two country clubs with golf courses plus three public courses, lots of scenic beauty, good fishing in numerous lakes and streams, shuffleboard and swimming. The Southern Highland Craft Guild sponsors handicrafts, and many outstanding craftsmen maintain workshops and classes in weaving, ceramics and woodcarving.

As to real estate, two- and three-bedroom homes in Beverly Hills, West Asheville and North Section sell at $35,000 to $50,000. In the Kimberly and Lake Park residential sections, three-bedroom homes were priced at $28,000 to $38,000. Relatively cheaper real estate can be obtained in the Piedmont counties near the Virginia border and in the smaller mountain communities. Quite a number of retired families live comfortably on small farms in the countryside around Asheville.

15

The Gulf Coast Country

The Gulf Coast country is an amphitheater-like region that includes the coastal area bordering the Gulf of Mexico from Alabama to Texas. This section of the United States has a personality all its own, with little resemblance to the interior of the states.

Few areas of the South have a more varied and colorful history than the Gulf Coast. Seven flags have flown over the territory since the French first established a settlement in 1699 at Biloxi. The influence of the French, Spanish and English is still evident in the Gulf Coast architecture and customs. Early Spanish and Civil War forts, presidential homes, legendary pirate hide-outs and Indian myths give charm and interest to this section of the nation.

Numerous bays, islands and streams along the Gulf Coast shoreline afford the fisherman wonderful opportunities to catch many species of fish as well as crabs, oysters and shrimp.

Everywhere are wonderful oak trees and Spanish moss, flowers, pine trees and the special atmosphere that makes this a good place to live and play the year round. The Gulf Coast is a way of living—a gentle, gracious, unhurried way that often seems unreal to visitors from other sections of the country. It has a reputation for good food, warm hospitality, fun and frivolity. Residents and visitors of the area can pursue a variety of outdoor sports and recreation at little expense and without traveling great distances.

Winter weather is normally mild. January, the coldest month, has an average mean temperature of fifty-two degrees. Snow is so rare that it causes considerable excitement. Summers are consistently warm with average mean temperatures around eighty-one degrees. Summer temperatures are usually checked by daily onshore sea breezes and the temperature is brought down to around seventy-two degrees at night. The average annual rainfall is about sixty inches, usually of the shower type. Long periods of rain are rare. While the area is located in the hurricane belt, one hurricane every fifteen years is the general average. Relative humidity averages 62 percent. The average number of clear days is 120 a year and partly cloudy days, 138. The growing season is 274 days or more.

On the Gulf Coast, prices are in general very reasonable. The mild winters permit lower costs in home construction and reduced costs for house heating. Vegetables are easily grown the year round. The abundance of fish, crab, oysters and shrimp reduces Gulf Coast food bills. The year-round outdoor living and the informality help cut down the clothing budget.

Alabama

Fairhope. Pop. 7,200 Alt. 125 ft. Baldwin County. On the eastern shore of Mobile Bay, an hour's drive from the city of Mobile, friendly Fairhope offers small-town comfort with big-town advantages. The area is cooled by breezes from the Gulf and the Bay in summer; in winter, temperatures reach freezing only a few times a year. Here you can swim from sandy beaches with shade trees growing to the water's edge. There is a huge new pier for saltwater fishing, crabbing, and a marina restaurant. Freshwater fishing is available within the town limits. Good hunting for wild fowl and small game is to be found in the immediate area. Fairhope has a night-lighted athletic field and tennis courts. There is a yacht club and over ninety-two clubs and organized groups covering social and civic activities, as well as the arts. The library is well stocked. Classes are held for the study of metal-craft, weaving, art, sculpture and creative writing. Golf is available nearby, at eleven courses within an hour's drive. Shuffleboard courts are maintained by the Tourist Club.

Fairhope has a single-tax plan under which some of the home and farm property falls. The lots or acreage are obtained under ninety-nine-year renewable leases. There is a good opportunity here to establish small rental cottages or courts. Another well-paying opportunity exists in the wholesale flower-blooming-pot-plant business with a big market in Mobile and the surrounding towns. Excellent opportunities also exist for establishing poultry farms. Chickens are now shipped in. Nearby Mobile would also be a good market for eggs and poultry.

The towns of *Daphne* and *Montrose,* a few miles southeast of Mobile, have become increasingly popular as year-round residential communities for people working in Mobile. Many retired families have located in this area. *Point Clear,* to the south, is a beautiful resort colony of summer homes, vacation cottages, and boasts the luxurious Grand Hotel.

Mobile. Pop. 232,000. Alt. 10 ft. Seat of Mobile County. The city of Mobile is located on the Mobile River at its entrance to Mobile Bay, thirty-one miles from the Gulf of Mexico. Mobile is regarded as the economic capital of sixty counties of the Greater Gulf area. It is a modern seacoast city where ocean steamers call from the world's great ports. This is a community noted for the friendliness of its citizens. Mean temperature in January is 61.1 degrees maximum to 41.3 degrees minimum. In July, mean temperatures are 90.5 maximum to 72.6 degrees minimum. Relative humidity at noon averages 58 percent and 68 percent at 6:00 P.M. Average wind velocity in winter months is eleven miles per hour and in summer seven miles per hour. Annual rainfall averages 66.98 inches.

During all seasons of the year, this area provides many types of recreation. Deep-sea and freshwater fishing are popular. The Alabama Deep Sea Fishing Rodeo is a big attraction during July and August. Wild game is hunted in the deep forest and swamps. Swimming facilities are found in the shores of the Bay and in nearby lakes. Mobile's thirty-five-mile Azalea Trail winding past antebellum homes attracts thousands of visitors during the late winter and early spring. Mardi Gras is celebrated during February or March.

More than two hundred churches provide services for all leading denominations. The Providence Hospital, the University of South Alabama Medical Center, the Doctors Hospital and the Mobile Infirmary are located in the city. Some citrus fruit is grown and there are many outdoor nurseries.

Mississippi

Ocean Springs. Pop. 13,500. Alt. 10 ft. Jackson County. This was the original site of Biloxi. When Biloxi was moved across the bay, the remaining community was called Ocean Springs, because of the mineral springs in the area. Ocean Springs, in addition to being a health resort and residential community, is also a vacation resort. Its climate and many opportunities for outdoor recreation, fishing, hunting, boating, swimming and similar pastimes bring visitors back year after year. A number of persons from many different states have found the Ocean Springs area a pleasant place in which to enjoy retirement life. Some of the popular activities are golf, square dancing and horseback riding. A few miles east of town is Gulf Island National Seashore, a perfect picnic area with facilities for camping, cooking and swimming, and headquarters during the summer for the Gulf Coast Marine Research Laboratory. Up-to-date churches, a community center, a score of clubs and organizations and the friendliness of the people offer good prospects for unhurried retirement living.

The Memorial Bridge across the bay connects Ocean Springs with Biloxi, the second largest city in Mississippi. Biloxi is the shipping center for shrimp, oysters and fish from the Gulf of Mexico. It is also the site of the Keesler Air Force Base, Electronics Center and a large Veteran's National Soldiers Home and Hospital. Here you can enjoy special pageants, parades and celebrations. At Ocean Springs you can live among beautiful moss-draped oaks and in homes set among camellias, azaleas and other flowers. The land is well suited to truck farming, pecan orchards and the growing of tung trees.

Gulfport. Pop. 46,000. Alt. 18 ft. Mississippi Gulf Coast. This new modern city with a deep-water port is destined to be one of the most popular winter and summer resort areas of the deep South. The mild climate (Mean annual temperature is 68 degrees), together with the cordiality of its residents, have won for Gulfport the title of the "Hospitality City." The average annual temperature is sixty-eight degrees, ranging from a minimum monthly average of fifty-one degrees in January to a maximum of eighty-two degrees in July.

Golf, tennis, swimming, city parks, sandy beaches, the new and modern library, the Recreational Center and a long pier extending out into the Gulf are a few of the facilities offered by Gulfport. Fourteen miles north of the city are a large recreational area and picnic grounds. The great number of lakes, rivers, bays and bayous within a few minutes' drive from Gulfport, in addition to deep-sea fishing, make this a fisherman's paradise. A little theater group and the Metropolitan Club are active. Gulfport, according to physicians, "has the makings of the finest spa in the U.S.A. Its mild climate and the purity of its water offer relief to suffers of asthma, chronic bronchitis, insomnia, organic heart disease and kidney ailments. These, of course, are not all cured at Gulfport, but sufferers report relief and comfort that they can obtain nowhere else." Artesian water from deep wells is said to be among the purest drinking water in the United States.

Long Beach. Pop. 8,000. This quiet and restful community of homes, three miles west of Gulfport, has a twenty-seven-mile-long sandy beach. The coldest month is 54 degrees, the hottest, 82.

Pass Christian. Pop. 3,881. Alt. 20 ft. Harrison County. This is a typical year-round Gulf resort town. For many years it has been the headquarters for a "Coast colony" of people from New Orleans. Pass Christian is, year-in and year-out, being rediscovered by tourists traveling the Old Spanish Trail. It was first settled as a colony of France over 250 years ago. The Pass, as it is affectionately referred to, has an atmosphere and a culture all its own. Oriental trees, shrubs and flowers thrive to the edge of the sea wall. Physicians have recommended this area for reasons of health for more than a century.

Some of the more magnificent old homes of the South will be found here. Pass Christian Reef is one of the most prolific oyster reefs in the country. Shrimp, crab and excellent salt-water fishing, as well as surf bathing and other water sports, are all part of life at the Pass.

Louisiana

New Orleans Area and the "Ozone Belt." Across Lake Pontchartrain from New Orleans is St. Tammany Parish, called the "Ozone Belt." Many people commute daily to New Orleans from the delightful residential towns of this parish. Residents of these towns, within an hour, have easy access to the recreational, cultural and rich atmosphere of the historic and cosmopolitan city of New Orleans. In favor of Louisiana is the fact that its personal income tax is among the lowest levied by any state.

The characteristics of the Ozone Belt are pine forests whose towering trees give off a fragrant balm, exuding the evaporation of pine oil, artesian waters of real purity and pleasing taste, springs that yield waters acknowledged to have high therapeutic value and the mild climate. The area is similar to the Ozone Belt of the Hartz Mountains in Germany. To such areas, on advice of physicians, go sufferers from diseases of the heart, the lungs and the respiratory system.

For generations St. Tammany Parish has been famous as a resort for convalescence and recuperation of invalids. This region is now also becoming a popular location for persons seeking a desirable spot for retirement living.

Temperatures during the winter months average sixty-three degrees maximum to forty-seven degrees minimum. During the summer months average temperatures are eighty-nine degrees maximum to seventy-five degrees minimum. No snow falls in this area. Annual rainfall measures sixty inches, distributed fairly evenly throughout the year. Relative humidity around noon is 62 percent.

Slidell, Covington, Hammond and *Abita Springs* are good retirement locations and are destined to become more popular as they become better known outside the state of Louisiana.

Slidell. Pop. 18,500. Alt. 11 ft. St. Tammany Parish. This is a suburban residential town just thirty-two miles from New Orleans, located near Lake Pontchartrain and Pearl River. Practically everyone owns his own home, and rentals are scarce. Frame dwelling costs are quite reasonable. Real estate taxes are low. Because of the mild climate and good water supply, homeowners have beautiful flower and vegetable gardens. Many grow a large variety of vegetables for the family table the year round. Fruit trees do very well, especially pear, fig, plum, mandarin and persimmon.

Covington. Pop. 6,754. Alt. 35 ft. Parish seat of St. Tammany Parish. A beautiful suburban-country town on the banks of the Bogue Falaya, a river with clear water and a sandy bottom. There are mild winters, high humidity and hot summers. Covington has many delightful homes and residential areas that stretch for miles along paved, shaded streets and rival those of much larger cities. Only a few blocks from the center of the town is Bogue Falaya State Park, a resort and recreation center for the city of New Orleans, providing swimming, water sports, hiking, picnicking and other forms of outdoor activities. Lake Pontchartrain and numerous smaller lakes and streams are within easy reach of fishermen and boatsmen. Many New Orleans businessmen live here and commute daily to their work.

Covington industries depend chiefly on the pine forests in the area. Where forests have been leveled, truck farms grow a variety of produce.

Covington has a library and many social clubs and organizations. Living costs are about average for the South or perhaps a bit lower because of the great variety of truck crops grown around the countryside. "This is a place that attracts artists, writers and those who are sensitive to their surroundings as well as many charming people who have taken up residence in Covington," is the comment of a citizen who has lived in Covington for many years.

Real estate has become rather expensive because the town is so desirable.

Abita Springs. Pop. 700. Alt. 56 ft. St. Tammany Parish. Here, where the sea breezes from the Gulf mingle with the ozone-laden air of the pine woods, Abita Springs affords an ideal place for a summer or winter residence to escape the rigors of a Northern climate. Abita Springs has been added to the Louisiana State Parks System, and plans are under way to make this one of the most attractive spots in the state. In the midst of rolling hills, covered with great pine trees, sweet gum, oak, magnolia and other trees, it makes a beautiful and enchanting spot for rest, recreation and retirement. There are several springs here, all noted for their health-giving qualities. The climate is mild and free from dampness and is highly recommended by physicians for the relief of respiratory ailments. The climate is said to be the equal and in many respects the superior of many parts of Southern California.

This lovely retirement spot is located about eight miles from the shores of Lake Pontchartrain, is sixty-five miles from New Orleans and is in the center of the Ozone Belt. Undeveloped resources give ample opportunity for enterprise and the profitable investment of capital. It is an ideal site for home seekers who wish to combine health and a profitable occupation. The climate is peculiarly adapted to farm products and fruit culture, especially figs, peaches, grapes, plums and strawberries. The area also offers great opportunities for livestock, poultry raising, flower and plant culture. In and near Abita Springs is good hunting for deer, wild turkey, squirrel and quail. Splendid fishing, camping, boating and swimming are also available.

Morgan City. Pop. 13,540. Alt. 6 ft. St. Mary Parish. About eighty-nine miles southeast from New Orleans surrounded by Lake Palourde, Grand Lake and the Atchafalaya River is the town of Morgan City. A correspondent writes: "Morgan City is probably the easiest place a man could find to sustain life. Anyone with fair vision and the ability to toddle to the waterfront, can, in a short time, catch enough shrimp and fish for an average family's meals. A branch of native willow, secured to a stake on shore, can be lowered into the stream, and in two hours will have harbored a multitude of shrimp, which can be shaken into a net and used for food or as live bait for larger fish, in the same stream. A small plot can be made to produce vegetables in almost every month of the year. Average temperature for January is fifty-two degrees, and for July, eighty-two degrees. These moderate temperatures are assured by the water that surrounds us, and our proximity to the Gulf of Mexico."

Morgan City offers a year-round recreation program under a trained director. The concert association brings in nationally known artists each winter. A fine library, very friendly people, numerous civic and social groups and clubs, a golf course and good hunting are a few other advantages that make this good retirement territory.

Texas

Austin. Pop. 306,000. Alt. 400 to 1,000 ft. Austin is the capital of Texas at the very heart of the state. It has a mild and pleasant climate, a university-town atmosphere and nearby lakes and hills, all of which make it a natural location for retirement living. The citizens of the "Friendly City," as Austin is called, include government officials, college professors and students, businessmen and more professional and semiprofessional people than most cities of similar size. The economic life of Austin, in addition to the activities of the state government and the University of

Texas, includes several regional offices of the federal government, many small manufacturing and processing plants, headquarters for state-wide associations, home offices of several insurance companies. In Austin and the adjacent territory are several springs and wells where water of the highest medicinal quality flows abundantly.

Living in the shadow of the University of Texas, residents of Austin have the opportunity of attending a wide assortment of concerts, plays, sporting events and other forms of entertainment. The Austin Symphony Orchestra, the Junior Symphony Orchestra and the Mixed Chorus Society present a series of complete programs. The Cultural Entertainment Committee of the University also sponsors a series of concerts and theatrical events monthly. A number of dramas and plays are sponsored by the Civic Theatre and other organizations. Works of well-known artists are exhibited at the Elisabeth Ney Museum. The O. Henry Memorial Museum contains the works of the famous short-story writer and other items of interest. Art classes are available for both children and adults in sketching, painting and ceramics. Adult education classes are offered by the city school system, and the University of Texas offers correspondence courses to all Texans who cannot come to the campus. The city library, state library and the library of the University of Texas have a total of over a million volumes. The city has 9 hospitals, 222 churches and a great number of the usual social and civic clubs and groups. Austin Municipal Park affords swimming, boating and fishing. Zilher Park has landscaped areas for picnicking. Pease Park and Wooldridge Park are also popular outdoor recreational areas. There are three golf courses.

The climate lacks the dampness of the coastal area. Winter temperatures seldom reach freezing, the lowest monthly average being forty-nine degrees. The daily summer temperature ranges from 73 to 94 degrees and the winter temperature from 42 to 62 degrees. Annual rainfall is thirty-four inches. The area enjoys sunshine for almost 300 days a year. Relative humidity averages 57 percent.

This combination of a generally mild climate and the picturesque, rolling countryside has encouraged many former university students, legislators, military personnel and others who have spent time in Austin to return to make it their permanent home. Within a short drive from Austin are five lakes and six major dams, which are becoming famous. They open up unlimited opportunities for resort and vacation developments. It is destined to become one of the South's most popular resort regions and the site for year-round homes. A 1975 survey by the U.S. Bureau of Labor Statistics designated Austin's living costs as the lowest of all the nation's cities surveyed. And, a national magazine named Austin as one of the nation's fourteen most "pleasant places to live."

El Paso. Pop. 350,000. Alt. 3,920 ft. Seat of El Paso County, Texas. The City of El Paso, "Sunshine Playground of the Border," located in the far western corner of Texas on the upper Rio Grande, is one of the leading cities of the Southwest. For many years El Paso has boasted of its five C's—climate, clothing, copper, cattle and cotton. The climate is basically warm and dry; humidity is extremely low. The average daily temperature during winter is fifty-seven degrees maximum to thirty-two degrees minimum. During the summer, the daily average is ninety-three degrees maximum to sixty-nine degrees minimum. The city has sunshine during 79 percent of daylight hours. There are, on the average, only thirty-four cloudy days per year. Rainfall averages nine inches a year. Relative humidity around noon averages 30 percent. The area is free from blizzards and cyclones. The climate is recommended by medical authorities for its health-giving attributes. Many people who suffer from various pulmonary diseases, such as asthma and tuberculosis, move to El Paso to regain their health.

The city and vicinity offer many scenic and historic attractions. These include old Spanish missions, Carlsbad Caverns, Indian ruins, Big Bend National Park and Old Mexico. Tourist expenditures are estimated to run as high as twenty-five million dollars annually. Throughout the year there are many events which attract more than local interest. These include the Sun Bowl Football Game, the Southwestern International Livestock Show and Rodeo, the Sun Carnival and bullfights across the border in Juarez. There are in El Paso some eighty-five active clubs and organizations, exclusive of fraternal orders. Among the important ones are the Coronado and El Paso Country Clubs with swimming pools, tennis courts, and eighteen-hole golf courses, a municipal golf course, the Skeet Shooters Association, symphony orchestra and the little theater. The University of Texas at El Paso with the El Paso Centennial Museum on its campus, Loretto Academy for Girls and the Cotton Memorial School of Art add college atmosphere to city life.

San Antonio. Pop. 786,000. Alt. 700 ft. Seat of Bexar County. Once a Spanish stronghold, San Antonio today is the headquarters of the largest military establishment in the United States. Once the capital of a province in New Spain, it is now the commercial and financial center of south and west Texas. The city's mild climate and sunny skies appeal alike to persons seeking retirement and to an expanding city population seeking happy and healthful living. The average winter temperature is fifty-nine degrees, with temperatures dropping to freezing only a few days each winter. The average summer temperature is 80 degrees with cool Gulf breezes on summer nights. Average humidity in summer months is 55 percent and in winter months, 45 percent. Average annual rainfall is twenty-seven inches. The sun shines during 50 percent of daylight hours in winter and during summer 70 percent.

The city's fifty-six parks and a recreation system of more than three thousand acres include facilities for golf, tennis, baseball and swimming pools. The Alamo Stadium is the scene of outstanding sporting events. At the Joe Freeman Coliseum, livestock shows, rodeos, ice shows and other events are popular. There are five hundred churches of leading denominations. San Antonio is a city of culture. Its symphony orchestra is well rated. There are a week-long opera season and a constant series of concerts, plays and other cultural diversions. There are numerous fine libraries, art galleries and museums, four universities, one college and two junior colleges, plus military academies and schools of music and art. There is much of historic interest to see, including the Alamo and several early missions. San Antonio is well known as a health resort and medical center. There is every indication of further steady increase in San Antonio's popularity as a retirement location.

Brownsville. Pop. 60,000. Alt. 35 ft. Seat of Cameron County. The only city in the United States which is a port of entry to Old Mexico by water, highway and air, Brownsville is on the shortest route to Mexico City for 70 percent of the people of the United States. Matamoros, Mexico, is just opposite Brownsville on the Rio Grande River.

Brownsville celebrates a four-day fiesta called Charro Days, when everyone wears a costume typical of some part of Latin America. Programs are sponsored throughout the year by the Knife and Fork Club and the Rotary Club featuring prominent lecturers on world topics. The Civic Music Association presents outstanding concert artists. There is a wide variety of social groups including the art league, garden clubs, study clubs and many civic organizations. The area affords freshwater, saltwater and channel fishing—you can catch fish any time of the year without driving more than thirty miles. Excellent hunting includes game in Mexico. Sailing, boating and bathing are popular in the Ship Channel and at the beaches at Padre Island, Boca Chica or Del Mar on the Gulf twenty-five miles from Brownsville. The Country Club provides an eighteen-hole golf course. Bullfights, dining and other recreational facilities in Mexico are just across the international toll bridges.

Almost every crop is grown in the Lower Rio Grande Valley. There are also good opportunities for small business enterprises. Several good opportunities exist for professional, service and retail enterprises. The attitude of the people is to encourage new industries, retail establishments, professions and small farmers. They are not anxious, however, to encourage such innovations as will destroy what they feel to be an admirable way of life.

The climate is pleasant throughout the year. Average winter temperatures are sixty-nine degrees maximum to fifty-one degrees minimum. During summer, temperatures average ninety degrees maximum to seventy-four degrees minimum, but cool breezes from the Gulf make living comfortable throughout the day and night. Rainfall averages twenty-seven inches annually. Relative humidity at noon is around 60 percent. The cost of living is considerably lower than in the North or East and lower than in the larger cities of the South. Tropical winters reduce the cost of fuel for house heating, and winters do not require heavy clothing.

The entire Lower Rio Grande Valley, of which Brownsville is the largest community, is rapidly achieving prominence as a good retirement area and housing is becoming hard to find. There are other fast-growing communities in the Valley.

McAllen. Pop. 35,000. Located in the lush tropical Lower Rio Grande Valley of Texas, across from large metropolitan city of Reynosa, Mexico. McAllen offers all the conveniences of nearby city life, but in a relaxing setting of palm trees, sunshine, citrus groves and recreational facilities.

Many excellent motels, golf courses, rental units for retirees and winter visitors. Tourist Clubs open during winter months. Over 12,000 now spend a major portion of the winter in the area.

McAllen is a summer and winter playground and a paradise for sportsmen who enjoy fresh or saltwater fishing and hunting of all varieties.

Good opportunities for winter visitor- and tourist-related businesses exist in this Mexican border city. They include motels, service firms, apartments, amusements, entertainment and seasonal facilities.

Harlingen. Pop. 41,207. This progressive, pleasant residential community offers advantages for quiet, enjoyable retirement living.

Harlingen's location, within minutes of the beautiful Gulf Coast and exciting Old Mexico, offers the visitor fishing, hunting, sightseeing and good dining. It is a semi-tropical vacation land where sunshine is the rule twelve months of the year.

Among the advantages specifically designed for retired residents and winter visitors is the Casa del Sol tourist complex, a million-dollar facility, offering a wide variety of recreational, hobby, and social activities. The Harlingen Tourist Club, operating from this facility, opens its membership to all retired new residents and winter visitors. A retirement subdivision with a Community House is available.

16

The Southwest

Arizona and New Mexico are both in mountainous and deep-canyon country. The altitude of the northern tablelands ranges from six thousand to twelve thousand feet; in the central parts of the states, altitudes are about five thousand feet. In general, these altitudes are too stimulating for elderly persons and may even be injurious to those with diminished vital powers.

In the southern section of Arizona, and to some extent in New Mexico, there are a few river valleys with altitudes varying from five hundred to two thousand feet with a mild, dry climate and an abundance of sunshine. These valleys are rapidly becoming well known as health resorts and popular vacation playgrounds. They deserve serious consideration as localities for retirement, particularly by those who prefer the inland, mountain-country type of living. Many will choose this area because of low humidity, dryness, sunshine, mild winter temperatures and proximity to natural mineral springs conducive to health building.

Winters are mild and sunny during the day and cool at

night. The mountains protect the area from a good part of the extreme cold from the north. December to February the mean monthly temperatures are fifty to sixty degrees for southern Arizona and forty-five degrees for southern New Mexico. At night, the temperature in New Mexico often drops below freezing. Snowfall is rare in the valley areas but is heavy at the higher altitudes.

The summers are long and hot, lasting from May to October, with wide variations in temperature between daylight hours and night. Temperatures of one hundred degrees and over occur very frequently during the day in the summer months. These high temperatures drop to about seventy-five degrees at night. Many homes and commercial buildings are equipped with summer air-conditioners or evaporative air-coolers. Persons who can afford it sometimes move to northern, higher elevations for the summer or to California to escape the summer heat.

The relative humidity, however, is very low, around 30 percent at noon. It often falls below 10 percent during the afternoon. This low humidity tends to mitigate the high summer temperatures and is responsible for the small number of heat prostrations throughout the area. In southern New Mexico relative humidity is slightly higher than in Arizona. There are two main rainy seasons. The first occurs during the winter months from November to March, the second and heavier from July through September when the area is subject to thunderstorms. Generally, there is less than twelve inches of annual rainfall in the southern areas. Winds are light, averaging only 5.8 miles per hour in southern Arizona but stronger in New Mexico, especially during the spring. The climate is considered beneficial for persons suffering from respiratory diseases and rheumatic illness.

Arizona

Tucson. Pop. 400,000. Alt. 2,400 ft. Seat of Pima County, Arizona. Located in the heart of a cactus- and mesquite-covered desert plateau, Tucson, "The Sunshine City," is surrounded by rugged mountains. Four flags have flown over the city—Spanish, Mexican, Confederate and Union. Winter temperature averages sixty-seven degrees maximum to thirty-seven degrees minimum. Snowfall in Tucson is rare, particularly accumulations exceeding an inch in depth. The summer season is long and hot, beginning in April and ending in October. Maximum temperatures above ninety degrees are the rule with daily minimums in the sixties. Annual rainfall is 10.53 inches. Relative humidity ranges from 15 to 30 percent. The sun shines during 87 percent of daylight hours. Mean speed of wind is 7.2 miles per hour.

The unusual setting of Tucson, its sunshine and dry climate are largely responsible for its growth as a resort and health city and for the fact that the number of permanent residents has more than doubled in the last decade. Many businessmen, professional men, writers, farmers and others who originally went to Tucson for a brief visit have returned to make it their permanent home. In spite of its health-resort character, Tucson does not appear to be a city populated by invalids. The really sick people are in hospitals and sanitariums. The other health seekers are those with sinus trouble, asthma, rheumatism, arthritis in stages that benefit from sunshine and dry air.

The University of Arizona is located here. There are varied cultural activities of the community. The university has attracted many people who need a desert climate for health reasons and yet want an intellectual environment. Artists and musicians have gathered there in great numbers. Nationally known guest artists appear with the Tucson Symphony Orchestra. The Arizona Civic Theater is active in drama presentations. Well-known speakers are heard on the Sunday Evening Forum program. The Tucson Opera Company and Arizona Ballet, as well as the Museum of Art round out a full cultural scene. The community offers a wide range of group activities, with several hundred civic, fraternal, social and special interest groups to choose from. Informality is the order of the day and night throughout the community.

Many retired and semi-retired people are moving to Tucson and enjoying the abundant sunshine and the many facilities designed for their comfort and pleasure. Along with moderately priced housing in all sections of the city, there are many retirement communities specifically for the "senior citizen." These include trailer parks, with their own shopping and recreational centers, cooperative apartment houses and residential areas. There are many clubs and recreation centers for senior citizens organized under community auspices. These feature shuffleboard, music, cards, square dancing, games, discussions, films, speakers, etc., and an opportunity for meeting people who are also from other parts of the country. Former residents of many states have formed "state" clubs which hold picnics and other social affairs. A local organization, TOCER (Tucson On Call Employment Reserve), for over 40 only, has been established to counsel and refer citizens on part-time and full-time employment.

For further information regarding facilities for senior citizens, write: Tucson Chamber of Commerce, 420 West Congress, Tucson, Arizona.

The combined elements of sun, warm, dry air and the low relative humidity have proved to be very beneficial to most respiratory infections, such as sinus, asthma and bronchitis, and to rheumatism, arthritis and allied diseases.

Many new residents claim never to have felt so well before. However, owing to the altitude, some severe heart conditions are adversely affected, and a few ailments are aggravated by occasional dust, an inevitable by-product of the dryness found on the desert.

Phoenix. Pop. 676,000. Alt. 1,080 ft. Seat of Maricopa County, Arizona. This is the capital of Arizona. It occupies an area of some 270 square miles on the broad plain of the Salt River Valley. Although reclaimed from a virtual desert, the city has developed surprising landscape beauty. The climate of Phoenix has been compared to that of the Upper Nile Valley of Egypt. In the winter months, daily maximum temperatures are around sixty-five degrees with minimums sometimes dropping below freezing, but afternoons are usually sunny and warm. The summer months frequently bring temperatures over one hundred degrees with night temperatures dropping to the low seventies. Relative humidity during daytime averages 30 percent, dropping to 15 percent in the afternoon. During recent years, summer air-conditioning has brought greater comfort to residents. Air-conditioning for homes and office buildings is now the rule for living in Phoenix.

The simplicity of living, the friendliness of the people, the interesting scenery surrounding the city, the dry air, the sense of freedom and relaxation and the rapidly expanding economic advantages have attracted new residents to Phoenix. The city has much to offer for retirement living and relaxation. There are fifty-three city parks, thirty motion picture theaters, radio and television stations, a city symphony orchestra and free lectures at five art galleries and two museums. All the usual civic, service and social clubs and groups are represented and active. All major sports activities are available, including golf, tennis, shuffleboard, swimming, fishing and hunting in nearby streams and mountains, rodeos, horse and dog racing and horseback riding. The Phoenix Technical School offers night classes for adults. Over two hundred churches care for the religious needs of all leading denominations. *Scottsdale,* a few minutes' drive from Phoenix, is a new and thriving resort community of 79,000 people.

Chandler (pop. 20,000), *Glendale* (pop. 66,000) and *Mesa* (pop. 100,000) are three communities, located within thirty minutes' drive from Phoenix, that offer the same climatic advantages with opportunities for less expensive living. Each community offers its own recreation and social activities at a quieter tempo and in a more rural atmosphere. Yet each community is within easy reach of the more active city life of Phoenix. These communities are trading centers of a rich agricultural area in the Salt River Valley noted for irrigated truck farms, citrus, date and fig groves. Arizona State University is only six miles from Mesa.

Residents talk about the variety of life available. You can: Climb out of your backyard pool . . . and go skiing within two hours . . . Mingle with a metropolitan throng, dine in a renowned restaurant, yet an hour later stand serenely in desert stillness. Drive for hours through mountain forests of pine, spruce, fir and aspen, then return home to plant palms, hibiscus and bougainvillea. Tour a modern library, art museum or computer center in the morning, visit a ghost town or prowl prehistoric ruins in the afternoon. Go to concerts and city recreation, or hunt deer, bear, cougar and javelinas, or go boating, prospecting or picnicking in desert or mountains *any* weekend.

Globe. Pop. 10,000. Alt. 3,500 ft. Seat of Gila County, Arizona. This is the "City of the Hills," whose main street lies in a canyon and whose pleasant homes overlook the tremendous vista of the Apache Indian Reservation and the Pinal Mountains. It is a thriving copper-mining town. You can enjoy plenty of outdoor life here, in a climate that is dry and sunny and somewhat of a compromise between the hot summers of the Southwest and the colder winters of the Northeast. Many physicians recommend this climate for asthma, sinus, bronchitis and other ailments. For fishing there are the Roosevelt Lake, the San Carlos Lake and the mountain streams. Hunters find deer, elk, antelope, turkey, dove and quail in the mountains. Globe is a center of early Indian culture and life. Many ancient ruins are still preserved.

Prescott. Pop. 16,888. Alt. 5,354 ft. Seat of Yavapai County, Arizona. This "Mile High City of Health" is one of the few Western cities that retains some of the flavor of the frontier days. It is located in an area of the nation's largest pine forest and is noted for the relief of many forms of allergic sensitivity, sinus and respiratory conditions. Many of its prominent citizens went to Prescott seeking relief from asthma and remained to make it their permanent residence. The results of a survey to determine the effects of the local climate on asthmatics indicate that, out of six thousand people questioned, one in every thirty-five had come to Prescott suffering from this ailment and 93 percent had found relief.

Winter temperatures average fifty degrees maximum to twenty-five degrees minimum. Due to the low humidity and light winds, these temperatures are not uncomfortable. Summer temperatures range from eighty-nine degrees maximum for short periods to fifty degrees about daybreak. Relative humidity ranges from a high of 66 percent in December to a low of 26 percent in June. Snowfall in winter usually amounts to twenty inches but disappears rapidly due to the dry air.

For recreation there are many scenic and picnic areas, such as Granite Basin, Granite Dells, Mingus Mountain, Castle Hot Springs and Thumb Butte. Miles of valleys, mountains and wilderness offer excellent fishing and hunting as well as all kinds of outdoor sports.

Cultural activities include the Prescott Fine Arts Association, community concerts, the Yavapai Symphony Association, Yavapai College with its lectures, theater, art, and dinner club. The outstanding annual events are the Frontier Days Rodeo in July, and the Smoki Indian Ceremonials in August.

New Mexico

Deming. Pop. 11,200. Alt. 4,321 ft. County seat of Luna County, New Mexico. Deming is located on a semi-arid mesa, in the heart of the 85 percent sunshine area. The mean temperature for the year is sixty degrees, ranging from an average high of seventy-nine degrees in July to an average low of forty-two degrees in December. Average relative humidity is 25 to 30 percent. Annual average rainfall is 8 inches. The climate is beneficial for arthritis, sinus disorders, tuberculosis, asthma and allergies, and for people susceptible to harsh, damp weather. Healthful sunshine is available 360 days of the year.

Cultural facilities consist of an excellent school system, thirty churches, a small but excellent library, community concerts, cantatas, annual talent shows and band concerts. For recreation there is the country club with public golf course and swimming pool, a municipal swimming pool and tennis courts, several parks with picnicking facilities, various fraternal and civic organizations and an active community house. Rock Hound State Park is fifteen miles southeast of Deming, and is the only state park to offer free rocks to rock hunters. Many gem-quality stones are found there. The Gila National Forest, largest in the United States, a vast sportsman's paradise, is ninety minutes drive away. Thirty-two miles south of Deming is the fascinating land of Old Mexico. Living expenses are about the same as those in the Midwest, and slightly lower than those in the

East. Taxes are lower and, on the whole, real estate costs less.

Truth or Consequences. Pop. 6,800. Alt. 4,200 ft. Sierra County, New Mexico. Formerly named Hot Springs, this town was made famous by Ralph Edwards and his radio program "Truth or Consequences." It is one of the health capitals of the nation. The healing waters of its hot mineral springs are famous for their value in the treatment of arthritis, rheumatic complaints and similar diseases. There are twenty regularly operated mineral spring bathhouses. The healing waters of Truth or Consequences are supplemented by a healthful climate with sunshine during 80 percent of daylight hours. The winter temperatures average forty-six degrees with a high of sixty and a low of twenty-eight degrees. In summer the average temperature is seventy-seven degrees with a high of ninety-two and a low of sixty-two degrees. Relative humidity averages between 10 and 15 percent. Annual rainfall is seven inches. Truth or Consequences is the home of the famous Carrie Tingley Hospital for Crippled Children. The community center is the gathering place for residents, tourists and visitors interested in card games, shuffleboard and dances. Elephant Butte Lake, three miles away, and nearby Caballo Reservoir offer boating, fishing, skiing and swimming. Two golf courses are open for residents and visitors. Other forms of recreation include sightseeing of historical locations, rock hunting and picnicking. There are churches of eighteen denominations, a well-stocked library, a good school system and many service and social clubs. Truth or Consequences is a good location for those seeking a retirement mecca, for those seeking relief from illness, for those seeking recreation.

Santa Fe. Pop. 45,900. Alt. 7,000 ft. Seat of Santa Fe County, New Mexico. This is a favorite retirement location, but not recommended for those suffering from heart diseases or nervous disorders. The high altitude accelerates respiration, increases the metabolic rate and tends to produce conditions of excitability. However, you will find many retired people living here. Winter temperatures average forty degrees maximum to twenty degrees minimum. An average of thirty inches of snow falls during the winter months. Relative humidity in winter averages 60 percent. Less than one inch of rain falls each month during the winter. There is no excessive heat in summer; the average highest temperature in July is eighty degrees and average lowest is fifty-seven degrees. Summer nights are cool enough to require wraps and covers. On an average, the sun shines during 74 percent of daylight hours. Living expenses in Santa Fe are not low, since nearly all food and merchandise are shipped in from outside the state.

Santa Fe has a thriving art colony, five fine museums and a state art gallery. The Community Concert Association, summer opera, cinema club and little theater provide opportunities to enjoy music and dramatic presentations. The Santa Fe Fiesta held over the Labor Day weekend is a colorful spectacle. There is excellent fishing in nearby trout streams and lakes. Hunters find a variety of game within a few miles of the city. For golfers there is an eighteen-hole municipal golf course. Santa Fe offers many interesting and educational sidelights on Indian culture and relics.

Real estate costs are relatively high. The sources of income are the state capital and federal government payrolls, the craft industries and the tourist trade. Recently some light industry has located in the city, and a research center is being established in an industrial park area south of town.

17

Social Security

Brief Summary of Program

Federal retirement, survivors and disability insurance is really a combination of two security plans. One is a contributory system to provide a pension when income is reduced upon retirement from work. The other is a life insurance system to replace earnings lost when a worker becomes disabled at a younger age or dies, leaving a dependent family. And in 1965, the Congress added a health insurance program to help pay the hospital and doctor bills for persons sixty-five and older, with an effective date of July 1, 1966.

During your working years, you pay a "premium" collected as a payroll tax, based on your wages up to $16,500 a year. The 1977 rate is 11.7 percent, of which the employee pays 5.85 percent and the employer contributes a like amount. This tax rate will increase periodically, until by 1986 both the employer and the employee will be paying at the rate of 6.45 percent. The taxes are deducted from your earnings each pay day.

A self-employed person pays 7.9 percent, and this will increase to 8.5 percent in 1987. Self-employed persons with net earnings of $400 or more in a year are required to report their earnings and pay the Social Security tax each year when they file their Federal individual tax return.

In addition to the taxes paid to support the retirement, survivors and disability cash benefits program, in 1966, a hospital insurance tax on earnings became payable. This began at 0.35 percent each for employer, employee and the self-employed, and will increase, by gradual steps, to 1.50 percent in 1986 and the years thereafter.

Wages and self-employment income are entered under a person's Social Security number by the Social Security Administration. This record of earnings is used to determine eligibility for benefits and the amount a person will receive.

The old-age benefits are payable to a retired person who is "fully insured" and has reached the age of sixty-two. If a worker becomes disabled before age sixty-five, he may qualify for monthly disability benefits. The "life insurance" payments are made to the widow and to certain dependents when an insured worker dies. In addition, a lump-sum death payment may be made to the widow or widower who was living in the same household with the worker at death; otherwise, it can go to pay the worker's burial expenses.

This, briefly, is what your federal Social Security program covers. There are many "ifs" and "buts" and variations, the most important of which will be covered in this chapter.

How to Estimate Your Monthly Payments

The exact amount of benefits payable on your Social Security record cannot be figured until a claim is filed on your record. But it is not hard to estimate how much will be payable to you and your dependents when you do qualify for benefits or how much would be paid to your dependents in the event of your death.

Benefits are based on average earnings. The amount will also depend on whether you start getting benefits at age sixty-two or decide to wait until later. Your monthly benefit will be lower if you choose to receive old-age benefits before you are sixty-five. Beginning with August, 1961, men have been able to start receiving old-age benefits at sixty-two; women have been able to do so since 1956.

Here is how to estimate the amount of old-age and survivors insurance benefits payable on the basis of your work under Social Security, if you are insured.

STEP 1. Pick your starting date. If you have worked under Social Security for at least a year and a half after 1950, you may use January 1, 1951, as a starting date in figuring your average earnings. Under the Social Security law your benefits may be based on your average earnings beginning with 1937, or beginning with 1951, whichever will give you the higher benefit. Because earnings levels have been higher in the last fifteen years or so than they were earlier, most people will get higher benefits based on their average earnings beginning with 1951, and this is the method explained in the following steps:

STEP 2. List your yearly earnings, for each year beginning with 1951 up to the present. List your expected earnings from now until you reach age sixty-two. List additional years if you plan to continue working after this age.

Don't include more than: $3,600 a year, 1951–1954; $4,200 a year, 1955–1958; $4,800 a year for 1959–1965; $6,600 for 1966 and 1967, $7,800 for 1968–1971; $9,000 for 1972; $10,-800 for 1973; $13,200 for 1974; $14,100 for 1975; $15,300 for 1976; and $16,500 for 1977.

STEP 3. Count the number of years after 1955 and up to, but not including, the year you reach age sixty-two. If the result is less than five, increase it to five.

STEP 4. Now, from the list you made under Step 1, select a

number of years equal to the number you figured in Step 2. Select those years in which your earnings were highest. You may select years after you reach sixty-two or sixty-five if your highest earnings were, or will be, in any of those years.

STEP 5. Total the earnings you have in your selected years. Divide this by the number of years selected in Step 2. *You now have your average yearly earnings,* after 1950.

If you die or become disabled at any age, your average earnings will be figured as if you became sixty-two in the year that you die or become disabled.

STEP 6. Check the chart of examples to see about what your benefits will be, depending on your age at the time you want benefits to start.

For estimates of monthly payments for average yearly earnings not listed in the chart, consult your local Social Security office.

How to Become "Insured"

To get Social Security retirement payments for yourself and benefits for your family, you must first have credit status for a certain amount of employment under Social Security.

The year is divided into calendar quarters and you get Social Security credit for one or more (but not more than four) of these quarters in a year. In general, this means a three-month period in which wages of $50 or more are paid. A self-employed person gets four "quarters of coverage" for a year in which his net earnings are $400 or more.

The exact number of credits you will need to get benefits after you reach age sixty-two, or die, or become disabled depends upon the date of your birth. No one is "fully insured" with credits less than a minimum of six quarters (1½ years) of work and no one needs more than forty quarters (10 years) of work.

Persons attaining retirement age and retiring after 1990

Examples of Monthly Social Security

Benefits can be paid to a:	$923 or less	$3,000
Retired worker at 65	107.90	223.20
Worker under 65 and disabled	107.90	223.20
Retired worker at 62	86.40	178.60
Wife or dependent husband at 65	54.00	111.60
Wife or dependent husband at 62	40.50	83.70
Wife under 65 and one child in her care	54.00	118.00
Widow or dependent widower at 65 (if worker never received reduced benefits)	107.90	223.20
Widow or dependent widower at 60 (if sole survivor)	77.20	159.60
Widow or dependent widower at 50 and disabled (if sole survivor)	56.80	111.70
Widow or widower caring for one child	161.90	334.80
Maximum family payment	161.90	341.20

Maximum earnings covered by Social Security were lower in past years and must be included in figuring your average earnings. This average determines your payment amount. Because of this, amounts shown in the last two columns generally

will need forty quarters of coverage. These credits can have been earned at any time after 1936 for workers and in self-employment after 1950. This rule covers most individuals. There is no age limit on earning credit status to qualify for benefits.

In general, the "fully insured" status provision means an individual must have contributed to the system about one-fourth of his normal working life, that is, ten years out of forty years of work.

Having a fully insured status means only that you are eligible for benefits. It does not mean that you qualify for maximum benefits. The amount will depend upon your

Payments (Effective June 1976)

Average Yearly Earnings after 1950

$4,000	$5,000	$6,000	$8,000*	$10,000*
262.60	304.50	344.10	427.80	474.00
262.60	304.50	344.10	427.80	474.00
210.10	243.60	275.30	342.30	379.20
131.30	152.30	172.10	213.90	237.00
98.50	114.30	129.10	160.50	177.80
186.20	257.40	287.20	321.00	355.60
262.60	304.50	344.10	427.80	474.00
187.80	217.80	246.10	305.90	339.00
131.40	152.40	172.20	214.00	237.10
394.00	456.80	516.20	641.80	711.00
448.80	561.90	631.30	748.70	829.50

won't be payable until future years. The maximum retirement benefit generally payable to a worker who is 65 in 1976 is $387.30.

average earnings. The more regularly you work under Social Security and the higher your earnings, the higher your benefits will be.

Qualifying for Payments

You qualify for primary old-age retirement benefits if you are fully insured, are over sixty-two and have filed a claim for benefits.

When a man retires, if his wife is sixty-two years of age or over, both of them can get Social Security benefits. A wife's benefit will equal one-half her husband's, if she is sixty-five. If a wife chooses to have her benefits before age sixty-five, the amount of her benefit will be permanently reduced.

A wife who is eligible for benefits based on her own employment earnings and also qualifies for benefits based on the earnings of her husband can receive the amount equal to the larger of the two benefits, but not both.

Additional family payments to a retired worker's dependents include: unmarried children under eighteen years of age; or between eighteen and twenty-two, if they are full-time students; unmarried children, 22 or over, who were disabled before they reached eighteen; a wife, regardless of her age, if she is caring for an entitled child under eighteen or disabled; a dependent husband. In each case the payment is one-half of the payment the qualified worker receives.

In the event of the worker's death, the eligible widow or widower and dependent children will receive three-fourths of the worker's benefit amount. The widow over 65 will receive benefits equal to 100 percent of what her husband received. If she chooses, a widow may elect benefits at age sixty at a permanently reduced rate. Dependent parents at sixty-two may be paid survivors' benefits.

Working While Getting Social Security Payments

You do not have to quit work completely to get Social Security benefits. If you earn $3,000 or less within a year (1977) as an employee of someone else, you will get all your benefits. If you earn more than $3,000, $1 of your benefits (or of your total family benefits) can be withheld for each $2 of your earnings above $3,000.

Here is an exception. No matter how much you earn, you and your dependents will not lose any benefits for those months in which you do not earn wages of more than $250.

If you are self-employed, you can be paid Social Security benefits for any month in which you do not render substantial services in self-employment, even though your net earnings from your business may be more than $3,000 for the year. In order to tell whether your services for the month are substantial, consult your local Social Security office for a ruling.

At any time during the year, if you are working for wages of more than $250 a month (or are rendering substantial services in self-employment) and expect your total earnings for the year to amount to more than $3,000, you should report this to your local Social Security office.

You will then receive, from your Social Security office, special post cards for reporting your estimated earnings of above $3,000 for the year.

When your report is received, the Social Security Administration will figure how much must be held back from your monthly benefit checks during the year. Benefits will be stopped for the number of months necessary, as based on your reported estimate of earnings. You should make as accurate an estimate of your yearly earnings as you can. If your estimate turns out to be too low, you will have to pay back some benefits at the end of the year. On the other hand, if you estimated too high and more of your benefits were withheld than need be, you will get a check for the unpaid amount you are entitled to, when the Social Security Administration receives your final annual report of what you actually did earn during the year.

If your earnings amounted to more than $3,000 for the year, you must also file an annual report with the Social Security Administration. The report is to be filed on or before April 15 of the following year. This report must be filed in addition to any income tax return you send to the District Director of Internal Revenue.

You do not need to file an annual report on your earnings if you reached the age of seventy-two before the beginning of the year or if you did not receive any benefit checks for any month of the year because of your work.

After you reach age seventy-two, you can get a Social Security check for every month, no matter how much you work or how much you earn.

Social Security insurance, like other forms of insurance, insures against specified risks, and it does not pay benefits unless the risk it insures against is realized. Old-Age, Survivors, and Disability Insurance pays benefits only if there is a loss of earnings resulting from retirement, disability or the death of an insured worker. One means of assuring that the purpose of the law is carried out is the test of retirement earnings, as explained above. It is not the purpose of the present Social Security program to pay benefits to a full-time worker just because he reaches age sixty-two. The purpose is to provide benefits to the aged who are substantially retired and to their dependents and survivors who do not have substantial income from work.

There is no retirement test on earnings for those over seventy-two. The test was dropped for these people because some wage earners and self-employed business men and professional people plan to go on working as long as they are able. After years of contributing to the Social Security fund, these people over seventy-two might otherwise never get anything for their Social Security taxes, even though they had paid taxes over a longer period than others in their age group who retired.

It is a source of wonder to many persons why retirees with good incomes from investments in stocks, bonds or real estate are paid Social Security benefits, without regard to a retirement test on income. The reason is that the Social Security program insures only against loss of earnings from work. The program is not intended to be a substitute for private savings, pension plans, and insurance protection.

Social Security is intended to be a foundation upon which other forms of income can be soundly built. If benefits were withheld from people who have an income from savings, there would be less incentive for people to save in order to build up the additional financial security they need in their old age.

Disability Benefits

If you become severely disabled before age sixty-five, you may qualify for monthly disability benefits. Certain members of your family may also be paid monthly benefits.

To be considered disabled under the Social Security law, you must have a condition so severe that it makes you unable to "engage in any substantial gainful activity," and is expected to last (or has lasted) at least twelve months or is expected to result in death.

To qualify for disability insurance payments, you generally must have Social Security credit for at least five years of work in a ten-year period preceding the disability. Younger disabled workers need credit for less work.

A disabled widow or dependent widow aged fifty to sixty may receive reduced monthly benefits on her deceased husband's account if her disability began within 7 years after her husband's death or within 7 years after she last received mother's benefits, whichever is later.

The amount of your disability insurance payment is the same as the amount of the old-age insurance benefit you would get if you were already age sixty-five. Figure your average yearly earnings as if you reached sixty-two at the time you became disabled. See the examples of old-age monthly payments in the table shown earlier in this chapter.

Events That Stop Benefits

Payments to a person receiving Social Security benefits of any kind are ended at the death of the person.

Payments to a child stop if that person marries.

Payments to a wife or dependent husband are ended if a divorce is granted.

Payments to a wife under 62 or widow or widower under 62 will stop when she no longer has in her care a child who is also entitled to monthly payments.

Payments as a survivor, relative or dependent are lost if the person receiving them becomes entitled to benefits earned in his own right that are greater than the amount received as a dependent or survivor.

Payments to a disabled person will stop if he or she is no longer disabled.

Kinds of Work Covered

Social Security now covers most jobs in which people work for wages and most work of self-employed persons. Some occupations, however, are covered only if certain conditions are met. Military service is covered like civilian employment.

Permanent maids, cooks, butlers, housekeepers, caretakers, gardeners, chauffeurs, and so forth, are all covered by Social Security. So is help-by-the-day. The test here is strictly in dollars. If you pay a domestic $50 or more in any calendar quarter, you must withhold 5.85 percent and add another 5.85 percent yourself. But only cash wages count. You file returns (Form 942) near the end of each calendar quarter with the District Director of Internal Revenue.

Practically the only employed persons excluded from Social Security are civilian employees of the Federal Government, who have a staff retirement system of their own, and persons with only small amounts of earnings.

Work done by a child under twenty-one for his parent, by a husband for his wife, or by a wife for her husband is not covered.

Things to Consider in Applying for Old-Age Benefits before Age Sixty-five.

In considering whether he wishes to apply for Social Security benefits before he reaches sixty-five, a man will want to weigh a number of factors, including his health, whether he is employed, his earning power and his family situation.

Just as in the case of a woman worker, a man who decides to take his benefits when he is sixty-two will get less per month than he would if he had waited until he was sixty-five. The amount of the reduction is five-ninths of 1 percent for each month a benefit will be paid before he reaches sixty-five.

This works out so that a man who takes his benefits at sixty-two will get 80 percent of the monthly benefit he would have been paid at sixty-five, about 86 percent at age sixty-three, and 93 percent at sixty-four.

On the other hand if you return to work after you start getting retirement checks, your added earnings will often result in higher benefits when you again stop working. Social Security will automatically refigure your benefit after the additional earnings are credited to your record.

How to Make a Claim for Benefits

There are four times when it is especially important to consult the Social Security office:

> About three months before you decide to retire,
> About three months before you reach age sixty-five, in order to sign up for health insurance.

344 THE RETIREMENT HANDBOOK

If a worker in your family dies.
If you are severely disabled.

Benefits are not paid automatically, and they are not paid retroactively for more than twelve months before application.

Certain supporting proofs must be supplied with your application for benefits. These are:

> Proof of age, for your own primary benefits, for a wife's or widow's benefits, for a dependent child's benefits. A birth certificate or a baptismal certificate or a hospital birth record are legal proof.
> Proof of marriage must be filed with a claim by a husband, wife, widow or widower.
> Proof of death is needed in claims for survivor's benefits.
> Proof of disability is required from your doctor or by a hospital or clinic where you have had treatment.
> Proof of burial expenses may be necessary for lump-sum death payments.

You do not have to delay in applying for Social Security benefits because you do not have some of the papers. Your local Social Security office will suggest other proofs that may be used.

18

The Medicare Program

The year 1965 earned its way into history if only for the amendments to the Social Security Act which provide medical and health care and other associated benefits for people aged sixty-five and over. Popularly known as Medicare, these amendments are comparable in significance to the adoption of the original Social Security bill in 1935.

There were years of debate and controversy over the basic philosophy behind the bill, as well as the specific measures proposed. It was about a generation ago that President Harry Truman expressed the basis of the need for legislation enabling health care for the aged.

President Truman said: "Millions of our citizens do not now have a full measure of opportunity to achieve and to enjoy good health. Millions do not now have protection or security against the economic effects of sickness. And the time has now arrived for action to help them attain that opportunity and to help get that protection."

President Lyndon B. Johnson took up the cudgel for the legislation soon after he took office. And on July 7, 1965, the Congress having approved the terms of the bill, President Johnson took his pen and flew out to Independence, Missouri, to pay tribute to President Truman's early efforts on the bill. In a memorable ceremony, President Johnson signed the bill in the company of President Truman—and the Medicare Amendment became law.

President Johnson commented: "The need for this action is plain. . . . There are more than 8 million (now about 20 million) Americans over the age of sixty-five. Most of them are threatened by illness and medical expenses they cannot afford. . . . This insurance will help pay for care in hospitals, in skilled nursing homes, or in the home. And under a separate plan it will meet the fees of the doctors."

These amendments, the broadest Social Security legislation in the nation's history, were designed to protect the workers of the nation and their families against the high cost of health care in old age. The cash contributions to Social Security were increased, partly to accommodate the new costs. There were also improvements in old-age and survivor's and disability insurance; there was better medical and income help for the needy.

Obviously these programs do not come entirely free, but by sharing the cost between employer and employee, as well as the federal and state governments, they are provided at rather bargain rates to the beneficiaries.

The basic plan provides for hospital insurance and other related health care. This plan allows in-patient hospital service up to 90 days per benefit period, with the patient paying $124 (1977) deductible and $31 a day from the sixty-first through the ninetieth day. There are 60 additional "reserve" hospital days, with the patient paying $62 a day. The plan also provides psychiatric hospital service up to 190 days during a lifetime.

The basic plan also provides protection against the cost of confinement in skilled nursing facilities. The plan covers up to 100 days in such a facility during a benefit period. The first 20 days are free. For the final 80 days, the individual pays $15.50 per day. To qualify for extended-care benefits, an individual must have been hospitalized for at least 3 days. In addition, the individual must enter the extended-care facility within 14 days of his discharge from the hospital and at the direction of a physician. He must need continuing skilled nursing care for further treatment of a condition for which he was treated in the hospital.

Medicare covers up to one hundred home visits by home health workers to patients subsequent to hospital discharge, if determined necessary by the physician and if the patient needs intermittent nursing care or physical or speech therapy.

Beyond the foregoing provisions of the basic plan, there is a voluntary supplementary plan that covers physicians' services and other care not covered by the basic plan.

The Supplementary Medicare Plan

The supplementary plan covers 80 percent of the reasonable charges for covered services, except for the first $60 in a calendar year. The services covered by this medical insurance include:

> Physicians' and surgeons' services, no matter where you receive the service, at home, in the doctor's office, in a clinic, or in a hospital.
>
> Home health visits: up to one hundred visits under an approved plan each year, with no need for prior hospitalization. This is in addition to the one hundred visits possible for you to receive under hospital insurance.
>
> Other medical and health services regardless of where rendered, including: outpatient hospital services; diagnostic tests (X-rays, laboratory services, and so

forth); X-ray or radium treatments; surgical dressings, splints, casts; certain ambulance services,
braces, artificial legs, arms, and eyes; rental of medical equipment such as iron lungs; and many other
medical items and services.

The law provides specific periods of time, called enrollment periods, during which you can sign up for supplementary benefits.

You will have protection as soon as you reach sixty-five
only if you apply during the three-month period just before
the month in which you reach sixty-five.

If you elect to join the supplementary plan, you partially
pay for it by a basic monthly premium of $7.20, $7.70
starting July 1977. The remaining cost is contributed from
federal general revenues.

The basic part of the Medicare legislation is financed
through a special-earnings tax paid by employer and employee or by the self-employed. The contributions go into
a special trust fund set up to handle the finances of the
program. Benefits for those who are not presently covered
under the regular Social Security structure or the Railroad
Retirement program will be financed from general funds of
the Treasury.

[NOTE: *Readers must check for changes in both Social Security
and Medicare made since this book went to press in Summer 1977.*]

Index

Supplemental Security
Income (SSI), 77
eligibility for, 78

Tapering-off work program,
44, 45
Taxes. *See also* Federal
income tax
death, 82
estate and gift, 87, 88
future legislation, 95
preferential advantages for
older people, 94, 95
after retirement, 51, 53
"Testamentary trust," 87
Texas, 315–321
Titian, 39
Townsend Movement, 52
Travel, 149
Truck crops, 196, 197
Truth or Consequences, New
Mexico, 330
Tryon, North Carolina, 302,
303
Tucson, Arizona, 324–326

United States Department of
Agriculture, 198, 200,
209, 225
United States Department of
Housing and Urban
Development (HUD), 116
United States Fish and
Wildlife Service, 202
United States Savings Bonds,
76, 77
United States Veterans
Administration, 62
University of Wisconsin, 28

Variable annuity plans, 64
Venice, Florida, 278, 279
Veterans Administration. *See*
United States Veterans
Administration
Veterans compensation, 78
Vitamins, 34
Vocational rehabilitation, 41
eligibility for, 42
services provided, 42
Volunteer work, 11, 148

Walnut Creek, California, 123
War veterans benefits, 62
Washington University, 28
Weather. *See also* Retirement
locations
desirable changes in, 234,
235
White House Conference on
Aging, 107
recommendations of, 95–97
White Sands Hotel, 115
Widows, 25, 65, 80, 81
training while wives, 85, 86
Willamette View Manor, 115
Wills, 82, 86, 87
importance of, 81
Wilmington, North Carolina,
298–300
Winter Park, Florida,
274–276
Wives
as partners in retirement,
13, 14, 19, 20, 79–81
training in management,
85, 86
working, 85